P9-CJM-951

THE CAMBRIDGE ANTHOLOGIES

GENERAL EDITOR: J. DOVER WILSON, LITT.D.

LITERARY FRIENDSHIPS
IN THE
AGE OF WORDSWORTH

LITERARY FRIENDSHIPS
IN THE
AGE OF WORDSWORTH

AN ANTHOLOGY
SELECTED AND EDITED
BY

R. C. BALD
Ph.D., Cambridge, Lecturer in English at
the University of Adelaide

820.9034
B190
WITHDRAW

100177

1967
OCTAGON BOOKS, INC.
New York

LIBRARY ST. MARY'S COLLEGE

First published 1932 by Cambridge University Press

Reprinted 1967
by permission of the Cambridge University Press

OCTAGON BOOKS, INC.
175 FIFTH AVENUE
NEW YORK, N. Y. 10010

LIBRARY OF CONGRESS CATALOG CARD NUMBER: 67-18748

Printed in U.S.A. by
NOBLE OFFSET PRINTERS, INC.
NEW YORK 3, N. Y.

CONTENTS

CONTENTS

CONTENTS

CONTENTS

CONTENTS

CONTENTS

CONTENTS

CONTENTS

CONTENTS

PREFACE

In compiling this companion to the study of the period of the Romantic Revival, the editor's aim has been to provide a background somewhat wider and more interesting than the usual bare statements of biographical facts concerning each author, which are all that are usually offered to the student or the general reader who does not care to go to the larger biographies or has not read widely enough to be familiar with the passages here presented. There is, however, no lack of material for such an anthology as this; the difficulty rather has been one of selection and compression. One principle, however, has been maintained throughout. Selections have been made from the works of the more important authors of the period, in order to present what they themselves said to or about one another; what their somewhat less distinguished friends said about them has had to be excluded. The few exceptions to this rule are easily explained: Dorothy Wordsworth was so much at one with her brother and with Coleridge during their most vital years that the extracts from her *Journals*, even apart from their very high intrinsic interest, have as much significance as if they had come from the pen of either of the other two; Haydon's account of his famous dinner party was too good to be omitted; and Crabb Robinson, prosaic as he often is, furnishes a day-by-day commentary such as is accessible nowhere else, and is too illuminating to be ignored. Explanatory notes have been kept down to the barest minimum; but a few biographical details concerning some of the minor personages who appear in these pages have been included in the Index.

Acknowledgments for permission to include copyright material are gratefully tendered to Messrs G. Bell & Sons, Ltd., Messrs William Heinemann, Ltd., Mr Roger Ingpen, Messrs Macmillan & Co., Ltd., Messrs Methuen & Co., Ltd., and Mr John Murray.

R. C. B.

Adelaide, June 1932

INTRODUCTION

I

ISOLATION, in the arts at least, is by no means as splendid as the popular phrase would have it. In all the great creative epochs there have been groups of men eagerly discussing the problems of life and art, exploring new ideas and new realms of technique, and generously sharing their results with one another. Athens, in the fifth century before Christ, and Florence, in the fifteenth century of our era, could never have achieved their pre-eminence in the history of Europe without the constant intercourse of the men who made them great; nor can anyone doubt that Shakespeare, no less than his opponent, profited by those "wit-combats betwixt him and Ben Jonson" at the Mermaid Tavern. Even Milton, who seems to stand alone more than any other figure in English literature, was in close contact with the greatest men and the greatest deeds of his age. The truth is that great men are stimulants to one another, and lead on lesser men to achievements which would have been impossible for them without these high examples and high incentives. Incomplete and thwarted achievement is the penalty of isolation.

Almost all the poets who are generally spoken of as the precursors of the Romantic Revival paid the penalty of isolation. Madness claimed Smart, Collins and Cowper; Gray "never spoke out"; Chatterton,

> the marvellous boy,
> The sleepless soul that perished in his pride,

took his own life. In the works of none of them can one find evidence of the eagerness of hope or the spur of emulation, for the isolation from which they suffered was the cruellest of all—the loneliness inflicted on them by a hard and unreceptive environment. The outbreak of the French Revolution, however, provided a new incentive to hope; youth and courage did the rest. Wordsworth and Coleridge together broke through the old barriers of prejudice and inertia, and twenty years later Shelley wrote: "The great writers of our age are, we have reason to suppose, the companions and forerunners of some unimagined change in our social condition or the opinions which cement it. The cloud of mind is discharging its collected lightning".

Since the days of Carlyle, historians, literary and otherwise, have alternatively stressed men and movements as the decisive factors in change and progress. The aim of this book is to hold the balance between the two tendencies, unnecessarily in conflict, and to show that, in so far as the Romantic Revival was a movement, the men who were its leaders were in constant and intimate contact with one another, and that their relations constitute some of the most delightful as well as some of the most important records in the annals of literary friendship. With the study of the records comes, too, the realization that without these friendships the work of almost every one of these men would have been, in some respects at least, different from what it was.

II

The extracts in this book cover the space of about half a century, yet, strangely enough, it contains but two vital "spots of time" when the most important creative work of the period was being done. The first of these extends from 1797 to 1805, when Coleridge wrote everything and Wordsworth practically everything by which they are remembered. The second period, from 1818 to 1823, is remarkable for an outburst of activity scarcely paralleled in the history of English literature; in prose, Lamb, Hazlitt and De Quincey, each of whose talents ripened slowly, suddenly reached maturity; and in poetry these same years saw the culmination of the powers of Byron, Shelley and Keats.

Nevertheless, the stream of friendship flowed steadily on through the whole period. It is true that there were occasional quarrels and misunderstandings, but these may be passed over lightly, for there was no breach that remained permanently unhealed. It is much more important to realize that, even during the years that were comparatively barren in literary production, men such as Lamb, Coleridge and Wordsworth were continually in touch with one another, and that the results of this constant intercourse were often revealed later. From 1805 to 1815, for instance, Coleridge was developing ideas in conversation that were not published until they had been thoroughly familiar to his friends for a decade, and during the same period Lamb, Hazlitt and De Quincey were storing up memories and experiences with which they afterwards enriched their writings.

It is inevitable that in such a book as this Lamb's letters should occupy a large space. Not only do they contain as much of his peculiar charm as his essays, but they also show that Lamb's wide tolerance and his genius for friendship made him the link that held together the men of the older generation. He had known Coleridge, Southey, Wordsworth and Hazlitt in the days before any of them became famous, and he kept their friendship throughout his life. The younger men he welcomed too, and his relations with such men as Procter and Hood bear eloquent testimony to the fact that age could never wither him; Shelley alone stood outside the bounds of his sympathies. It was around Leigh Hunt, however, that the most famous of the younger men congregated; to his warm-hearted encouragement Keats undoubtedly owed a great debt, and Shelley formed a friendship with him that only death could break. Hunt also had the distinction of being the only member of the London or the Lake groups who was on friendly terms with Byron before he left England for ever.

Byron is one of the four men who seem to stand aloof from the others. He esteemed his rank and position more than his literary achievements, and has recorded that the literary men whose friendship he valued were Moore, Rogers and Scott, who were men of the world as well as men of letters. Even Byron, however, could not help respecting the genuineness of Shelley's unworldly idealism, and, in spite of the protests of his friends, twice found his company a stimulus and an incentive at times when life had become stale and unprofitable for him. Both Scott and Landor were removed by distance from the centre of literary activities, but Scott's generous friendliness for Wordsworth, his admiration for Byron and his staunch support of Southey are pleasant to record. It is pleasant, too, to remember that he wrote to Lamb inviting him to Abbotsford; but, although the two men never met, they always regarded one another with the warmest respect. Landor did not meet most of his famous contemporaries till late in life, and then most of his relations were with an altogether younger generation; his long-standing friendship with Southey is the only one that covers the period of this book. Landor had seen and perhaps spoken to Shelley in Pisa, but at that period he "would not see a single English person; says he is glad that the country produces people of worth, but will have nothing to do with them"; in spite of this, however, both Hunt and Hazlitt received unexpectedly warm welcomes at his villa at Fiesole not long afterwards. Blake, alone of the great writers of the age, stood aloof from his contemporaries in true isolation. He lived in a world apart, into which none but such as he could enter.

III

This book is primarily a record of friendships, but it remains to suggest very briefly the effects which these friendships had on the thought and work of the men who shared them.

It is practically impossible to overestimate the importance of the constant companionship of Coleridge with Dorothy and William Wordsworth at Nether Stowey and Alfoxden during 1797 and 1798. Here the volume of *Lyrical Ballads* was planned, and Wordsworth's theory of poetic diction was worked out. It is true that Coleridge was as incapable of writing *We Are Seven* (as *The Three Graves* showed) as Wordsworth was of writing *The Ancient Mariner*, yet every poem in the *Lyrical Ballads* was fully discussed by the three, and its significance clearly realized, for the *Lyrical Ballads* were written in pursuance of a definite plan to illustrate the twin powers of poetry, "the power of exciting the sympathy of the reader by a faithful adherence to the truth of nature, and the power of giving the interest of novelty by the modifying colours of the imagination. The sudden charm, which accidents of light and shade, which moonlight or sun-set diffused over a known and familiar landscape, appeared to represent the practicability of combining both". By carrying their plan into execution Wordsworth and Coleridge permanently enlarged the scope of English poetry and ultimately brought about a revolution in taste and feeling, the results of which are still felt.

Although Coleridge claimed that the ideas expressed in the famous Preface to the second edition of the *Lyrical Ballads* were as much his as Wordsworth's, he was startled by the criticism with which they met, and he soon began to re-examine their principles. As early as 1802 he wrote to Southey: "Although Wordsworth's Preface is half a child of my brain, and arose out of conversations so frequent that, with few exceptions, we could scarcely either of us, perhaps, say which first started any particular thought...yet I am far from going all lengths with Wordsworth....On the contrary, I rather suspect that somewhere or other there is a radical difference in our theoretical opinions respecting poetry; this I shall endeavour to go to the bottom of". Here is the germ, which was developed and elaborated in conversation during the intervening years, of the most vital and interesting chapters of the *Biographia Literaria*. Coleridge's influence, indeed, was probably more personal than that of any of his contemporaries. The circulation of *Christabel* in manuscript influenced Scott and Byron; his talk helped to clarify the thought of the young Hazlitt, who, though estranged from Coleridge in later years, acknowledged that he was "the only man who ever taught me anything"; and he gathered around him a knot of disciples who took up and spread his philosophical and theological ideas, although they were never, or only imperfectly, recorded in print by Coleridge himself.

In their younger days Lamb, Southey and Coleridge were all eager explorers of the neglected writers of the sixteenth and seventeenth centuries, but, for the greater part of the period, Lamb was undoubtedly the guide and director of his fellows. His tattered but well-read collection of old books was at the disposal of his friends, especially Coleridge; his enthusiasm for the Elizabethan dramatists and the less known authors of the seventeenth century, which is so evident in his *Specimens* and in his essays, was often the subject of his talk. A slight example will show how Lamb's influence was spread. Hazlitt's famous account of one of Lamb's "Thursday nights" represents him as reading "with suffused features and a faltering tongue" Donne's elegy *On his Mistress*. One is not surprised to find Leigh Hunt, who was present, writing later to Shelley, asking him airily "Do you know Donne?" and then following up with a quotation from this very poem.[1] Naturally, some of Lamb's friends owed more to him than others did. While it is interesting to find Wordsworth seeking Lamb's advice about a course of reading among the Elizabethan dramatists, it is not known whether he carried it out, and, if he did, it had little influence on his poetry. Hazlitt, on the other hand, probably owed much more to Lamb than he realized, for one has only to compare Lamb's paper on Hogarth with Hazlitt's seventh lecture on the *English Comic Writers* to perceive that Hazlitt had often heard Lamb talking about the Hogarth prints that were hung round his room. Similarly, Lamb is in the background of many of the *Lectures on the English Poets* and almost all of the *Lectures on the Dramatic Poetry of the Age of Queen Elizabeth*. Coleridge, indeed, went so far as to say, rather unkindly, that some of Hazlitt's criticisms of Shakespeare were "round and round imitations of Charles Lamb's exquisite criticisms", and, because they did not "progress and evolve, but only spun upon themselves", lacked an essential criterion of genius.[2]

[1] Hunt's letter to Shelley is dated Sept. 20, 1819. Mr E. V. Lucas, in his *Life of Charles Lamb*, believes that the evening's conversation recorded by Hazlitt occurred about 1814; Hunt, however, was in prison then. It is possible, of course, that Lamb read out or talked of the poem on more than one occasion, or that Hazlitt's essay is to some extent an imaginary reconstruction, built up from his recollections of many such evenings.

[2] It is interesting to note that Coleridge is himself here borrowing from one of Lamb's criticisms. Lamb, comparing the styles of Shakespeare and Fletcher in a note to his *Specimens*, had said: "Noble as this whole passage is, it must be confessed that the manner of it, compared with Shakespeare's finest scenes, is faint and languid. Its motion is circular, not progressive; each line revolves on itself in a sort of separate orbit".

Hazlitt, Byron and Shelley were, during the greater part of their careers, out of sympathy with Wordsworth and Southey, whom they regarded as political renegades and castigated in such works as *The Spirit of the Age*, *The Vision of Judgment*, and *Peter Bell the Third*. Nevertheless, Shelley had cherished an early admiration for Wordsworth's poetry, and later, even though it disappointed him at first, he studied *The Excursion* carefully. The Third Canto of *Childe Harold*, written when Byron and Shelley were together in Switzerland, shows that Wordsworth's influence had even penetrated to Byron, who could not remain unaffected by Shelley's interest in the Lake poet. Keats, too, was for a time an enthusiastic admirer of Wordsworth, and often repeated the *Lines written above Tintern Abbey* and the *Ode on Intimations of Immortality*; he was proud also of meeting Wordsworth, but Wordsworth's influence is implicit rather than explicit in his work.

The influence of Keats's friendship with Hunt on *Endymion* is well known: it was responsible for the more unfortunate passages of that poem, and helped to provoke the savage reviews in the *Quarterly* and in *Blackwood's Magazine*, which were for so long supposed to have hastened Keats's death. Keats, however, outgrew Hunt's influence and turned to Hazlitt, with his more trenchant judgments, for correction: "I am convinced that there are three things to rejoice at in this Age," he wrote to Haydon, "*The Excursion*, Your Pictures, and Hazlitt's depth of Taste", and later, when he was convinced that he needed more than anything else the mental discipline of a philosophical training, it was to Hazlitt that he proposed to turn for advice and guidance. Hunt also influenced Shelley, although never so strongly as he had influenced Keats. "I am sending you a poem in the style you like", Shelley wrote to him of *Rosalind and Helen*, and later, when *Julian and Maddalo* was written, he wrote: "You will find the little piece, I think, in some degree consistent with your own ideas of the manner in which poetry ought to be written. I have employed a certain familiar style of language to express the actual way in which people talk with each other". Yet of the two men it was definitely Shelley who was the more vital spirit, and, when he died, it was left to Hunt to reverence his memory with the unflagging devotion of a disciple.

In conclusion, it is hardly necessary to say that too much stress must not be laid on the mutual influences that have just been suggested. Without them, the essential originality of each of the great writers of the period would have remained unchanged. However, these influences helped to determine the channels into which the creative effort of the period was poured; and life would have been less stimulating, work less congenial, and mental activity more restricted for each of the writers of the age without the friendships and the intercourse recorded in this book.

CHRIST'S HOSPITAL, 1782–99

Lamb and Coleridge entered Christ's Hospital together in 1782, and Leigh Hunt followed them in 1791. Lamb left school in 1789, and by 1792 was in the East India House; Coleridge passed from Christ's Hospital to Jesus College, Cambridge, in 1791, and Hunt, already the author of a volume of *Juvenilia*, left school in 1799.

Lamb's Elia essay *Christ's Hospital Five and Thirty Years Ago* is written to supplement an earlier essay on his old school, and for the greater part of it he is writing from the point of view of Coleridge, the lonely little boy from a distant Devonshire village, in order to contrast Coleridge's situation with his own, which had been explained in the earlier essay.

I

The Frost performs its secret ministry,
Unhelped by any wind. The owlet's cry
Came loud—and hark, again! loud as before.
The inmates of my cottage, all at rest,
Have left me to that solitude, which suits
Abstruser musings: save that at my side
My cradled infant slumbers peacefully.
'Tis calm indeed! so calm, that it disturbs
And vexes meditation with its strange
And extreme silentness. Sea, hill, and wood,
This populous village! Sea, and hill, and wood,
With all the numberless goings-on of life,
Inaudible as dreams! the thin blue flame
Lies on my low-burnt fire, and quivers not;
Only that film which fluttered on the grate
Still flutters there, the sole unquiet thing.
Methinks, its motion in this hush of nature
Gives it dim sympathies with me who live,
Making it a companionable form,
Whose puny flaps and freaks the idling Spirit
By its own moods interprets, everywhere

LIBRARY ST. MARY'S COLLEGE

Echo or mirror seeking of itself,
And makes a toy of Thought.

But O! how oft,
How oft, at school, with most believing mind,
Presageful, have I gazed upon the bars,
To watch that fluttering *stranger*! and as oft,
With unclosed lids, already had I dreamt
Of my sweet birth-place, and the old church-tower,
Whose bells, the poor man's only music, rang
From morn to evening, all the hot Fair-day,
So sweetly, that they stirred and haunted me
With a wild pleasure, falling on mine ear
Most like articulate sounds of things to come!
So gazed I, till the soothing things, I dreamt,
Lulled me to sleep, and sleep prolonged my dreams!
And so I brooded all the following morn,
Awed by the stern preceptor's face, mine eye
Fixed with mock study on my swimming book:
Save if the door half opened, and I snatched
A hasty glance, and still my heart leaped up,
For still I hoped to see the *stranger's* face,
Townsman, or aunt, or sister more beloved,
My play-mate when we both were clothed alike!

Dear Babe, that sleepest cradled by my side,
Whose gentle breathings, heard in this deep calm,
Fill up the interspersed vacancies
And momentary pauses of the thought!
My babe so beautiful! it thrills my heart
With tender gladness, thus to look at thee,
And think that thou shalt learn far other lore,
And in far other scenes! For I was reared
In the great city, pent 'mid cloisters dim,
And saw nought lovely but the sky and stars.

COLERIDGE: *Frost at Midnight* (1798)

II

In Mr Lamb's *Works*, published a year or two since, I find a magnificent eulogy on my old school,[1] such as it was, or now appears to him to have been, between the years 1782 and 1789. It happens, very oddly, that my own standing at Christ's was nearly corresponding with his; and with all gratitude to him for his enthusiasm for the cloisters, I think he has contrived to bring together whatever can be said in praise of them, dropping all the other side of the argument most ingeniously.

I remember L. at school; and can well recollect that he had some peculiar advantages, which I and others of his schoolfellows had not. His friends lived in town, and were near at hand; and he had the privilege of going to see them, almost as often as he wished, through some invidious distinction, which was denied to us. The present worthy sub-treasurer to the Inner Temple can explain how that happened. He had his tea and hot rolls in a morning, while we were battening upon our quarter of a penny loaf—our *crug*—moistened with attenuated small beer, in wooden piggins, smacking of the pitched leathern jack it was poured from. Our Monday's milk porritch, blue and tasteless, and the pease soup of Saturday, coarse and choking, were enriched for him with a slice of "extraordinary bread and butter", from the hot-loaf of the Temple. The Wednesday's mess of millet, somewhat less repugnant (we had three banyan to four meat days in the week)—was endeared to his palate with a lump of double-refined, and a smack of ginger (to make it go down the more glibly) or the fragrant cinnamon. In lieu of our *half-pickled* Sundays, or *quite fresh* boiled beef on Thursdays (strong as *caro equina*), with detestable marigolds floating in the pail to poison the broth—our scanty mutton scrags on Fridays—and rather more savoury, but grudging, portions of the same flesh, rotten-roasted or rare, on the Tuesdays (the only dish which excited our appetites, and disappointed our stomachs, in almost

[1] *Recollections of Christ's Hospital.*

equal proportion)—he had his hot plate of roast veal, or the more tempting griskin (exotics unknown to our palates), cooked in the paternal kitchen (a great thing), and brought him daily by his maid or aunt! I remember the good old relative (in whom love forbade pride) squatting down upon some odd stone in a by-nook of the cloisters, disclosing the viands (of higher regale than those cates which the ravens ministered to the Tishbite); and the contending passions of L. at the unfolding. There was love for the bringer; shame for the thing brought, and the manner of its bringing; sympathy for those who were too many to share in it; and, at top of all, hunger (eldest, strongest of the passions!) predominant, breaking down the stony fences of shame, and awkwardness, and a troubling over-consciousness.

I was a poor friendless boy. My parents, and those who should care for me, were far away. Those few acquaintances of theirs, which they could reckon upon as being kind to me in the great city, after a little forced notice, which they had the grace to take of me on my first arrival in town, soon grew tired of my holiday visits. They seemed to them to recur too often, though I thought them few enough; and, one after another, they all failed me, and I felt myself alone among six hundred playmates.

O the cruelty of separating a poor lad from his early homestead! The yearnings which I used to have towards it in those unfledged years! How, in my dreams, would my native town (far in the west) come back, with its church, and trees, and faces! How I would wake weeping, and in the anguish of my heart exclaim upon sweet Calne in Wiltshire!

To this late hour of my life, I trace impressions left by the recollection of those friendless holidays. The long warm days of summer never return but they bring with them a gloom from the haunting memory of those *whole-day leaves*, when, by some strange arrangement, we were turned out, for the live-long day, upon our own hands, whether we had friends to go to, or none. I remember those bathing-excursions to the New River, which L. recalls with such relish, better, I think, than he can—for he was a home-seeking lad, and did not much care for such water-pastimes:—How merrily we would sally forth into the fields; and strip under the first warmth of the sun; and wanton like young dace in the streams; getting us appetites for noon, which those of us that were penniless (our scanty morning crust long since exhausted) had not the means of allaying—while the cattle, and the birds, and the fishes, were at feed about us, and we had nothing to satisfy our cravings—the very beauty of the day, and the exercise of the pastime, and the sense of liberty, setting a keener edge upon them!—How faint and languid, finally, we would return, towards night-fall, to our desired morsel, half-rejoicing, half-reluctant, that the hours of our uneasy liberty had expired!

It was worse in the days of winter, to go prowling about the streets objectless—shivering at cold windows of print shops, to extract a little amusement; or haply, as a last resort, in the hopes of a little novelty, to pay a fifty-times repeated visit (where our individual faces should be as well known to the warden as those of his own charges) to the Lions in the Tower—to whose levée, by courtesy immemorial, we had a prescriptive title to admission.

L.'s governor (so we called the patron who presented us to the foundation) lived in a manner under his paternal roof. Any complaint which he had to make was sure of being attended to. This was understood at Christ's, and was an effectual screen to him against the severity of masters, or worse tyranny of the monitors. The oppressions of these young brutes are heart-sickening to call to recollection. I have been called out of my bed, and *waked for the purpose*, in the coldest winter nights—and this not once, but night after night—in my shirt, to receive the discipline of a leathern thong, with eleven other sufferers, because it pleased my callow overseer, when there has been any talking heard after we were gone to bed, to make the six last beds in the dormitory, where the youngest children of us slept, answerable for an offence they neither dared to commit, nor had the power to hinder.—The same execrable tyranny drove the younger part of us from the fires, when our feet were perishing with snow; and, under the cruellest penalties, forbade the indulgence of a drink of water, when we lay in sleepless summer nights, fevered with the season and the day's sports.

LAMB: *Christ's Hospital Five and Thirty Years Ago*

III

Come back into memory, like as thou wert in the day-spring of thy fancies, with hope like a fiery column before thee—the dark pillar not yet turned—Samuel Taylor Coleridge—Logician, Metaphysician, Bard!—How have I seen the casual passer through the Cloisters stand still, entranced with admiration (while he weighed the disproportion between the *speech* and the *garb* of the young Mirandula), to hear thee unfold, in thy deep and sweet intonations, the mysteries of Jamblichus, or Plotinus (for even in those years thou waxedst not pale at such philosophic draughts), or reciting Homer in his Greek, or Pindar——while the walls of the old Grey Friars re-echoed to the accents of the *inspired charity-boy*!—Many were the "wit-combats" (to dally awhile with the words of old Fuller) between him and C. V. Le G——, "which two I behold like a Spanish great galleon, and an English man of war: Master Coleridge, like the former, was built far higher in learning, solid, but slow in his performances. C. V. L., with the English man of war, lesser in bulk, but lighter in sailing, could turn with all times, tack about, and take advantage of all winds, by the quickness of his wit and invention".

LAMB: *Christ's Hospital Five and Thirty Years Ago*

IV

The Upper Grammar School was divided into four classes or forms. The two under ones were called Little and Great Erasmus; the two upper were occupied by the Grecians and Deputy Grecians. We used to think the title of Erasmus taken from the great scholar of that name; but the sudden appearance of a portrait among us, bearing to be the likeness of a certain Erasmus Smith, Esq., shook us terribly in this opinion, and was a hard trial of our gratitude. We scarcely relished this perpetual company of our benefactor, watching us, as he seemed to do, with his omnipresent eyes. I believe he was a rich merchant, and that the forms of Little and Great Erasmus were really named after him. It was but a poor consolation to think that he himself, or his great-uncle, might have been named after Erasmus. Little Erasmus learned Ovid; Great Erasmus, Virgil, Terence, and the Greek Testament. The Deputy Grecians were in Homer, Cicero, and Demosthenes; the Grecians, in the Greek plays and the mathematics.

When a boy entered the Upper School, he was understood to be in the road to the University, provided he had inclination and talents for it; but, as only one Grecian a year went to College, the drafts out of Great and Little Erasmus into the writing-school were numerous. A few also became Deputy Grecians without going farther, and entered the world from that form. Those who became Grecians always went to the University, though not always into the Church; which was reckoned a departure from the contract. When I first came to school, at seven years old, the names of the Grecians were Allen, Favell, Thomson, and Le Grice, brother of the Le Grice above mentioned, and now a clergyman in Cornwall. Charles Lamb had lately been Deputy Grecian; and Coleridge had left for the University.

The master, inspired by his subject with an eloquence beyond himself, once called him, "that sensible fool, Collĕrĭdge", pronouncing the word like a dactyl. Coleridge must have alternately delighted and bewildered him. The compliment, as to the bewildering, was returned, if not the delight. The pupil, I am told, said he dreamt of the master all his life, and that his dreams were horrible.

I do not remember seeing Coleridge when I was a child. Lamb's visits to the school, after he left it, I remember well, with his fine intelligent face. Little did I think I should have the pleasure of sitting with it in after-times as an old friend, and seeing it careworn and still finer. Allen,[1] the Grecian,

[1] Allen went to Oxford when Coleridge went to Cambridge, and it was in his rooms at University College that Coleridge first met Southey.

was so handsome, though in another and more obvious way, that running one day against a barrow-woman in the street, and turning round to appease her in the midst of her abuse, she said, "Where are you driving to, you great hulking, good-for-nothing—beautiful fellow, God bless you!" Le Grice the elder was a wag, like his brother, but more staid. He went into the Church, as he ought to do, and married a rich widow. He published a translation, abridged, of the celebrated pastoral of Longus; and report at school made him the author of a little anonymous tract on the *Art of Poking the Fire*.

LEIGH HUNT: *Autobiography*

PANTISOCRACY

This amusing letter from Coleridge to Southey, with its jumble of love, poetry and pantisocracy, illustrates excellently the youthful enthusiasms of the two undergraduate poets. Their plan was to found a pantisocratic colony on communistic lines in America, and among the recruits were to be the two sisters, Sara and Edith Fricker, mentioned in the letter, whom they shortly afterwards married.

10 o'clock, Thursday morning, *September* 18, 1794.

Well, my dear Southey! I am at last arrived at Jesus. My God! how tumultuous are the movements of my heart. Since I quitted this room what and how important events have been evolved! America! Southey! Miss Fricker! Yes, Southey, you are right. Even Love is the creature of strong motive. I certainly love her. I *think* of her incessantly and with unspeakable tenderness,—with that inward melting away of soul that symptomatizes it.

Pantisocracy! Oh, I shall have such a scheme of it! My head, my heart, are all alive. I have drawn up my arguments in battle array; they shall have the *tactician* excellence of the mathematician with the enthusiasm of the poet. The head shall be the mass; the heart the fiery spirit that fills, informs, and agitates the whole. Harwood—pish! I say nothing of him.

SHAD GOES WITH US. HE IS MY BROTHER! I am longing to be with you. Make Edith my sister. Surely, Southey, we shall be *frendotatoi meta frendous*—most friendly where all are friends. She must, therefore, be more emphatically my sister.

Brookes and Beardmore, as I suspected, have spread my opinions in mangled forms at Cambridge. Caldwell, the most pantisocratic of aristocratics, has been laughing at me. Up I arose, terrible in reasoning. He fled from me, because "he could not answer for his own sanity, sitting so near a madman of genius". He told me that the strength of my imagination had intoxicated my reason, and that the acuteness of my reason had given a directing influence to my imagination. Four months ago the remark would not have been more elegant than just. Now it is nothing.

I like your sonnets[1] exceedingly—the best of any I have yet seen. "Though to the eye fair is the extended vale" should be "to the eye though fair the extended vale" I by no means disapprove of discord introduced to produce *effect*, nor is my ear so fastidious as to be angry with it where it could not have been avoided without weakening the sense. But discord for discord's sake is rather too licentious.

"Wild wind" has no other but alliterative beauty; it applies to a storm, not to the autumnal breeze that makes the trees rustle mournfully. Alter it to "That rustle to the sad wind moaningly".

"'Twas a long way and tedious", and the three last lines are marked beauties—unlaboured strains poured soothingly along from the feeling simplicity of heart. The next sonnet is altogether exquisite, the circumstance common yet new to poetry, the moral accurate and full of soul. "I never saw", etc., is most exquisite. I am almost ashamed to write the following, it is so inferior. Ashamed? No, Southey! God knows my heart! I am *delighted* to feel you superior to me in genius as in virtue.

No more my visionary soul shall dwell
On joys that were; no more endure to weigh

[1] The poems referred to are nos. vi and viii of Southey's *Sonnets*. Although he altered his original drafts, he did not accept Coleridge's emendations.

The shame and anguish of the evil day.
Wisely forgetful! O'er the ocean swell
Sublime of Hope, I seek the cottag'd dell
Where Virtue calm with careless step may stray,
And, dancing to the moonlight roundelay,
The wizard Passions weave an holy spell.
Eyes that have ach'd with sorrow! ye shall weep
Tears of doubt-mingled joy, like theirs who start
From precipices of distemper'd sleep,
On which the fierce-eyed fiends their revels keep,
And see the rising sun, and feel it dart
New rays of pleasance trembling to the heart.

I have heard from Allen, and write the third letter to him. Yours is the second. Perhaps you would like two sonnets I have written to my Sally. When I have received an answer from Allen I will tell you the contents of his first letter.

My compliments to Heath.

I will write you a huge, big letter next week. At present I have to transact the tragedy business, to wait on the Master, to write to Mrs Southey, Lovell, etc., etc.

God love you, and

S. T. Coleridge

LAMB'S TRAGEDY

To Coleridge

P.M. *September* 27, 1796.

My dearest Friend,—White or some of my friends or the public papers by this time may have informed you of the terrible calamities that have fallen on our family. I will only give you the outlines. My poor dear dearest sister in a fit of insanity has been the death of her own mother. I was at hand only time enough to snatch the knife out of her grasp. She is at present in a madhouse, from whence I fear she must be moved to an hospital. God has preserved to me my senses,—I eat and drink and sleep, and have my judgment I believe very sound. My poor father was slightly wounded, and I am left to take care of him and my aunt. Mr Norris of the Bluecoat School has been very very kind to us, and we have no other friend, but thank God I am very calm and composed, and able to do the best that remains to do. Write,—as religious a letter as possible—but no mention of what is gone and done with.—With me "the former things are passed away", and I have something more to do [than] to feel——

God almighty have us all in his keeping.—

C. Lamb

Mention nothing of poetry. I have destroyed every vestige of past vanities of that kind. Do as you please, but if you publish, publish mine (I give free leave) without name or initial, and never send me a book, I charge you.

Your own judgment will convince you not to take any notice of this yet to your dear wife.—You look after your family,—I have my reason and strength left to take care of mine. I charge you, don't think of coming to see me. Write. I will not see you if you come. God almighty love you and all of us.——

NETHER STOWEY AND ALFOXDEN, 1797–8

Wordsworth probably met Coleridge at Bristol in 1795, two years after his return from France, and at a time when he was still trying to assuage his bitter disappointment at the turn taken by the Revolution in France by absorption in the ideals expressed by Godwin in his *Political Justice*. Meanwhile, Coleridge had seen his last hopes of pantisocracy fade, and he was sorely disappointed at what seemed to him to be Southey's cooling ardour. The friendship between the poets soon grew, and on July 2, 1797, Coleridge brought Wordsworth and his sister with him to Nether Stowey, and, as the first letter describes, settled them at Alfoxden, about four miles away from the cottage in which he was living.

I

Coleridge *to* Southey

[*July*, 1797.]

. . . I have been on a visit to Wordsworth's at Racedown, near Crewkerne, and I brought him and his sister back with me, and here I have *settled* them. By a combination of curious circumstances a gentleman's seat, with a park and woods, elegantly and completely furnished, with nine lodging rooms, three parlours, and a hall, in the most beautiful and romantic situation by the seaside, four miles from Stowey,—this we have got for Wordsworth at the *rent of twenty-three pounds a year, taxes included*! The park and woods are *his* for all purposes *he* wants them, and the large gardens are altogether and entirely his. Wordsworth is a very great man, the only man of whom *at all times* and *in all modes of excellence* I feel myself inferior, the only one, I mean, whom *I have yet met with*, for the London *literati* appear to me to be very much like little potatoes, that is, *no great things*, a compost of nullity and dullity.

Charles Lamb has been with me for a week. He left me Friday morning. The second day after Wordsworth came to me, dear Sara accidentally emptied a skillet of boiling milk on my foot, which confined me during the whole time of C. Lamb's stay and still prevents me from all *walks* longer than a furlong. While Wordsworth, his sister, and Charles Lamb were out one evening, sitting in the arbour of T. Poole's garden which communicates with mine I wrote these lines, with which I am pleased...

Well, they are gone, and here must I remain,
This lime-tree bower my prison! I have lost
Beauties and feelings, such as would have been
Most sweet to my remembrance even when age
Had dimmed mine eyes to blindness! They, meanwhile,
Friends, whom I never more may meet again,
On springy heath, along the hill-top edge,
Wander in gladness, and wind down, perchance,
To that still roaring dell, of which I told;
The roaring dell, o'erwooded, narrow, deep,
And only speckled by the mid-day sun;
Where its slim trunk the ash from rock to rock
Flings arching like a bridge;—that branchless ash,
Unsunned and damp, whose few poor yellow leaves
Ne'er tremble in the gale, yet tremble still,
Fanned by the water-fall! and there my friends
Behold the dark green file of long lank weeds,
That all at once (a most fantastic sight!)
Still nod and drip beneath the dripping edge
Of the blue clay-stone.

Now, my friends emerge
Beneath the wide wide Heaven—and view again

The many-steepled tract magnificent
Of hilly fields and meadows, and the sea,
With some fair bark, perhaps, whose sails light up
The slip of smooth clear blue betwixt two Isles
Of purple shadow! Yes! they wander on
In gladness all; but thou, methinks, most glad,
My gentle-hearted Charles! for thou hast pined
And hungered after Nature, many a year,
In the great City pent, winning thy way
With sad yet patient soul, through evil and pain
And strange calamity! Ah! slowly sink
Behind the western ridge, thou glorious Sun!
Shine in the slant beams of the sinking orb,
Ye purple heath-flowers! richlier burn, ye clouds!
Live in the yellow light, ye distant groves!
And kindle, thou blue Ocean! So my friend
Struck with deep joy may stand, as I have stood,
Silent with swimming sense; yea, gazing round
On the wide landscape, gaze till all doth seem
Less gross than bodily; and of such hues
As veil the Almighty Spirit, when yet he makes
Spirits perceive his presence.

A delight
Comes sudden on my heart, and I am glad
As I myself were there! Nor in this bower,
This little lime-tree bower, have I not marked
Much that has soothed me. Pale beneath the blaze
Hung the transparent foliage; and I watched
Some broad and sunny leaf, and loved to see
The shadow of the leaf and stem above,
Dappling its sunshine! And that walnut-tree
Was richly tinged, and a deep radiance lay
Full on the ancient ivy, which usurps
Those fronting elms, and now, with blackest mass
Makes their dark branches gleam a lighter hue
Through the late twilight: and though now the bat
Wheels silent by, and not a swallow twitters,
Yet still the solitary humble-bee
Sings in the bean-flower! Henceforth I shall know
That Nature ne'er deserts the wise and pure;
No plot so narrow, be but Nature there,
No waste so vacant, but may well employ
Each faculty of sense, and keep the heart
Awake to Love and Beauty! and sometimes
'Tis well to be bereft of promised good,

That we may lift the soul, and contemplate
With lively joy the joys we cannot share.
My gentle-hearted Charles! when the last rook
Beat its straight path along the dusky air
Homewards, I blest it! deeming its black wing
(Now a dim speck, now vanishing in light)
Had cross'd the mighty orb's dilated glory,
While thou stood'st gazing; or when all was still,
Flew creaking o'er thy head, and had a charm
For thee, my gentle-hearted Charles, to whom
No sound is dissonant which tells of Life.[1]

I would make shift by some means or other to visit you, if I thought that you and Edith Southey would return with me. I think—indeed, I am almost certain—that I could get a one-horse chaise free of all expense. I have driven back Miss Wordsworth over forty miles of execrable roads, and have been always very cautious, and am now no inexpert whip. And Wordsworth, at whose house I now am for change of air, has commissioned me to offer you a suite of rooms at this place, which is called "All-foxen"; and so divine and wild is the country that I am sure it would increase your stock of images, and three weeks' absence from Christchurch will endear it to you; and Edith Southey and Sara may not have another opportunity of seeing one another, and Wordsworth is very solicitous to know you, and Miss Wordsworth is a most exquisite young woman in her mind and heart. I pray you write me immediately, directing Stowėy, near Bridgewater, as before.

God bless you and your affectionate

S. T. Coleridge

II

Lamb *to* Coleridge

[Probably *July* 19 or 26, 1797.]

I am scarcely yet so reconciled to the loss of you, or so subsided into my wonted uniformity of feeling, as to sit calmly

[1] I have ventured to give the text of this poem as it appears in Coleridge's *Poems* under the title *This Lime Tree Bower My Prison*, and not in its original form as it appeared in the letter.

down to think of you and write to you. But I reason myself into the belief that those few and pleasant holidays shall not have been spent in vain. I feel improvement in the recollection of many a casual conversation. The names of Tom Poole, of Wordsworth and his good sister, with thine and Sara's, are become "familiar in my mouth as household words". You would make me very happy, if you think W. has no objection, by transcribing for me that inscription of his. I have some scattered sentences ever floating in my memory, teasing me that I cannot remember more of it. You may believe that I will make no improper use of it. Believe me I can think now of many subjects on which I had planned gaining information from you; but I forgot my "treasure's worth" while I possessed it. Your leg is now become to me a matter of much more importance—and many a little thing, which when I was present with you seemed scarce to *indent* my notice, now presses painfully on my remembrance. Is the Patriot come yet? Are Wordsworth and his sister gone yet? I was looking out for John Thelwall all the way from Bridgewater, and had I met him, I think it would have moved me almost to tears. You will oblige me too by sending me my great-coat, which I left behind in the oblivious state the mind is thrown into at parting—is it not ridiculous that I sometimes envy that great-coat lingering so cunningly behind?—at present I have none—so send it me by a Stowey waggon, if there be such a thing, directing for C. L., No. 45, Chapel-Street, Pentonville, near London. But above all, *that Inscription*!—it will recall to me the tones of all your voices—and with them many a remembered kindness to one who could and can repay you all only by the silence of a grateful heart. I could not talk much, while I was with you, but my silence was not sullenness, nor I hope from any bad motive; but, in truth, disuse has made me awkward at it. I know I behaved myself, particularly at Tom Poole's and at Cruikshank's, most like a sulky child; but company and converse are strange to me. It was kind in you all to endure me as you did.

Are you and your dear Sara—to me also very dear, because very kind—agreed yet about the management of little Hartley?

and how go on the little rogue's teeth? I will see White to-morrow, and he shall send you information on that matter; but as perhaps I can do it as well after talking with him, I will keep this letter open.

My love and thanks to you and all of you.

C. L.

III

1798.

February 5th.—Walked to Stowey with Coleridge, returned by Woodlands; a very warm day. In the continued singing of birds distinguished the notes of a blackbird or thrush. The sea overshadowed by a thick dark mist, the land in sunshine. The sheltered oaks and beeches still retaining their brown leaves. Observed some trees putting out red shoots. Query: What trees are they?

12*th.*—Walked alone to Stowey. Returned in the evening with Coleridge. A mild, pleasant, cloudy day.

13*th.*—Walked with Coleridge through the wood. A mild and pleasant morning, the near prospect clear. The ridges of the hills fringed with wood, showing the sea through them like the white sky, and still beyond the dim horizon of the distant hills hanging as it were in one undetermined line between sea and sky.

14*th.*—Gathered sticks with William in the wood, he being unwell and not able to go further. The young birch trees of a bright red, through which gleams a shade of purple. Sat down in a thick part of the wood. The near trees still, even to their topmost boughs, but a perpetual motion in those that skirt the wood. The breeze rose gently; its path distinctly marked, till it came to the very spot where we were.

17*th.*—A deep snow upon the ground. Wm. and Coleridge walked to Mr Bartholomew's, and to Stowey. Wm. returned, and we walked through the wood into the Coombe to fetch some eggs. The sun shone bright and clear. A deep stillness in the thickest part of the wood, undisturbed except by the occasional dropping of the snow from the holly boughs; no other sound but that of the water, and the slender notes of a redbreast, which sang at intervals on the outskirts of the southern side of the wood. There the bright green moss was bare at the roots of the trees, and the little birds were upon it. The whole appearance of the wood was enchanting; and each tree, taken singly, was beautiful. The branches of the hollies pendent with their white burden, but still showing their bright red berries, and their glossy green leaves. The bare branches of the oaks thickened by the snow.

22nd.—Coleridge came in the morning to dinner. Wm. and I walked after dinner to Woodlands; the moon and two planets; sharp and frosty. Met a razor-grinder with a soldier's jacket on, a knapsack on his back, and a boy to drag his wheel. The sea very black, and making a loud noise as we came through the wood, loud as if disturbed, and the wind was silent.

23rd.—William walked with Coleridge in the morning. I did not go out.

27th.—I walked to Stowey in the evening. Wm. and Basil went with me through the wood. The prospect bright, yet *mildly* beautiful. The sea big and white, swelled to the very shores, but round and high in the middle. Coleridge returned with me, as far as the wood. A very bright moonlight night. Venus almost like another moon. Lost to us at Alfoxden long before she goes down the large white sea.

March 6th.—A pleasant morning, the sea white and bright, and full to the brim. I walked to see Coleridge in the evening. William went with me to the wood. Coleridge very ill. It was a mild, pleasant afternoon, but the evening became very foggy; when I was near Woodlands, the fog overhead became thin, and I saw the shapes of the Central Stars. Again it closed, and the whole sky was the same.

7th.—William and I drank tea at Coleridge's. A cloudy sky. Observed nothing particularly interesting—the distant prospect obscured. One only leaf upon the top of a tree—the sole remaining leaf—danced round and round like a rag blown by the wind.

11th.—A cold day. The children went down towards the sea. William and I walked to the top of the hills above Holford. Met the blacksmith. Pleasant to see the labourer on Sunday jump with the friskiness of a cow upon a sunny day.

18*th.*—The Coleridges left us. A cold, windy morning. Walked with them half way. On our return, sheltered among the hollies, during a hail-shower. The withered leaves danced with the hailstones. William wrote a description of the storm.[1]

19*th.*—Wm. and Basil and I walked to the hill-tops, a very cold bleak day. We were met on our return by a severe hailstorm. William wrote some lines describing a stunted thorn.[2]

23*rd.*—Coleridge dined with us. He brought his ballad[3] finished. We walked with him to the Miner's house. A beautiful evening, very starry, the horned moon.

April 2nd.—A very high wind. Coleridge came to avoid the smoke; stayed all night. We walked in the wood, and sat under the trees. The half of the wood perfectly still, while the wind was making a loud noise behind us. The still trees only gently bowed their heads, as if listening to the wind. The hollies in the thick wood unshaken by the blast; only, when it came with a greater force, shaken by the rain drops falling from the bare oaks above.

18*th.*—Walked in the wood, a fine sunny morning, met Coleridge returned from his brother's. He dined with us. We drank tea, and then walked with him nearly to Stowey.

20*th.*—Walked in the evening up the hill dividing the Coombes. Came home the Crookham way, by the thorn, and "the little muddy pond". Nine o'clock at our return. William all the morning engaged in wearisome composition. The moon crescent. *Peter Bell* begun.

24*th.*—Walked a considerable time in the wood. Sat under the trees, in the evening walked on the top of the hill, found Coleridge on our return and walked with him towards Stowey.

May 6th, Sunday.—Expected the painter, and Coleridge. A rainy morning—very pleasant in the evening. Met Cole-

[1] The lines beginning "A whirl-blast from behind the hill".

[2] The opening stanzas of *The Thorn.*

[3] *The Rime of the Ancient Mariner.*

ridge as we were walking out. Went with him to Stowey; heard the nightingale; saw a glow-worm.

Wednesday, 16th May.—Coleridge, William and myself set forward to the Chedder rocks; slept at Bridgewater.

DOROTHY WORDSWORTH'S *Journal*

IV

HAZLITT'S FIRST ACQUAINTANCE WITH POETS

My father was a Dissenting Minister at W[e]m in Shropshire; and in the year 1798 (the figures that compose that date are to me like the "dreaded name of Demogorgon") Mr Coleridge came to Shrewsbury, to succeed Mr Rowe in the spiritual charge of a Unitarian Congregation there. He did not come till late on the Saturday afternoon before he was to preach; and Mr Rowe, who himself went down to the coach in a state of anxiety and expectation, to look for the arrival of his successor, could find no one at all answering the description but a round-faced man in a short black coat (like a shooting jacket) which hardly seemed to have been made for him, but who seemed to be talking at a great rate to his fellow-passengers. Mr Rowe had scarce returned to give an account of his disappointment, when the round-faced man in black entered, and dissipated all doubts on the subject, by beginning to talk. He did not cease while he staid; nor has he since, that I know of. He held the good town of Shrewsbury in delightful suspense for three weeks that he remained there, "fluttering the *proud Salopians* like an eagle in a dove-cote"; and the Welsh mountains that skirt the horizon with their tempestuous confusion, agree to have heard no such mystic sounds since the days of

> High-born Hoel's harp or soft Llewellyn's lay!

As we passed along between W[e]m and Shrewsbury, and I eyed their blue tops seen through the wintry branches, or the red rustling leaves of the sturdy oak-trees by the road-side, a sound was in my ears as of a Siren's song; I was stunned, startled with it, as from deep sleep; but I had no notion then that I should ever be able to express my admiration to others in motley imagery or quaint allusion, till the light of his genius shone into my soul, like the sun's rays glittering in the puddles of the road. I was at that time dumb, inarticulate, helpless, like a worm by the way-side, crushed, bleeding, lifeless; but now, bursting from the deadly bands that bound them,

With Styx nine times round them,

my ideas float on winged words, and as they expand their plumes, catch the golden light of other years. My soul has indeed remained in its original bondage, dark, obscure, with longings infinite and unsatisfied; my heart, shut up in the prison-house of this rude clay, has never found, nor will it ever find, a heart to speak to; but that my understanding also did not remain dumb and brutish, or at length found a language to express itself, I owe to Coleridge. But this is not to my purpose.

My father lived ten miles from Shrewsbury, and was in the habit of exchanging visits with Mr Rowe, and with Mr Jenkins of Whitchurch (nine miles farther on) according to the custom of Dissenting Ministers in each other's neighbourhood. A line of communication is thus established, by which the flame of civil and religious liberty is kept alive, and nourishes its smouldering fire unquenchable, like the fires in the Agamemnon of Æschylus, placed at different stations, that waited for ten long years to announce with their blazing pyramids the destruction of Troy. Coleridge had agreed to come over to see my father, according to the courtesy of the country, as Mr Rowe's probable successor; but in the meantime I had gone to hear him preach the Sunday after his arrival. A poet and a philosopher getting up into a Unitarian pulpit to preach the Gospel, was a romance in these degenerate days, a sort of revival of the primitive spirit of Christianity, which was not to be resisted.

It was in January, 1798, that I rose one morning before daylight, to walk ten miles in the mud, and went to hear this celebrated person preach. Never, the longest day I have to live, shall I have such another walk as this cold, raw, comfortless one, in the winter of the year 1798. *Il y a des impressions que ni le tems ni les circonstances peuvent effacer. Dusse-je vivre des siècles entiers, le doux tems de ma jeunesse ne peut renaître pour moi, ni s'effacer jamais dans ma mémoire.* When I got there, the organ was playing the 100th psalm, and, when it was done, Mr Coleridge rose and gave out his text, "And he went up into the mountain to pray, HIMSELF, ALONE". As he gave out this text, his voice "rose like a stream of rich distilled perfumes", and when he came to the two last words, which he pronounced loud, deep, and distinct, it seemed to me, who was then young, as if the sounds had echoed from the bottom of the human heart, and as if that prayer might have floated in solemn silence through the universe. The idea of St John came into mind, "of one crying in the wilderness, who had his loins girt about, and whose food was locusts and wild honey". The preacher then launched into his subject, like an eagle dallying with the wind. The sermon was upon peace and war; upon church and state—not their alliance, but their separation—on the spirit of the world and the spirit of Christianity, not as the same, but as opposed to one another. He talked of those who had "inscribed the cross of Christ on banners dripping with human gore". He made a poetical and pastoral excursion,—and to shew the fatal effects of war, drew a striking contrast between the simple shepherd boy, driving his team afield, or sitting under the hawthorn, piping to his flock, "as though he should never be old", and the same poor country-lad, crimped, kidnapped, brought into town, made drunk at an alehouse, turned into a wretched drummer-boy, with his hair sticking on end with powder and pomatum, a long cue at his back, and tricked out in the loathsome finery of the profession of blood.

Such were the notes our once-lov'd poet sung.

And for myself, I could not have been more delighted if I had heard the music of the spheres. Poetry and Philosophy had met together. Truth and Genius had embraced, under the eye and with the sanction of Religion. This was even beyond my hopes. I returned home well satisfied. The sun that was still labouring pale and wan through the sky, obscured by thick mists, seemed an emblem of the *good cause*; and the cold dank drops of dew that hung half melted on the beard of the thistle, had something genial and refreshing in them; for there was a spirit of hope and youth in all nature, that turned every thing into good. The face of nature had not then the brand of JUS DIVINUM on it:

Like to that sanguine flower inscrib'd with woe.

On the Tuesday following, the half-inspired speaker came. I was called down into the room where he was, and went half-hoping, half-afraid. He received me very graciously, and I listened for a long time without uttering a word. I did not suffer in his opinion by my silence. "For those two hours", he afterwards was pleased to say, "he was conversing with W. H.'s forehead!" His appearance was different from what I had anticipated from seeing him before. At a distance, and in the dim light of the chapel, there was to me a strange wildness in his aspect, a dusky obscurity, and I thought him pitted with the small-pox. His complexion was at that time clear, and even bright—

As are the children of yon azure sheen.

His forehead was broad and high, light as if built of ivory, with large projecting eyebrows, and his eyes rolling beneath them like a sea with darkened lustre. "A certain tender bloom his face o'erspread", a purple tinge as we see it in the pale thoughtful complexions of the Spanish portrait-painters, Murillo and Velasquez. His mouth was gross, voluptuous, open, eloquent; his chin good-humoured and round; but his nose, the rudder of the face, the index of the will, was small, feeble, nothing—like what he has done. It might seem that the genius of his face as from a height surveyed and projected him (with sufficient capacity and huge aspiration) into the world unknown of thought and imagination, with nothing to support or guide his veering purpose, as if Columbus had launched his adventurous course for the New World in a scallop, without oars or compass. So at least I comment on it after the event. Coleridge in his person was rather above the common size, inclining to the corpulent, or like Lord Hamlet, "somewhat fat and pursy". His hair (now, alas! grey) was then black and glossy as the raven's, and fell in smooth masses over his forehead. This long pendulous hair is peculiar to enthusiasts, to those whose minds tend heavenward; and is traditionally inseparable (though of a different colour) from the pictures of Christ. It ought to belong, as a character, to all who preach *Christ crucified*, and Coleridge was at that time one of those!...

No two individuals were ever more unlike than were the host and his guest. A poet was to my father a sort of nondescript: yet whatever added grace to the Unitarian cause was to him welcome. He could hardly have been more surprised or pleased, if our visitor had worn wings. Indeed, his thoughts had wings; and as the silken sounds rustled round our little wainscoted parlour, my father threw back his spectacles over his forehead, his white hairs mixing with its sanguine hue; and a smile of delight beamed across his rugged cordial face, to think that Truth had found a new ally in Fancy! Besides, Coleridge seemed to take considerable notice of me; and that of itself was enough. He talked very familiarly, but agreeably, and glanced over a variety of subjects. At dinner-time he grew more animated, and dilated in a very edifying manner on Mary Wolstonecraft and Mackintosh. The last, he said, he considered (on my father's speaking of his *Vindiciæ Gallicæ* as a capital performance) as a clever scholastic man—a master of the topics,—or as the ready warehouseman of letters, who knew exactly where to lay his hand on what he wanted, though the goods were not his own. He thought him no match for Burke, either in style or matter. Burke was a metaphysician, Mackintosh a mere logician. Burke was an orator (almost a poet) who reasoned in figures, because he had an eye for nature: Mackintosh, on the other hand, was a rhetorician, who had only an eye to common-places. On this I ventured to say that I had always entertained a great opinion of Burke, and that (as far as I could find) the speaking of him with contempt might be made the test of a vulgar democratical mind. This was the first observation I ever made to Coleridge, and he said it was a very just and striking one. I remember the leg of Welsh mutton and the turnips on the table that day had the finest flavour imaginable. Coleridge added that Mackintosh and Tom Wedgwood (of whom, however, he spoke highly) had expressed a very indifferent opinion of his friend Mr Wordsworth, on which he remarked to them—"He strides on so far before you, that he dwindles in the distance!" Godwin had once boasted to him of having carried on an argument with Mackintosh for three hours with dubious success; Coleridge told him—"If there had been a man of genius in the room, he would have settled the question in five minutes". He asked me if I had ever seen Mary Wolstonecraft, and I said, I had once for a few moments, and that she seemed to me to turn off Godwin's objections to something she advanced with quite a playful, easy air. He replied, that "this was only one instance of the ascendancy which people of imagination exercised over those of mere intellect". He did not rate Godwin very high[1] (this was caprice or prejudice, real or affected) but he had a great idea of Mrs Wolstonecraft's powers of conversation, none at all of her talent for book-making. We talked a little about Holcroft. He had been asked if he was not much struck *with* him, and he said, he thought himself in more danger of being struck *by* him. I complained that he would not let me get on at all, for he required a definition of every the commonest word, exclaiming, "What do you mean by a *sensation*, Sir? What do you mean by an *idea*?" This, Coleridge said, was barricadoing the road to truth:—it was setting up a turnpike-gate at every step we took. I forget a great number of things, many more than I remember; but the day passed off pleasantly, and the next morning Mr Coleridge was to return to Shrewsbury. When I came down to breakfast, I found that he had just received a letter from his friend T. Wedgwood, making

[1] He complained in particular of the presumption of attempting to establish the future immortality of man "without" (as he said) "knowing what Death was or what Life was"—and the tone in which he pronounced these two words seemed to convey a complete image of both. [Hazlitt.]

him an offer of 150*l*. a-year if he chose to waive his present pursuit, and devote himself entirely to the study of poetry and philosophy. Coleridge seemed to make up his mind to close with this proposal in the act of tying on one of his shoes. It threw an additional damp on his departure. It took the wayward enthusiast quite from us to cast him into Deva's winding vales, or by the shores of old romance. Instead of living at ten miles distance, of being the pastor of a Dissenting congregation at Shrewsbury, he was henceforth to inhabit the Hill of Parnassus, to be a Shepherd on the Delectable Mountains. Alas! I knew not the way thither, and felt very little gratitude for Mr Wedgwood's bounty. I was presently relieved from this dilemma; for Mr Coleridge, asking for a pen and ink, and going to a table to write something on a bit of card, advanced towards me with undulating step, and giving me the precious document, said that that was his address, *Mr Coleridge, Nether-Stowey, Somersetshire*; and that he should be glad to see me there in a few weeks' time, and, if I chose, would come half-way to meet me. I was not less surprised than the shepherd-boy (this simile is to be found in Cassandra) when he sees a thunder-bolt fall close at his feet. I stammered out my acknowledgments and acceptance of this offer (I thought Mr Wedgwood's annuity a trifle to it) as well as I could; and this mighty business being settled, the poet-preacher took leave, and I accompanied him six miles on the road. It was a fine morning in the middle of winter, and he talked the whole way. The scholar in Chaucer is described as going

——Sounding on his way.

So Coleridge went on his. In digressing, in dilating, in passing from subject to subject, he appeared to me to float in air, to slide on ice. He told me in confidence (going along) that he should have preached two sermons before he accepted the situation at Shrewsbury, one on Infant Baptism, the other on the Lord's Supper, shewing that he could not administer either, which would have effectually disqualified him for the object in view. I observed that he continually crossed me on the way by shifting from one side of the foot-path to the other. This struck me as an odd movement; but I did not at that time connect it with any instability of purpose or involuntary change of principle, as I have done since. He seemed unable to keep on in a strait line. He spoke slightingly of Hume (whose Essay on Miracles he said was stolen from an objection started in one of South's sermons—*Credat Judæus Apella!*). I was not very much pleased at this account of Hume, for I had just been reading, with infinite relish, that completest of all metaphysical *choke-pears*, his *Treatise on Human Nature*, to which the *Essays*, in point of scholastic subtlety and close reasoning, are mere elegant trifling, light summer-reading. Coleridge even denied the excellence of Hume's general style, which I think betrayed a want of taste or candour. He however made me amends by the manner in which he spoke of Berkeley. He dwelt particularly on his *Essay on Vision* as a masterpiece of analytical reasoning. So it undoubtedly is. He was exceedingly angry with Dr Johnson for striking the stone with his foot, in allusion to this author's Theory of Matter and Spirit, and saying, "Thus I confute him, Sir". Coleridge drew a parallel (I don't know how he brought about the connection) between Bishop Berkeley and Tom Paine. He said the one was an instance of a subtle, the other of an acute mind, than which no two things could be more distinct. The one was a shop-boy's quality, the other the characteristic of a philosopher. He considered Bishop Butler as a true philosopher, a profound and conscientious thinker, a genuine reader of nature and of his own mind. He did not speak of his *Analogy*, but of his *Sermons at the Rolls' Chapel*, of which I had never heard. Coleridge somehow always contrived to prefer the *unknown* to the *known*. In this instance he was right. The *Analogy* is a tissue of sophistry, of wire-drawn, theological special-pleading; the *Sermons* (with the Preface to them) are in a fine vein of deep, matured reflection, a candid appeal to our observation of human nature, without pedantry and without bias. I told Coleridge I had written a few remarks, and was sometimes foolish enough to believe that I had made a discovery on the same subject (the *Natural Disinterestedness of the Human Mind*)

—and I tried to explain my view of it to Coleridge, who listened with great willingness, but I did not succeed in making myself understood. I sat down to the task shortly afterwards for the twentieth time, got new pens and paper, determined to make clear work of it, wrote a few meagre sentences in the skeleton-style of a mathematical demonstration, stopped half-way down the second page; and, after trying in vain to pump up any words, images, notions, apprehensions, facts, or observations, from that gulph of abstraction in which I had plunged myself for four or five years preceding, gave up the attempt as labour in vain, and shed tears of helpless despondency on the blank unfinished paper. I can write fast enough now. Am I better than I was then? Oh no! One truth discovered, one pang of regret at not being able to express it, is better than all the fluency and flippancy in the world. Would that I could go back to what I then was! Why can we not revive past times as we can revisit old places? If I had the quaint Muse of Sir Philip Sidney to assist me, I would write a *Sonnet to the Road between W[e]m and Shrewsbury*, and immortalise every step of it by some fond enigmatical conceit. I would swear that the very milestones had ears, and that Harmer-hill stooped with all its pines, to listen to a poet, as he passed! I remember but one other topic of discourse in this walk. He mentioned Paley, praised the naturalness and clearness of his style, but condemned his sentiments, thought him a mere time-serving casuist, and said that "the fact of his work on Moral and Political Philosophy being made a text-book in our Universities was a disgrace to the national character". We parted at the six-mile stone; and I returned homeward pensive but much pleased. I had met with unexpected notice from a person, whom I believed to have been prejudiced against me. "Kind and affable to me had been his condescension, and should be honoured ever with suitable regard." He was the first poet I had known, and he certainly answered to that inspired name. I had heard a great deal of his powers of conversation, and was not disappointed. In fact, I never met with any thing at all like them, either before or since. I could easily credit the accounts which were circulated of his holding forth to a large party of ladies and gentlemen, an evening or two before, on the Berkeleian Theory, when he made the whole material universe look like a transparency of fine words; and another story (which I believe he has somewhere told himself) of his being asked to a party at Birmingham, of his smoking tobacco and going to sleep after dinner on a sofa, where the company found him to their no small surprise, which was increased to wonder when he started up of a sudden, and rubbing his eyes, looked about him, and launched into a three-hours' description of the third heaven, of which he had had a dream, very different from Mr Southey's Vision of Judgment, and also from that other Vision of Judgment, which Mr Murray, the Secretary of the Bridge-street Junto, has taken into his especial keeping!

On my way back, I had a sound in my ears, it was the voice of Fancy: I had a light before me, it was the face of Poetry. The one still lingers there, the other has not quitted my side! Coleridge in truth met me half-way on the ground of philosophy, or I should not have been won over to his imaginative creed. I had an uneasy, pleasurable sensation all the time, till I was to visit him. During those months the chill breath of winter gave me a welcoming; the vernal air was balm and inspiration to me. The golden sunsets, the silver star of evening, lighted me on my way to new hopes and prospects. *I was to visit Coleridge in the spring.* This circumstance was never absent from my thoughts, and mingled with all my feelings. I wrote to him at the time proposed, and received an answer postponing my intended visit for a week or two, but very cordially urging me to complete my promise then. This delay did not damp, but rather increased my ardour. In the meantime, I went to Llangollen Vale, by way of initiating myself in the mysteries of natural scenery; and I must say I was enchanted with it. I had been reading Coleridge's description of England in his fine *Ode on the Departing Year*, and I applied it, *con amore*, to the objects before me. That valley was to me (in a manner) the cradle of a new existence: in the river that winds through it, my spirit was baptised in the waters of Helicon!

I returned home, and soon after set out on my journey with unworn heart and untired feet. My way lay through Worcester and Gloucester, and by Upton, where I thought of Tom Jones and the adventure of the muff. I remember getting completely wet through one day, and stopping at an inn (I think it was at Tewkesbury) where I sat up all night to read Paul and Virginia. Sweet were the showers in early youth that drenched my body, and sweet the drops of pity that fell upon the books I read! I recollect a remark of Coleridge's upon this very book, that nothing could shew the gross indelicacy of French manners and the entire corruption of their imagination more strongly than the behaviour of the heroine in the last fatal scene, who turns away from a person on board the sinking vessel, that offers to save her life, because he has thrown off his clothes to assist him in swimming. Was this a time to think of such a circumstance! I once hinted to Wordsworth, as we were sailing in his boat on Grasmere lake, that I thought he had borrowed the idea of his *Poems on the Naming of Places* from the local inscriptions of the same kind in Paul and Virginia. He did not own the obligation, and stated some distinction without a difference, in defence of his claim to originality. Any the slightest variation would be sufficient for this purpose in his mind; for whatever *he* added or omitted would inevitably be worth all that any one else had done, and contain the marrow of the sentiment. I was still two days before the time fixed for my arrival, for I had taken care to set out early enough. I stopped these two days at Bridgewater, and when I was tired of sauntering on the banks of its muddy river, returned to the inn, and read Camilla. So have I loitered my life away, reading books, looking at pictures, going to plays, hearing, thinking, writing on what pleased me best. I have wanted only one thing to make me happy; but wanting that, have wanted everything!

I arrived, and was well received. The country about Nether Stowey is beautiful, green and hilly, and near the sea-shore. I saw it but the other day, after an interval of twenty years, from a hill near Taunton. How was the map of my life spread out before me, as the map of the country lay at my feet! In the afternoon, Coleridge took me over to All-Foxden, a romantic old family-mansion of the St Aubins, where Wordsworth lived. It was then in the possession of a friend of the poet's, who gave him the free use of it. Somehow that period (the time just after the French Revolution) was not a time when *nothing was given for nothing*. The mind opened, and a softness might be perceived coming over the heart of individuals, beneath "the scales that fence" our self-interest. Wordsworth himself was from home, but his sister kept house, and set before us a frugal repast; and we had free access to her brother's poems, the *Lyrical Ballads*, which were still in manuscript, or in the form of *Sybilline Leaves*. I dipped into a few of these with great satisfaction, and with the faith of a novice. I slept that night in an old room with blue hangings, and covered with the round-faced family-portraits of the age of George I and II, and from the wooded declivity of the adjoining park that overlooked my window, at the dawn of day, could

——hear the loud stag speak.

In the outset of life (and particularly at this time I felt it so) our imagination has a body to it. We are in a state between sleeping and waking, and have indistinct but glorious glimpses of strange shapes, and there is always something to come better than what we see. As in our dreams the fulness of the blood gives warmth and reality to the coinage of the brain, so in youth our ideas are clothed, and fed, and pampered with our good spirits; we breathe thick with thoughtless happiness, the weight of future years presses on the strong pulses of the heart, and we repose with undisturbed faith in truth and good. As we advance, we exhaust our fund of enjoyment and of hope. We are no longer wrapped in *lamb's-wool*, lulled in Elysium. As we taste the pleasures of life, their spirit evaporates, the sense palls; and nothing is left but the phantoms, the lifeless shadows of what *has been*!

That morning, as soon as breakfast was over, we strolled out into the park, and seating ourselves on the trunk of an old ash-tree that stretched along the ground, Coleridge read aloud, with a sonorous and musical voice, the ballad of *Betty Foy*. I was not critically or sceptically inclined. I saw touches of truth and nature, and took the rest for granted. But in the *Thorn*, the *Mad Mother*, and the *Complaint of a Poor Indian Woman*, I felt that deeper power and pathos which have been since acknowledged,

> In spite of pride, in erring reason's spite,

as the characteristics of this author; and the sense of a new style and a new spirit in poetry came over me. It had to me something of the effect that arises from the turning up of the fresh soil, or of the first welcome breath of Spring,

> While yet the trembling year is unconfirmed.

Coleridge and myself walked back to Stowey that evening, and his voice sounded high

> Of Providence, foreknowledge, will, and fate,
> Fix'd fate, free-will, foreknowledge absolute,

as we passed through echoing grove, by fairy stream or waterfall, gleaming in the summer moonlight! He lamented that Wordsworth was not prone enough to believe in the traditional superstitions of the place, and that there was a something corporeal, a *matter-of-fact-ness*, a clinging to the palpable, or often to the petty, in his poetry, in consequence. His genius was not a spirit that descended to him through the air; it sprung out of the ground like a flower, or unfolded itself from a green spray, on which the gold-finch sang. He said, however (if I remember right), that this objection must be confined to his descriptive pieces, that his philosophic poetry had a grand and comprehensive spirit in it, so that his soul seemed to inhabit the universe like a palace, and to discover truth by intuition, rather than by deduction. The next day Wordsworth arrived from Bristol at Coleridge's cottage. I think I see him now. He answered in some degree to his friend's description of him, but was more gaunt and Don Quixote-like. He was quaintly dressed (according to the *costume* of that unconstrained period) in a brown fustian

LIBRARY ST. MARY'S COLLEGE

jacket and striped pantaloons. There was something of a roll, a lounge in his gait, not unlike his own Peter Bell. There was a severe, worn pressure of thought about his temples, a fire in his eye (as if he saw something in objects more than the outward appearance), an intense high narrow forehead, a Roman nose, cheeks furrowed by strong purpose and feeling, and a convulsive inclination to laughter about the mouth, a good deal at variance with the solemn, stately expression of the rest of his face. Chantry's bust wants the marking traits; but he was teazed into making it regular and heavy: Haydon's head of him, introduced into the *Entrance of Christ into Jerusalem,* is the most like his drooping weight of thought and expression. He sat down and talked very naturally and freely, with a mixture of clear gushing accents in his voice, a deep guttural intonation, and a strong tincture of the northern *burr,* like the crust on wine. He instantly began to make havoc of the half of a Cheshire cheese on the table, and said triumphantly that "his marriage with experience had not been so unproductive as Mr Southey's in teaching him a knowledge of the good things of this life". He had been to see the *Castle Spectre* by Monk Lewis, while at Bristol, and described it very well. He said "it fitted the taste of the audience like a glove". This *ad captandum* merit was however by no means a recommendation of it, according to the severe principles of the new school, which reject rather than court popular effect. Wordsworth, looking out of the low, latticed window, said, "How beautifully the sun sets on that yellow bank!" I thought within myself, "With what eyes these poets see nature!" and ever after, when I saw the sun-set stream upon the objects facing it, conceived I had made a discovery, or thanked Mr Wordsworth for having made one for me! We went over to All-Foxden again the day following, and Wordsworth read us the story of Peter Bell in the open air; and the comment made upon it by his face and voice was very different from that of some later critics! Whatever might be thought of the poem, "his face was as a book where men might read strange matters", and he announced the fate of his hero in prophetic tones. There is a *chaunt* in the recitation both of Coleridge and Wordsworth, which acts as a spell upon the hearer, and disarms the judgment. Perhaps they have deceived themselves by making habitual use of this ambiguous accompaniment. Coleridge's manner is more full, animated, and varied; Wordsworth's more equable, sustained, and internal. The one might be termed more *dramatic*, the other more *lyrical*. Coleridge has told me that he himself liked to compose in walking over uneven ground, or breaking through the straggling branches of a copse-wood; whereas Wordsworth always wrote (if he could) walking up and down a straight gravel-walk, or in some spot where the continuity of his verse met with no collateral interruption. Returning that same evening, I got into a metaphysical argument with Wordsworth, while Coleridge was explaining the different notes of the nightingale to his sister, in which we neither of us succeeded in making ourselves perfectly clear and intelligible. Thus I passed three weeks at Nether Stowey and in the neighbourhood, generally devoting the afternoons to a delightful chat in an arbour made of bark by the poet's friend Tom Poole, sitting under two fine elm-trees, and listening to the bees humming round us, while we quaffed our *flip*. It was agreed, among other things, that we should make a jaunt down the Bristol-Channel, as far as Linton. We set off together on foot, Coleridge, John Chester, and I. This Chester was a native of Nether Stowey, one of those who were attracted to Coleridge's discourse as flies are to honey, or bees in swarming-time to the sound of a brass pan. He "followed in the chase, like a dog who hunts, not like one that made up the cry". He had on a brown cloth coat, boots, and corduroy breeches, was low in stature, bow-legged, had a drag in his walk like a drover, which he assisted by a hazel switch, and kept on a sort of trot by the side of Coleridge, like a running footman by a state coach, that he might not lose a syllable or sound that fell from Coleridge's lips. He told me his private opinion, that Coleridge was a wonderful man. He scarcely opened his lips, much less offered an opinion the whole way: yet of the three, had I to chuse during that journey, I would be John Chester. He afterwards followed Coleridge into Germany, where the Kantean philosophers were puzzled how to bring him under any of their categories. When he sat down at table with his idol, John's felicity was complete; Sir Walter Scott's, or Mr Blackwood's, when they sat down at the same table with the King, was not more so. We passed Dunster on our right, a small town between the brow of a hill and the sea. I remember eying it wistfully as it lay below us: contrasted with the woody scene around, it looked as clear, as pure, as *embrowned* and ideal as any landscape I have seen since, of Gaspar Poussin's or Domenichino's. We had a long day's march—(our feet kept time to the echoes of Coleridge's tongue)—through Minehead and by the Blue Anchor, and on to Linton, which we did not reach till near midnight, and where we had some difficulty in making a lodgment. We however knocked the people of the house up at last, and we were repaid for our apprehensions and fatigue by some excellent rashers of fried bacon and eggs. The view in coming along had been splendid. We walked for miles and miles on dark brown heaths overlooking the Channel, with the Welsh hills beyond, and at times descended into little sheltered valleys close by the seaside, with a smuggler's face scowling by us, and then had to ascend conical hills with a path winding up through a coppice to a barren top, like a monk's shaven crown, from one of which I pointed out to Coleridge's notice the bare masts of a vessel on the very edge of the horizon and within the red-orbed disk of the setting sun, like his own spectre-ship in the *Ancient Mariner*. At Linton the character of the sea-coast becomes more marked and rugged. There is a place called the *Valley of Rocks* (I suspect this was only the poetical name for it) bedded among precipices overhanging the sea, with rocky caverns beneath, into which the waves dash, and where the sea-gull for ever wheels its screaming flight. On the tops of these are huge stones thrown transverse, as if an earthquake had tossed them there, and behind these is a fretwork of perpendicular rocks, something like the *Giant's Causeway*. A thunder-storm came on while we were at the inn, and Coleridge was running out bare-headed to enjoy the commotion of the elements in the

Valley of Rocks, but as if in spite, the clouds only muttered a few angry sounds, and let fall a few refreshing drops. Coleridge told me that he and Wordsworth were to have made this place the scene of a prose-tale, which was to have been in the manner of, but far superior to, the *Death of Abel*, but they had relinquished the design. In the morning of the second day, we breakfasted luxuriously in an old-fashioned parlour, on tea, toast, eggs, and honey, in the very sight of the bee-hives from which it had been taken, and a garden full of thyme and wild flowers that had produced it. On this occasion Coleridge spoke of Virgil's Georgics, but not well. I do not think he had much feeling for the classical or elegant. It was in this room that we found a little worn-out copy of the *Seasons*, lying in a window-seat, on which Coleridge exclaimed, "*That* is true fame!" He said Thomson was a great poet, rather than a good one; his style was as meretricious as his thoughts were natural. He spoke of Cowper as the best modern poet. He said the *Lyrical Ballads* were an experiment about to be tried by him and Wordsworth, to see how far the public taste would endure poetry written in a more natural and simple style than had hitherto been attempted; totally discarding the artifices of poetical diction, and making use only of such words as had probably been common in the most ordinary language since the days of Henry II. Some comparison was introduced between Shakespear and Milton. He said "he hardly knew which to prefer. Shakespear appeared to him a mere stripling in the art; he was as tall and as strong, with infinitely more activity than Milton, but he never appeared to have come to man's estate; or if he had, he would not have been a man, but a monster". He spoke with contempt of Gray, and with intolerance of Pope. He did not like the versification of the latter. He observed that "the ears of these couplet-writers might be charged with having short memories, that could not retain the harmony of whole passages". He thought little of Junius as a writer; he had a dislike of Dr Johnson; and a much higher opinion of Burke as an orator and politician, than of Fox or Pitt. He however thought him very inferior in richness of style and imagery to some of our elder prose-writers, particularly Jeremy Taylor. He liked Richardson, but not Fielding; nor could I get him to enter into the merits of *Caleb Williams.*[1] In short, he was profound and discriminating with respect to those authors whom he liked, and where he gave his judgment fair play; capricious, perverse, and prejudiced in his antipathies and distastes. We loitered on the "ribbed sea-sands", in such talk as this, a whole morning, and I recollect met with a curious sea-weed, of which John Chester told us the country name! A fisherman gave Coleridge an account of a boy that had been drowned the day before, and that they had tried to save him at the risk of their own lives. He said "he did not know how it was that they ventured, but, Sir, we have a *nature* towards one another". This expression, Coleridge remarked to me, was a fine illustration of that theory of disinterestedness which I (in common with Butler) had adopted. I broached to him an argument of mine to prove that *likeness* was not mere association of ideas. I said that the mark in the sand put one in mind of a man's foot, not because it was part of a former impression of a man's foot (for it was quite new) but because it was like the shape of a man's foot. He assented to the justness of this distinction (which I have explained at length elsewhere, for the benefit of the curious) and John Chester listened; not from any interest in the subject, but because he was astonished that I should be able to suggest any thing to Coleridge that he did not already know. We returned on the third morning, and Coleridge remarked the silent cottage-smoke curling up the valleys where, a few evenings before, we had seen the lights gleaming through the dark.

In a day or two after we arrived at Stowey, we set out, I on my return home, and he for Germany. It was a Sunday morning, and he was to preach that day for Dr Toulmin of

[1] He had no idea of pictures, of Claude or Raphael, and at this time I had as little as he. He sometimes gives a striking account at present of the Cartoons at Pisa, by Buffamalco and others; of one in particular, where Death is seen in the air brandishing his scythe, and the great and mighty of the earth shudder at his approach, while the beggars and the wretched kneel to him as their deliverer. He would of course understand so broad and fine a moral as this at any time. [Hazlitt.]

Taunton. I asked him if he had prepared anything for the occasion? He said he had not even thought of the text, but should as soon as we parted. I did not go to hear him,—this was a fault,—but we met in the evening at Bridgewater. The next day we had a long day's walk to Bristol, and sat down, I recollect, by a well-side on the road, to cool ourselves and satisfy our thirst, when Coleridge repeated to me some descriptive lines from his tragedy of Remorse; which I must say became his mouth and that occasion better than they, some years after, did Mr Elliston's and the Drury-lane boards,—

> Oh memory! shield me from the world's poor strife,
> And give those scenes thine everlasting life.

I saw no more of him for a year or two, during which period he had been wandering in the Hartz Forest in Germany; and his return was cometary, meteorous, unlike his setting out. It was not till some time after that I knew his friends Lamb and Southey. The last always appears to me (as I first saw him) with a common-place book under his arm, and the first with a *bon-mot* in his mouth. It was at Godwin's that I met him with Holcroft and Coleridge, where they were disputing fiercely which was the best—*Man as he was, or man as he is to be.* "Give me", says Lamb, "man as he is *not* to be." This saying was the beginning of a friendship between us, which I believe still continues.—Enough of this for the present.

> But there is matter for another rhyme,
> And I to this may add a second tale.

HAZLITT: *My First Acquaintance with Poets*

V

DOROTHY WORDSWORTH

Child of my parents! Sister of my soul!
Thanks in sincerest verse have been elsewhere
Poured out for all the early tenderness
Which I from thee imbibed: and 'tis most true
That later seasons owed to thee no less;

For, spite of thy sweet influence and the touch
Of kindred hands that opened out the springs
Of genial thought in childhood, and in spite
Of all that unassisted I had marked
In life or nature of those charms minute
That win their way into the heart by stealth,
(Still to the very going-out of youth)
I too exclusively esteemed *that* love,
And sought *that* beauty, which, as Milton sings,
Hath terror in it. Thou didst soften down
This over-sternness; but for thee, dear Friend!
My soul, too reckless of mild grace, had stood
In her original self too confident,
Retained too long a countenance severe;
A rock with torrents roaring, with the clouds
Familiar, and a favourite of the stars:
But thou didst plant its crevices with flowers,
Hang it with shrubs that twinkle in the breeze,
And teach the little birds to build their nests
And warble in its chambers. At a time
When Nature, destined to remain so long
Foremost in my affections, had fallen back
Into a second place, pleased to become
A handmaid to a nobler than herself,
When every day brought with it some new sense
Of exquisite regard for common things,
And all the earth was budding with these gifts
Of more refined humanity, thy breath,
Dear Sister! was a kind of gentler spring
That went before my steps.

WORDSWORTH: *The Prelude*, Bk xiv

VI

COLERIDGE

Whether to me shall be allotted life,
And, with life, power to accomplish aught of worth,
That will be deemed no insufficient plea
For having given the story of myself,
Is all uncertain: but, beloved Friend!
When, looking back, thou seest, in clearer view
Than any liveliest sight of yesterday,
That summer, under whose indulgent skies,
Upon smooth Quantock's airy ridge we roved
Unchecked, or loitered 'mid her sylvan combs,
Thou in bewitching words, with happy heart,
Didst chaunt the vision of that Ancient Man,
The bright-eyed Mariner, and rueful woes
Didst utter of the Lady Christabel;
And I, associate with such labour, steeped
In soft forgetfulness the livelong hours,
Murmuring of him who, joyous hap, was found,
After the perils of his moonlight ride,
Near the loud waterfall; or her who sate
In misery near the miserable Thorn;—
When thou dost to that summer turn thy thoughts,
And hast before thee all which then we were,
To thee, in memory of that happiness,
It will be known, by thee at least, my Friend!
Felt, that the history of a Poet's mind
Is labour not unworthy of regard:
To thee the work shall justify itself.

WORDSWORTH: *The Prelude*, Bk xiv

LAMB AND SOUTHEY

Southey, to whom Coleridge had introduced Lamb in the early days of pantisocracy at the Salutation Tavern, was Lamb's principal correspondent during 1798 and 1799. Southey, like Lamb, was an inveterate reader of old books, as the beginning of the first letter shows.

I

November 8, 1798.

...I perfectly accord with your opinion of old Wither. Quarles is a wittier writer, but Wither lays more hold of the heart. Quarles thinks of his audience when he lectures; Wither soliloquizes in company from a full heart. What wretched stuff are the "Divine Fancies" of Quarles! Religion appears to him no longer valuable than it furnishes matters for quibbles and riddles; he turns God's grace into wantonness. Wither is like an old friend, whose warm-heartedness and estimable qualities make us wish he possessed more genius, but at the same time make us willing to dispense with that want. I always love Wither, and sometimes admire Quarles. Still that portrait poem is a fine one; and the extract from "Shepherds' Hunting" places him in a starry height far above Quarles. If you wrote that review in the *Critical Review*, I am sorry you are so sparing of praise to the *Ancient Marinere*. So far from calling it as you do, with some wit, but more severity, a "Dutch Attempt", &c., I call it a right English attempt, and a successful one, to dethrone German sublimity. You have selected a passage fertile in unmeaning miracles, but have passed by fifty passages as miraculous as the miracles they celebrate. I never so deeply felt the pathetic as in that part,

> A spring of love gush'd from my heart,
> And I bless'd them unaware.

It stung me into high pleasure through sufferings. Lloyd does not like it; his head is too metaphysical, and your taste too correct; at least I must allege something against you both, to excuse my own dotage—

> So lonely 'twas, that God himself
> Scarce seem'd there to be!—&c., &c.

But you allow some elaborate beauties: you should have extracted 'em. The *Ancient Marinere* plays more tricks with the mind than that last poem, which is yet one of the finest written. But I am getting too dogmatical; and before I degenerate into abuse, I will conclude with assuring you that I am

Sincerely yours,

C. Lamb

II

October 31, 1799.

Dear Southey,—I have but just got your letter, being returned from Herts, where I have passed a few red-letter days with much pleasure. I would describe the county to you, as you have done by Devonshire; but alas! I am a poor pen at that same. I could tell you of an old house with a tapestry bedroom, the "Judgment of Solomon" composing one panel, and "Actæon spying Diana naked" the other. I could tell of an old marble hall, with Hogarth's prints, and the Roman Cæsars in marble hung round. I could tell of a *wilderness*, and of a village church, and where the bones of my honoured grandam lie; but there are feelings which refuse to be translated, sulky aborigines, which will not be naturalized in another soil. Of this nature are old family faces, and scenes of infancy.

I have given your address, and the books you want, to the Arches; they will send them as soon as they can get them, but they do not seem quite familiar to their names. I have seen Gebor! Gebor aptly so denominated from Geborish, *quasi* Gibberish. But Gebor hath some lucid intervals. I remember darkly one beautiful simile veiled in uncouth phrases about the youngest daughter of the Ark. I shall have nothing to communicate, I fear, to the Anthology. You shall have some fragments of my play,[1] if you desire them; but I think I would rather print it whole. Have you seen it, or shall I lend you a copy? I want your opinion of it.

I must get to business; so farewell. My kind remembrances to Edith.

C. Lamb

THE LAKES

The Wordsworths, after a tour of Germany with Coleridge, settled at Dove Cottage, near Grasmere, at the end of 1799, and in August of the next year Coleridge took Greta Hall at Keswick. Here he was joined by Southey in 1803.

I

1800.

Wednesday (*27th June*).—A very rainy day. I made a shoe. Wm. and John went to fish in Langdale. In the evening I went above the house, and gathered flowers, which I planted, foxgloves, etc. On Sunday Mr and Mrs Coleridge came. The day was very warm. We sailed to the foot of Loughrigg. They staid with us three weeks, and till the Thursday following, from 1st till the 23rd of July. On the Friday preceding their departure, we drank tea at the island. The weather was delightful, and on the Sunday we made a great fire, and drank tea in Bainriggs with the Simpsons. I accompanied Mrs C. to Wytheburne, and returned with W. to tea at Mr Simpson's. It was exceedingly hot, but the day after, Friday 24th July, still hotter. All the morning I was engaged in unpacking our Somersetshire goods. The house was a hot oven. I was so weary, I could not walk: so I went out, and sate with Wm. in the orchard. We had a delightful half-hour in the warm still evening.

Monday (*28th July*).—Received a letter from Coleridge enclosing one from Mr Davy about the *Lyrical Ballads.*

[1] *John Woodvil.*

Intensely hot. . . . William went into the wood, and altered his poems.

Thursday (*31st July*).—All the morning I was busy copying poems. Gathered peas, and in the afternoon Coleridge came. He brought the second volume of the Anthology. The men went to bathe, and we afterwards sailed down to Loughrigg. Read poems on the water, and let the boat take its own course. We walked a long time upon Loughrigg. I returned in the grey twilight. The moon just setting as we reached home.

Friday, 1st August.—In the morning I copied *The Brothers*. Coleridge and Wm. went down to the lake. They returned, and we all went together to Mary Point, where we sate in the breeze, and the shade, and read Wm.'s poems. Altered *The Whirlblast*, etc. We drank tea in the orchard.

Saturday Morning, 2nd.—Wm. and Coleridge went to Keswick. John went with them to Wytheburn, and staid all day fishing, and brought home 2 small pikes at night. I accompanied them to Lewthwaite's cottage, and on my return papered Wm.'s rooms. . . . About 8 o'clock it gathered for rain, and I had the scatterings of a shower, but afterwards the lake became of a glassy calmness, and all was still. I sate till I could see no longer, and then continued my work in the house.

Sunday, 31st.—. . . A great deal of corn is cut in the vale, and the whole prospect, though not tinged with a general autumnal yellow, yet softened down into a mellowness of colouring, which seems to impart softness to the forms of hills and mountains. At 11 o'clock Coleridge came, when I was walking in the still clear moonshine of the garden. He came over Helvellyn. Wm. was gone to bed, and John also, worn out with his ride round Coniston. We sate and chatted till half-past three,. . . Coleridge reading a part of *Christabel.* Talked much about the mountains, etc., etc.

Friday, 3rd October.—Very rainy all the morning. Wm. walked to Ambleside after dinner. I went with him part of the way. He talked much about the object of his essay for the second volume of "L. B.". . . .

N.B.—When William and I returned from accompanying Jones, we met an old man almost double. He had on a coat, thrown over his shoulders, above his waistcoat and coat. Under this he carried a bundle, and had an apron on and a night-cap. His face was interesting. He had dark eyes and a long nose. John, who afterwards met him at Wytheburn, took him for a Jew. He was of Scotch parents, but had been born in the army. He had had a wife, and "she was a good woman, and it pleased God to bless us with ten children". All these were dead but one, of whom he had not heard for many years, a sailor. His trade was to gather leeches, but now leeches were scarce, and he had not strength for it. He lived by begging, and was making his way to Carlisle, where he should buy a few godly books to sell. He said leeches were very scarce, partly owing to this dry season, but many years they had been scarce. He supposed it owing to their being much sought after, that they did not breed fast, and were of slow growth. Leeches were formerly 2*s.* 6*d.* per 100; they are now 30*s.* He had been hurt in driving a cart, his leg broken, his body driven over, his skull fractured. He felt no pain till he recovered from his first insensibility. It was then late in the evening, when the light was just going away.

Saturday, 4th October 1800.—A very rainy, or rather showery and gusty, morning; for often the sun shines. Thomas Ashburner could not go to Keswick. Read a part of Lamb's play.[1] The language is often very beautiful, but too imitative in particular phrases, words, etc. The characters, except Margaret's, unintelligible, and, except Margaret's, do not show themselves in action. Coleridge came in while we were at dinner, very wet. We talked till twelve o'clock. He had sate up all the night before, writing essays for the newspaper. ...Exceedingly delighted with the second part of *Christabel*.

Sunday Morning, 5th October.—Coleridge read *Christabel* a second time; we had increasing pleasure. Wm. and I were employed all the morning in writing an addition to the Preface. Wm. went to bed, very ill after working after dinner. Coleridge and I walked to Ambleside after dark with the letter. Returned to tea at 9 o'clock. Wm. still in bed, and very ill. Silver How in both lakes.

[1] *John Woodvil.*

Monday.—A rainy day. Coleridge intending to go, but did not go off. We walked after dinner to Rydale. After tea read *The Pedlar*. Determined not to print *Christabel* with the L. B.

Tuesday.—Coleridge went off at eleven o'clock. I went as far as Mr Simpson's. Returned with Mary.

DOROTHY WORDSWORTH'S *Journal*

II

LAMB *to* WORDSWORTH

January 30, 1801.

Thanks for your Letter and Present. I had already borrowed your second volume.[1] What most please me are, the Song of Lucy... *Simon's sickly daughter* in the Sexton made me *cry*. Next to these are the description of the continuous Echoes in the story of Joanna's laugh, where the mountains and all the scenery absolutely seem alive—and that fine Shakesperian character of the Happy Man, in the Brothers,

> ...that creeps about the fields,
> Following his fancies by the hour, to bring
> Tears down his cheek, or solitary smiles
> Into his face, *until the Setting Sun*
> *Write Fool upon his forehead.*

I will mention one more: the delicate and curious feeling in the wish for the Cumberland Beggar, that he may have about him the melody of Birds, altho' he hear them not. Here the mind knowingly passes a fiction upon herself, first substituting her own feelings for the Beggar's, and, in the same breath detecting the fallacy, will not part with the wish....

I am sorry that Coleridge has christened his Ancient Marinere "a poet's Reverie"—it is as bad as Bottom the Weaver's declaration that he is not a Lion but only the scenical representation of a Lion. What new idea is gained by this Title, but one subversive of all credit, which the tale should

[1] The second edition of *Lyrical Ballads*, containing the famous *Preface* and a second volume of new poems, was published in 1800.

force upon us, of its truth? For me, I was never so affected with any human Tale. After first reading it, I was totally possessed with it for many days—I dislike all the miraculous part of it, but the feelings of the man under the operation of such scenery dragged me along like Tom Piper's magic whistle. I totally differ from your idea that the Marinere should have had a character and profession. This is a Beauty in Gulliver's Travels, where the mind is kept in a placid state of little wonderments; but the Ancient Marinere undergoes such Trials, as overwhelm and bury all individuality or memory of what he was, like the state of a man in a Bad dream, one terrible peculiarity of which is: that all consciousness of personality is gone. Your other observation is I think as well a little unfounded: the Marinere from being conversant in supernatural events *has* acquired a supernatural and strange cast of *phrase*, eye, appearance, &c. which frighten the wedding guest. You will excuse my remarks, because I am hurt and vexed that you should think it necessary, with a prose apology, to open the eyes of dead men that cannot see. To sum up a general opinion of the second vol.—I do not feel any one poem in it so forcibly as the Ancient Marinere, the Mad Mother, and the Lines at Tintern Abbey in the first.—I could, too, have wished the Critical preface had appeared in a separate treatise. All its dogmas are true and just, and most of them new, *as* criticism. But they associate a *diminishing* idea with the Poems which follow, as having been written for *Experiment* on the public taste, more than having sprung (as they must have done) from living and daily circumstances.—I am prolix, because I am gratified in the opportunity of writing to you, and I don't well know when to leave off. I ought before this to have reply'd to your very kind invitation into Cumberland. With you and your Sister I could gang any where. But I am afraid whether I shall ever be able to afford so desperate a Journey. Separate from the pleasure of your company, I don't much care if I never see a mountain in my life. I have passed all my days in London, until I have formed as many and intense local attachments, as any of you mountaineers can have done with dead nature. The Lighted shops of the Strand and Fleet Street, the innumerable trades, tradesmen and customers, coaches, waggons, playhouses, all the bustle and wickedness round about Covent Garden, the very women of the Town, the Watchmen, drunken scenes, rattles,—life awake, if you awake, at all hours of the night, the impossibility of being dull in Fleet Street, the crowds, the very dirt & mud, the Sun shining upon houses and pavements, the print shops, the old book stalls, parsons cheap'ning books, coffee houses, steams of soups from kitchens, the pantomimes, London itself a pantomime and a masquerade,—all these things work themselves into my mind and feed me, without a power of satiating me. The wonder of these sights impells me into night-walks about her crowded streets, and I often shed tears in the motley Strand from fulness of joy at so much Life.—All these emotions must be strange to you. So are your rural emotions to me. But consider, what must I have been doing all my life, not to have lent great portions of my heart with usury to such scenes?——

My attachments are all local, purely local. I have no passion (or have had none since I was in love, and then it was the spurious engendering of poetry & books) to groves and vallies. The rooms where I was born, the furniture which has been before my eyes all my life, a book case which has followed me about (like a faithful dog, only exceeding him in knowledge) wherever I have moved—old chairs, old tables, streets, squares, where I have sunned myself, my old school,—these are my mistresses. Have I not enough, without your mountains? I do not envy you. I should pity you, did I not know, that the Mind will make friends of any thing. Your sun & moon and skys and hills & lakes affect me no more, or scarcely come to me in more venerable characters, than as a gilded room with tapestry and tapers, where I might live with handsome visible objects. I consider the clouds above me but as a roof, beautifully painted but unable to satisfy the mind, and at last, like the pictures of the apartment of a connoisseur, unable to afford him any longer a pleasure. So fading upon me, from disuse, have been the Beauties of

Nature, as they have been confinedly called; so ever fresh & green and warm are all the inventions of men and assemblies of men in this great city. I should certainly have laughed with dear Joanna.

Give my kindest love, *and my sister's*, to D. & your*self* and a kiss from me to little Barbara Lewthwaite.

C. Lamb

Thank you for Liking my Play!!

III

1802.

Friday, 7th May.—William had slept uncommonly well, so, feeling himself strong, he fell to work at *The Leech Gatherer*; he wrote hard at it till dinner time, then he gave over, tired to death—he had finished the poem. I was making Derwent Coleridge's frocks. After dinner we sate in the orchard. It was a thick, hazy, dull air. The thrush sang almost continually; the little birds were more than usually busy with their voices. The sparrows are now fully fledged. The nest is so full that they lie upon one another; they sit quietly in their nest with closed mouths. I walked to Rydale after tea, which we drank by the kitchen fire. The evening very dull; a terrible kind of threatening brightness at sunset above Easedale. The sloe-thorn beautiful in the hedges, and in the wild spots higher up among the hawthorns. No letters. William met me. He had been digging in my absence, and cleaning the well. We walked up beyond Lewthwaites. A very dull sky; coolish; crescent moon now and then. I had a letter brought me from Mrs Clarkson while we were walking in the orchard. I observed the sorrel leaves opening at about nine o'clock. William went to bed tired with thinking about a poem.

Sunday Morning, 9th May.—The air considerably colder to-day, but the sun shone all day. William worked at *The Leech Gatherer* almost incessantly from morning till tea-time. I copied *The Leech Gatherer* and other poems for Coleridge. I was oppressed and sick at heart, for he wearied himself to death. After tea he wrote two stanzas in the manner of

Thomson's *Castle of Indolence*, and was tired out. Bad new of Coleridge.

Monday, 10*th May*.—A fine clear morning, but coldish. William is still at work, though it is past ten o'clock; he will be tired out, I am sure. My heart fails in me. He worked a little at odd things, but after dinner he gave over. An affecting letter from Mary H.[1] We sate in the orchard before dinner. ...I wrote to Mary H....I wrote to Coleridge, sent off reviews and poems. Went to bed at twelve o'clock. William did not sleep till three o'clock.

Friday, 21*st May*.—A very warm gentle morning, a little rain. William wrote two sonnets on Buonaparte, after I had read Milton's sonnets to him. In the evening he went with Mr Simpson with Borthwick's boat to gather ling in Bainrigg's. I plashed about the well, was much heated, and I think I caught cold.

DOROTHY WORDSWORTH'S *Journal*

IV

September 24, 1802.

My dear Manning,—Since the date of my last letter, I have been a traveller. A strong desire seized me of visiting remote regions. My first impulse was to go and see Paris. It was a trivial objection to my aspiring mind, that I did not understand a word of the language, since I certainly intend some time of my life to see Paris, and equally certainly intend never to learn the language; therefore that could be no objection. However, I am very glad I did not go, because you had left Paris (I see) before I could have set out. I believe, Stoddart promising to go with me another year, prevented that plan. My next scheme (for to my restless ambitious mind London was become a bed of thorns) was to visit the far-famed peak in Derbyshire, where the Devil sits, they say, without breeches. *This* my purer mind rejected as indelicate. And my final resolve was, a tour to the lakes. I set out with Mary to Keswick, without giving Coleridge any notice, for, my time

[1] Mary Hutchinson, afterwards Wordsworth's wife.

being precious, did not admit of it. He received us with all the hospitality in the world, and gave up his time to show us all the wonders of the country. He dwells upon a small hill by the side of Keswick, in a comfortable house, quite enveloped on all sides by a net of mountains: great floundering bears and monsters they seem'd, all couchant and asleep. We got in in the evening, travelling in a post chaise from Penrith, in the midst of a gorgeous sunshine, which transmuted all the mountains into colours, purple, &c., &c. We thought we had got into fairy land. But that went off (and it never came again; while we stayed we had no more fine sunsets); and we entered Coleridge's comfortable study just in the dusk, when the mountains were all dark with clouds upon their heads. Such an impression I never received from objects of sight before, nor do I suppose that I can ever again. Glorious creatures, fine old fellows, Skiddaw, &c. I never shall forget ye, how ye lay about that night, like an intrenchment; gone to bed, as it seemed for the night, but promising that ye were to be seen in the morning. Coleridge had got a blazing fire in his study, which is a large, antique, ill-shaped room, with an old fashioned organ, never play'd upon, big enough for a church, shelves of scattered folios, an Eolian harp, and an old sofa, half bed, &c. And all looking out upon the fading view of Skiddaw, and his broad-breasted brethren: what a night! Here we staid three full weeks, in which time I visited Wordsworth's cottage, where we stayed a day or two with the Clarksons (good people, and most hospitable, at whose house we tarried one day and night), and saw Lloyd. The Wordsworths were gone to Calais. They have since been in London, and past much time with us: he is now gone into Yorkshire to be married. So we have seen Keswick, Grasmere, Ambleside, Ulswater (where the Clarksons live), and a place at the other end of Ulswater; I forget the name; to which we travelled on a very sultry day, over the middle of Helvellyn. We have clambered up to the top of Skiddaw, and I have waded up the bed of Lodore. In fine, I have satisfied myself, that there is such a thing as that which tourists call *romantic*, which I very much suspected before: they make such a spluttering about it, and toss their splendid epithets around them, till they give as dim a light as at four o'clock next morning the lamps do after an illumination. Mary was excessively tired, when she got about half way up Skiddaw, but we came to a cold rill (than which nothing can be imagined more cold, running over cold stones), and with the reinforcement of a draught of cold water, she surmounted it most manfully. O, its fine black head, and the bleak air atop of it, with a prospect of mountains all about and about, making you giddy; and then Scotland afar off, and the border countries so famous in song and ballad! It was a day that will stand out, like a mountain, I am sure, in my life. But I am returned (I have now been come home near three weeks—I was a month out), and you cannot conceive the degradation I felt at first, from being accustomed to wander free as air among mountains, and bathe in rivers without being controul'd by any one, to come home and *work*. I felt very *little*. I had been dreaming I was a very great man. But that is going off, and I find I shall conform in time to that state of life to which it has pleased God to call me. Besides, after all, Fleet Street and the Strand are better places to live in for good and all than amidst Skiddaw. Still, I turn back to those great places where I wandered about, participating in their greatness. After all, I could not *live* in Skiddaw. I could spend a year, two, three years among them, but I must have a prospect of seeing Fleet Street at the end of that time, or I should mope and pine away, I know. Still, Skiddaw is a fine creature....

Farewell, my dear fellow,

C. Lamb

V

Coleridge's *Dejection* appeared in the *Morning Post* for October 4, 1802, on Wordsworth's wedding day. Although it was hardly appropriate to the occasion, it was undoubtedly intended as a tribute to him, for in the MSS. the "Lady" of the text printed here is replaced by "William" or "Wordsworth".

DEJECTION: AN ODE

Written April 4, 1802

Late, late yestreen I saw the new Moon,
With the old Moon in her arm;
And I fear, I fear, my Master dear!
We shall have a deadly storm.

Ballad of Sir Patrick Spence

I

Well! If the Bard was weather-wise, who made
The grand old ballad of Sir Patrick Spence,
This night, so tranquil now, will not go hence
Unroused by winds that ply a busier trade
Than those which mould yon cloud in lazy flakes,
Or the dull sobbing draft, that moans and rakes
Upon the strings of this Æolian lute,
Which better far were mute.
For lo! the New-moon winter-bright!
And overspread with phantom light,
(With swimming phantom light o'erspread,
But rimmed and circled by a silver thread)
I see the old Moon in her lap, foretelling
The coming-on of rain and squally blast.
And oh! that even now the gust were swelling,
And the slant night-shower driving loud and fast!
Those sounds which oft have raised me, whilst they awed,
And sent my soul abroad,
Might now perhaps their wonted impulse give,
Might startle this dull pain, and make it move and live!

II

A grief without a pang, void, dark, and drear,
A stifled, drowsy, unimpassioned grief,
Which finds no natural outlet, no relief,
In word, or sigh, or tear—
O Lady! in this wan and heartless mood,
To other thoughts by yonder throstle wooed,
All this long eve, so balmy and serene,
Have I been gazing on the western sky,
And its peculiar tint of yellow green:
And still I gaze—and with how blank an eye!
And those thin clouds above, in flakes and bars,
That give away their motion to the stars;
Those stars, that glide behind them or between,
Now sparkling, now bedimmed, but always seen:
Yon crescent Moon, as fixed as if it grew
In its own cloudless, starless lake of blue;
I see them all so excellently fair,
I see, not feel, how beautiful they are!

III

My genial spirits fail;
And what can these avail
To lift the smothering weight from off my breast?
It were a vain endeavour,
Though I should gaze for ever
On that green light that lingers in the west:
I may not hope from outward forms to win
The passion and the life whose fountains are within.

IV

O Lady! we receive but what we give,
And in our life alone does Nature live:
Ours is her wedding-garment, ours her shroud!
And would we aught behold, of higher worth,
Than that inanimate cold world allowed
To the poor loveless ever-anxious crowd,

Ah! from the soul itself must issue forth
A light, a glory, a fair luminous cloud
Enveloping the Earth—
And from the soul itself must there be sent
A sweet and potent voice, of its own birth,
Of all sweet sounds the life and element!

V

O pure of heart! thou need'st not ask of me
What this strong music in the soul may be!
What, and wherein it doth exist,
This light, this glory, this fair luminous mist,
This beautiful and beauty-making power.
Joy, virtuous Lady! Joy that ne'er was given,
Save to the pure, and in their purest hour,
Life, and Life's effluence, cloud at once and shower,
Joy, Lady! is the spirit and the power,
Which wedding Nature to us gives in dower,
A new Earth and new Heaven,
Undreamt of by the sensual and the proud—
Joy is the sweet voice, Joy the luminous cloud—
We in ourselves rejoice!
And thence flows all that charms or ear or sight,
All melodies the echoes of that voice,
All colours a suffusion from that light.

VI

There was a time when, though my path was rough,
This joy within me dallied with distress,
And all misfortunes were but as the stuff
Whence Fancy made me dreams of happiness:
For hope grew round me, like the twining vine,
And fruits and foliage not my own seemed mine.
But now afflictions bow me down to earth:
Nor care I that they rob me of my mirth;
But oh! each visitation
Suspends what nature gave me at my birth,
My shaping spirit of Imagination.

For not to think of what I needs must feel,
  But to be still and patient, all I can;
And haply by abstruse research to steal
  From my own nature all the natural man—
  This was my sole resource, my only plan:
Till that which suits a part infects the whole,
And now is almost grown the habit of my soul.

VII

Hence, viper thoughts, that coil around my mind,
    Reality's dark dream!
I turn from you, and listen to the wind,
  Which long has raved unnoticed. What a scream
Of agony by torture lengthened out
That lute sent forth! Thou Wind, that rav'st without,
  Bare crag, or mountain-tairn, or blasted tree,
Or pine-grove whither woodman never clomb,
Or lonely house, long held the witches' home,
  Methinks were fitter instruments for thee,
Mad Lutanist! who in this month of showers,
Of dark-brown gardens and of peeping flowers,
Mak'st Devils' yule with worse than wintry song
The blossoms, buds, and timorous leaves among.
  Thou Actor, perfect in all tragic sounds!
Thou mighty Poet, even to frenzy bold!
    What tell'st thou now about?
    'Tis of the rushing of an host in rout,
  With groans of trampled men, with smarting wounds—
At once they groan with pain, and shudder with the cold!
But hush! there is a pause of deepest silence!
  And all that noise, as of a rushing crowd,
With groans, and tremulous shudderings—all is over—
  It tells another tale, with sounds less deep and loud!
    A tale of less affright,
    And tempered with delight,
As Otway's self had framed the tender lay,
    'Tis of a little child
    Upon a lonesome wild,

Not far from home, but she hath lost her way:
And now moans low in bitter grief and fear,
And now screams loud, and hopes to make her mother hear.

VIII

'Tis midnight, but small thoughts have I of sleep:
Full seldom may my friend such vigils keep!
Visit her, gentle Sleep! with wings of healing,
   And may this storm be but a mountain-birth,
May all the stars hang bright above her dwelling,
   Silent as though they watched the sleeping Earth!
      With light heart may she rise,
      Gay fancy, cheerful eyes,
   Joy lift her spirit, joy attune her voice;
To her may all things live, from pole to pole,
Their life the eddying of her living soul!
   O simple spirit, guided from above,
Dear Lady! friend devoutest of my choice,
Thus mayest thou ever, evermore rejoice.

COLERIDGE

WORDSWORTH'S SCOTTISH TOUR, 1803

I

Saturday, September 17th.—The morning very fine. We rose early and walked through the glen of Roslin, past Hawthornden, and considerably further, to the house of Mr Walter Scott at Lasswade....

Arrived at Lasswade before Mr and Mrs Scott had risen, and waited some time in a large sitting-room. Breakfasted with them, and stayed till two o'clock, and Mr Scott accompanied us back almost to Roslin, having given us directions respecting our future journey, and promised to meet us at Melrose two days after.

Monday, September 19th.—We rose early, and went to Melrose, six miles before breakfast....After breakfast we went out, intending to go to the Abbey, and in the street met Mr Scott, who gave us a cordial greeting, and conducted us thither himself. He was here on his own ground, for he is familiar with all that is known of the authentic history of Melrose and the popular tales connected with it. He pointed out many pieces of beautiful sculpture in obscure corners which would have escaped our notice. . . . Mr Scott went with us into the gardens and orchards of a Mr Riddel, from which we had a very sweet view of the Abbey through trees, the town being entirely excluded. Dined with Mr Scott at the inn; he was now travelling to the assizes at Jedburgh in his character of Sheriff of Selkirk, and on that account, as well as for his own sake, he was treated with great respect, a small part of which was vouchsafed to us as his friends, though I could not persuade the woman to show me the beds, or to make any sort of promise till she was assured from the Sheriff himself that he had no objection to sleep in the same room with William.

Tuesday, September 20th.—Mr Scott departed very early for Jedburgh, and we soon followed, intending to go by Dryburgh to Kelso. It was a fine morning. We went without breakfast, being told that there was a public-house at Dryburgh. The road was very pleasant, seldom out of sight of the Tweed for any length of time, though not often close to it. The valley is not so pleasantly defined as between Peebles and Cloven ford, yet so soft and beautiful, and in many places pastoral, but that peculiar and pensive simplicity which I have spoken of before was wanting, yet there was a fertility chequered with wildness which to many travellers would be more than a compensation. The reaches of the vale were shorter, the turnings more rapid, the banks often clothed with wood. In one place was a lofty scar, at another a green promontory, a small hill skirted by the river, the hill irregular and green, and scattered over with trees. We wished we could have brought Melrose to that spot, and mentioned this to Mr Scott, who told us that the monks had first their abode there, and raised a temporary building of wood.

DOROTHY WORDSWORTH'S *Journal*

II

WORDSWORTH *to* SCOTT

Grasmere, *October* 16, 1803.

We had a delightful journey home, delightful weather, and a sweet country to travel through. We reached our little cottage in high spirits, and thankful to God for all his bounties. My wife and child were both well, and as I need not say, we had all of us a happy meeting. . . . We passed Branxholme—your Branxholme, we supposed—about four miles on this side of Hawick. It looks better in your poem than in its present realities. The situation, however, is delightful, and makes amends for an ordinary mansion. The whole of the Teviot and the pastoral steeps about Mosspaul pleased us exceedingly. The Esk below Langholm is a delicious river, and we saw it to great advantage. We did not omit noticing Johnnie Armstrong's Keep; but his hanging place, to our great regret, we missed. We were, indeed, most truly sorry that we could not have you along with us into Westmoreland. The country was in its full glory—the verdure of the valleys, in which we are so much superior to you in Scotland, but little tarnished by the weather, and the trees putting on their most beautiful looks. My sister was quite enchanted, and we often said to each other, What a pity Mr Scott is not with us! . . . I had the pleasure of seeing Coleridge and Southey at Keswick. Southey, whom I never saw much of before, I liked much: he is very pleasant in his manner, and a man of great reading in old books, poetry, chronicles, memoirs, etc., etc., particularly Spanish and Portuguese. . . . My sister and I often talk of the happy days that we spent in your company. Such things do not occur often in life. If we live we shall meet again; that is my consolation when I think of these things. Scotland and England sound like division, do what ye can; but we really are but neighbours, and if you were no further off, and in Yorkshire, we should think so. Farewell. God prosper you and all that belongs to you.—Your sincere friend, for such I will call myself, though slow to use a word of such solemn meaning to any one,

W. Wordsworth

DE QUINCEY AS UNDERGRADUATE

I

It was either late in 1804 or early in 1805, according to my present computations, that I had obtained from a literary friend a letter of introduction to Mr Lamb. All that I knew of his works was his play of *John Woodvil*, which I had bought in Oxford, and perhaps *I* only had bought throughout that great University, at the time of my matriculation there, about the Christmas of 1803. Another book fell into my hands on that same morning, I recollect—the *Gebir* of Mr Walter Savage Landor, which astonished me by the splendour of its descriptions (for I had opened accidentally upon the sea-nymph's marriage with Tamor, the youthful brother of Gebir)—and I bought this also. Afterwards, when placing these two most unpopular of books on the same shelf with the other far holier idols of my heart, the joint poems of Wordsworth and Coleridge as then associated in the *Lyrical Ballads*—poems not equally unknown, perhaps a *little* better known, but only with the result of being more openly scorned, rejected—I could not but smile internally at the fair prospect I had of congregating a library which no man had read but myself. *John Woodvil* I had almost studied, and Miss Lamb's pretty *High-Born Helen*, and the ingenious imitations of Burton; these I had read, and, to a certain degree, must have admired, for some parts of them had settled without effort in my memory. I had read also the *Edinburgh* notice of them; and with what contempt may be supposed from the fact that my veneration for Wordsworth transcended all that I felt for any created being, past or present; insomuch that, in the summer, or spring rather, of that same year, and full eight months before I first went to Oxford, I had ventured to address a letter to him, through his publishers, the Messrs Longman (which letter, Miss Wordsworth in after years assured me, they believed to be the production of some person much older than I represented myself), and that in due time I had been honoured by a long answer from Wordsworth; an honour which, I well remember, kept me awake, from mere excess of pleasure, through a long night in June 1803.

DE QUINCEY: *London Reminiscences*

II

FIRST MEETING WITH LAMB

I had been told that he was never to be found at home except in the evenings; and to have called then would have been, in a manner, forcing myself upon his hospitalities and at a moment when he might have confidential friends about him; besides that, he was sometimes tempted away to the theatres. I went, therefore, to the India House; made inquiries amongst the servants; and, after some trouble (for *that* was early in his Leadenhall Street career, and possibly he was not much known), I was shown into a small room, or else a small section of a large one (thirty-four years affects one's remembrance of some circumstances) in which was a very lofty writing-desk, separated by a still higher railing from that part of the floor on which the profane—the laity, like myself—were allowed to approach the *clerus*, or clerkly rulers of the room. Within the railing sat, to the best of my remembrance, six quill-driving gentlemen; not gentlemen whose duty or profession it was merely to drive the quill, but who were then driving it—*gens de plume*, such *in esse*, as well as *in posse*—in act as well as habit; for, as if they supposed me a spy sent by some superior power to report upon the situation of affairs as surprised by me, they were all too profoundly immersed in their oriental studies to have any sense of my presence. Consequently, I was reduced to a necessity of announcing myself and my errand. I walked, therefore, into one of the two open doorways of the railing, and stood closely by the high stool of him who occupied the first place within the little aisle. I touched his arm, by way of recalling him from his lofty Leadenhall speculations to this sublunary world; and, presenting my letter, asked if that gentleman (pointing to the address) were really a citizen of the present room; for I had been repeatedly misled, by the directions given me, into wrong rooms. The gentleman smiled; it was a smile not to be forgotten. This was Lamb. . . .

DE QUINCEY: *London Reminiscences*

SOUTHEY TO COLERIDGE

In the spring of 1804 Coleridge left England for Malta, in the hope of regaining some of his lost health in a southern climate. He was unsuccessful, but he remained abroad until 1806.

June 11, 1804, Keswick.

Dear Coleridge,

The first news of you was from Lamb's letter, which arrived when I was in London. I saw, also, your letter to Stuart, and heard of one to Tobin, before I returned and found my own. Ere this you are at Malta. What an infectious thing is irregularity! Merely because it was uncertain when a letter could set off, I have always yielded to the immediate pressure of other employment; whereas, had there been a day fixed for the mail, to have written would then have been a fixed business, and performed like an engagement.

I was worn to the very bone by fatigue in London,—more walking in one day than I usually take in a month; more waste of breath than serves for three months' consumption in the country; add to this a most abominable cold, affecting chest, head, eyes, and nose. It was impossible to see half the persons whom I wished to see, and ought to have seen, without prolonging my stay to an inconvenient time, and an unreasonable length of absence from home. I called upon Sir George [Beaumont] unsuccessfully, and received a note that evening, saying he would be at home the following morning; then I saw him, and his lady, and his pictures, and afterwards met him the same day at dinner at Davy's. As he immediately left town, this was all our intercourse; and, as it is not likely that he will visit the Lakes this year, probably will be all.

I went to the Exhibition merely to see your picture, which perfectly provoked me. Hazlitt's[1] does look as if you were on your trial, and certainly had stolen the horse; but then you did it cleverly,—it had been a deep, well-laid scheme, and it was no fault of yours that you had been detected. But this portrait by Northcote looks like a grinning idiot; and the worst is, that it is just like enough to pass for a good likeness, with those who only know your features imperfectly. Dance's drawing has that merit at least, that nobody would ever suspect you of having been the original. Poole's business will last yet some weeks. As the Abstract is printed, I can give you the very important result: one in eight through Great Britain receives permanent parish pay;—what is still more extraordinary, and far more consolatory, one in nine is engaged in some benefit society,—a prodigious proportion, if you remember that, in this computation, few women enter, and no children.

I dined with Sotheby, and met there Henley, a man every way to my taste. Sotheby was very civil, and as his civility has not that smoothness so common among the vagabonds of fashion, I took it in good part. He is what I should call a clever man. Other lions were Price, the picturesque man, and Davies Giddy, whose face ought to be perpetuated in marble for the honour of mathematics. Such a forehead I never saw. I also met Dr [Burney] at dinner; who, after a long silence, broke out into a discourse upon the properties of the conjunction *Quam*. Except his quamical knowledge, which is as profound as you will imagine, he knows nothing but bibliography, or the science of title-pages, impresses, and dates. It was a relief to leave him, and find his brother, the captain, at Rickman's, smoking after supper, and letting out puffs at one corner of his mouth and puns at the other. The captain hath a son,[2]—begotten, according to Lamb, upon a mermaid; and thus far is certain, that he is the queerest fish out of water. A paralytic affection in childhood has kept one side

[1] In the previous year Hazlitt had visited the Lakes and painted portraits of Coleridge and Wordsworth.

[2] Martin Burney.

of his face stationary, while the other has continued to grow, and the two sides form the most ridiculous whole you can imagine; the boy, however, is a sharp lad, the inside not having suffered....

God bless you!

R. S.

LAMB TO WORDSWORTH

October 13, 1804.

Dear Wordsworth,

I have not forgotten your commissions. But the truth is, and why should I not confess it? I am not plethorically abounding in Cash at this present. Merit, God knows, is very little rewarded; but it does not become me to speak of myself. My motto is "Contented with little, yet wishing for more". Now the books you wish for would require some pounds, which I am sorry to say I have not by me: so I will say at once, if you will give me a draft upon your town-banker for any sum you propose to lay out, I will dispose of it to the very best of my skill in choice old books, such as my own soul loveth. In fact, I have been waiting for the liquidation of a debt to enable myself to set about your commission handsomely, for it is a scurvy thing to cry Give me the money first, and I am the first of the family of the Lambs that have done it for many centuries: but the debt remains as it was, and my old friend that I accommodated has generously forgot it!

The books which you want I calculate at about £8.

Ben Jonson is a Guinea Book. Beaumont & Fletcher in folio, the right folio, not now to be met with; the octavos are about £3. As to any other old dramatists, I do not know where to find them except what are in Dodsley's old plays, which are about £3 also: Massinger I never saw but at one shop, but it is now gone, but one of the editions of Dodsley contains about a fourth (the best) of his plays. Congreve and the rest of King Charles's moralists are cheap and accessible. The works on Ireland I will enquire after, but I fear, Spenser's is not to be had apart from his poems; I never saw it. But you may depend upon my sparing no pains to furnish you as complete a library of old Poets & Dramatists as will be prudent to buy; for I suppose you do not include the £20 edition of Hamlet, single play, which Kemble has. Marlow's plays and poems are totally vanished; only one edition of Dodsley retains one, and the other two, of his plays: but John Ford is the man after Shakespear. Let me know your will and pleasure soon: for I have observed, next to the pleasure of buying a bargain for one's self is the pleasure of persuading a friend to buy it. It tickles one with the image of an imprudency without the penalty usually annex'd.

C. Lamb

MR H——

I

December 11, 1806.

Mary's love to all of you—I wouldn't let her write.

Dear Wordsworth,—*Mr H.* came out last night, and failed. I had many fears; the subject was not substantial enough. John Bull must have solider fare than a *letter*. We are pretty stout about it; have had plenty of condoling friends; but, after all, we had rather it should have succeeded. You will see the prologue in most of the morning papers. It was received with such shouts as I never witnessed to a prologue. It was attempted to be encored. How hard!—a thing I did merely as a task, because it was wanted, and set no great store by; and *Mr H.*!! The number of friends we had in the house—my brother and I being in public offices, &c.—was astonishing, but they yielded at length to a few hisses.

A hundred hisses! (Damn the word, I write it like kisses—how different!)—a hundred hisses outweigh a thousand claps. The former come more directly from the heart. Well 'tis withdrawn, and there is an end.

Better luck to us. C. Lamb

P.S. Pray, when any of you write to the Clarksons, give our kind loves, and say we shall not be able to come and see them at Christmas, as I shall have but a day or two, and tell them we bear our mortification pretty well.

II

We often make life unhappy in wishing things to have turned out otherwise than they did, merely because that is possible to the imagination, which is impossible in fact. I remember, when Lamb's farce was damned (for damned it was, that's certain), I used to dream every night for a month after (and then I vowed I would plague myself no more about it) that it was revived at one of the minor or provincial theatres with great success, that such and such retrenchments or alterations had been made in it, and that it was thought *it might do at the other House*. I had heard indeed (this was told in confidence to Lamb) that *Gentleman* Lewis was present on the night of its performance, and had said that if he had had it he would have made it, by a few judicious curtailments, "the most popular little thing that had been brought out for some time". How often did I conjure up in recollection the full diapason of applause at the end of the *Prologue*, and hear my ingenious friend in the first row of the pit roar with laughter at his own wit! Then I dwelt with forced complacency on some part in which it had succeeded in doing well: then we would consider (in concert) whether the long tedious opera of the *Travellers*, which preceded it, had not tired people beforehand, so that they had no spirits left for the quaint and sparkling "wit skirmishes" of the dialogue; and we all agreed it might have gone down after a tragedy, except Lamb himself, who swore he had no hopes of it from the beginning, and that he knew the name of the hero when it came to be discovered could not be got over. *Mr H——*, thou wert damned! Bright shone the morning on the play-bills that announced thy appearance, and the streets were filled with the buzz of persons asking one another if they would go to see *Mr H——*, and answer—that they would certainly; but before night the gaiety, not of the author, but of his friends and the town, was eclipsed, for thou wert damned! Hadst thou been anonymous thou haply mightst have lived. But thou didst come to an untimely end for thy tricks, and for want of a better name to pass them off!

HAZLITT: *On Great and Little Things*

TO WILLIAM WORDSWORTH

COMPOSED ON THE NIGHT AFTER HIS RECITATION OF A POEM ON THE GROWTH OF AN INDIVIDUAL MIND.[1]

Friend of the wise! and Teacher of the Good!
Into my heart have I received that Lay
More than historic, that prophetic Lay
Wherein (high theme by thee first sung aright)
Of the foundations and the building up
Of a Human Spirit thou hast dared to tell
What may be told, to the understanding mind
Revealable; and what within the mind
By vital breathings secret as the soul
Of vernal growth, oft quickens in the heart
Thoughts all too deep for words!—

Theme hard as high!
Of smiles spontaneous, and mysterious fears
(The first-born they of Reason and twin-birth)
Of tides obedient to external force,
And currents self-determined, as might seem,
Or by some inner Power; of moments awful,
Now in thy inner life, and now abroad,
When power streamed from thee, and thy soul received
The light reflected, as a light bestowed—
Of fancies fair, and milder hours of youth,
Hyblean murmurs of poetic thought
Industrious in its joy, in vales and glens
Native or outland, lakes and famous hills!

[1] *The Prelude*, which had been completed during Coleridge's absence from England, was read to him by Wordsworth one night near the end of 1806, soon after his return.

Or on the lonely high-road, when the stars
Were rising; or by secret mountain-streams,
The guides and the companions of thy way!
—Of more than Fancy, of the Social Sense
Distending wide, and man beloved as man,
Where France in all her towns lay vibrating
Like some becalmèd bark beneath the burst
Of Heaven's immediate thunder, when no cloud
Is visible, or shadow on the main.
For thou wert there, thine own brows garlanded,
Amid the tremor of a realm aglow,
Amid a mighty nation jubilant,
When from the general heart of human kind
Hope sprang forth like a full-born Deity!
——Of that dear Hope afflicted and struck down,
So summoned homeward, thenceforth calm and sure
From the dread watch-tower of man's absolute self,
With light unwaning on her eyes, to look
Far on—herself a glory to behold,
The Angel of the vision! Then (last strain)
Of Duty, chosen Laws controlling choice,
Action and joy!—An Orphic song indeed,
A song divine of high and passionate thoughts
To their own music chaunted!

O great Bard!
Ere yet that last strain dying awed the air,
With stedfast eye I viewed thee in the choir
Of ever-enduring men. The truly great
Have all one age, and from one visible space
Shed influence! They, both in power and act,
Are permanent, and Time is not with them,
Save as it worketh for them, they in it.
Nor less a sacred Roll, than those of old,
And to be placed, as they, with gradual fame
Among the archives of mankind, thy work
Makes audible a linked lay of Truth,
Of Truth profound a sweet continuous lay,

LIBRARY ST. MARY'S COLLEGE

Not learnt, but native, her own natural notes!
Ah! as I listen'd with a heart forlorn,
The pulses of my being beat anew:
And even as life returns upon the drowned,
Life's joy rekindling roused a throng of pains—
Keen pangs of Love, awakening as a babe
Turbulent, with an outcry in the heart;
And fears self-willed, that shunned the eye of hope;
And hope that scarce would know itself from fear;
Sense of past youth, and manhood come in vain,
And genius given, and knowledge won in vain;
And all which I had culled in wood-walks wild,
And all which patient toil had reared, and all,
Commune with thee had opened out—but flowers
Strewed on my corse, and borne upon my bier,
In the same coffin, for the self-same grave!

That way no more! and ill beseems it me,
Who came a welcomer in herald's guise,
Singing of glory and futurity,
To wander back on such unhealthful road,
Plucking the poisons of self-harm! And ill
Such intertwine beseems triumphal wreaths
Strew'd before thy advancing!

Nor do thou,
Sage Bard! impair the memory of that hour
Of thy communion with my nobler mind
By pity or grief, already felt too long!
Nor let my words import more blame than needs.
The tumult rose and ceased: for Peace is nigh
Where wisdom's voice has found a listening heart
Amid the howl of more than wintry storms,
The halcyon hears the voice of vernal hours
Already on the wing.

Eve following eve,
Dear tranquil time, when the sweet sense of Home
Is sweetest! moments for their own sake hailed

And more desired, more precious, for thy song,
In silence listening, like a devout child,
My soul lay passive, by thy various strain
Driven as in surges now beneath the stars,
With momentary stars of my own birth,
Fair constellated foam, still darting off
Into the darkness; now a tranquil sea,
Outspread and bright, yet swelling to the moon.

And when—O Friend! my comforter and guide!
Strong in thyself, and powerful to give strength!—
Thy long sustainèd Song finally closed,
And thy deep voice had ceased—yet thou thyself
Wert still before my eyes, and round us both
That happy vision of beloved faces—
Scarce conscious, and yet conscious of its close
I sate, my being blended in one thought
(Thought was it? or aspiration? or resolve?)
Absorbed, yet hanging still upon the sound—
And when I rose, I found myself in prayer.

COLERIDGE

THE LAKE POETS

I

COLERIDGE

I had received directions for finding out the house where Coleridge was visiting; and, in riding down a main street of Bridgewater, I noticed a gateway corresponding to the description given me. Under this was standing, and gazing about him, a man whom I will describe. In height he might seem to be about five feet eight (he was, in reality, about an inch and a half taller, but his figure was of an order which drowns the height); his person was broad and full, and tended even to corpulence; his complexion was fair, though not what painters technically style fair, because it was associated with black hair; his eyes were large, and soft in their expression;

and it was from the peculiar appearance of haze or dreaminess which mixed with their light that I recognized my object. This was Coleridge. I examined him steadfastly for a minute or more; and it struck me that he saw neither myself nor any other object in the street. He was in a deep reverie; for I had dismounted, made two or three trifling arrangements at an inn-door, and advanced close to him, before he had apparently become conscious of my presence. The sound of my voice, announcing my own name, first awoke him; he started, and for a moment seemed at a loss to understand my purpose or his own situation; for he repeated rapidly a number of words which had no relation to either of us. There was no *mauvaise honte* in his manner, but simple perplexity, and an apparent difficulty in recovering his position amongst daylight realities. This little scene over, he received me with a kindness of manner so marked that it might be called gracious. The hospitable family with whom he was domesticated were distinguished for their amiable manners and enlightened understandings: they were descendants from Chubb, the philosophic writer, and bore the same name. For Coleridge they all testified deep affection and esteem—sentiments in which the whole town of Bridgewater seemed to share; for in the evening, when the heat of the day had declined, I walked out with him; and rarely, perhaps never, have I seen a person so much interrupted in one hour's space as Coleridge, on this occasion, by the courteous attentions of young and old.

Coleridge led me to a drawing-room, rang the bell for refreshments, and omitted no point of a courteous reception. He told me that there would be a very large dinner party on that day, which, perhaps, might be disagreeable to a perfect stranger; but, if not, he could assure me of a most hospitable welcome from the family. I was too anxious to see him under all aspects to think of declining this invitation. That point being settled, Coleridge, like some great river, the Orellana, or the St Lawrence, that, having been checked and fretted by rocks or thwarting islands, suddenly recovers its volume of waters and its mighty music, swept at once, as if returning to his natural business, into a continuous strain of eloquent dissertation, certainly the most novel, the most finely illustrated, and traversing the most spacious fields of thought by transitions the most just and logical, that it was possible to conceive. What I mean by saying that his transitions were "just" is by way of contradistinction to that mode of conversation which courts variety through links of *verbal* connections. Coleridge, to many people, and often I have heard the complaint, seemed to wander; and he seemed then to wander the most when, in fact, his resistance to the wandering instinct was greatest—viz., when the compass and huge circuit by which his illustrations moved travelled farthest into remote regions before they began to revolve. Long before this coming round commenced most people had lost him, and naturally enough supposed that he had lost himself. They continued to admire the separate beauty of the thoughts, but did not see their relations to the dominant theme. Had the conversation been thrown upon paper, it might have been easy to trace the continuity of the links; just as in Bishop Berkeley's "Siris", from a pedestal so low and abject, so culinary, as Tar Water, the method of preparing it, and its medicinal effects, the dissertation ascends, like Jacob's ladder, by just gradations, into the Heaven of Heavens and the thrones of the Trinity. But Heaven is there connected with earth by the Homeric chain of gold; and, being subject to steady examination, it is easy to trace the links; whereas, in conversation, the loss of a single word may cause the whole cohesion to disappear from view. However, I can assert, upon my long and intimate knowledge of Coleridge's mind, that logic the most severe was as inalienable from his modes of thinking as grammar from his language.

De Quincey: *Literary Reminiscences*

II

DOVE COTTAGE

Twice, as I have said, did I advance as far as the lake of Coniston; which is about eight miles from the church of Grasmere, and once I absolutely went forwards from Coniston to the very gorge of Hammerscar, from which the whole Vale of Grasmere suddenly breaks upon the view in a style of almost theatrical surprise, with its lovely valley stretching before the eye in the distance, the lake lying immediately below, with its solemn ark-like island of four and a half acres in size seemingly floating on its surface, and its exquisite outline on the opposite shore, revealing all its little bays and wild sylvan margin, feathered to the edge with wild flowers and ferns. In one quarter, a little wood, stretching for about half a mile towards the outlet of the lake; more directly in opposition to the spectator, a few green fields; and beyond them, just two bowshots from the water, a little white cottage gleaming from the midst of trees, with a vast and seemingly never-ending series of ascents rising above it to the height of more than three thousand feet. That little cottage was Wordsworth's from the time of his marriage, and earlier; in fact, from the beginning of the century to the year 1808. Afterwards, for many a year, it was mine.

DE QUINCEY: *Literary Reminiscences*

III

WORDSWORTH

I was ushered up a little flight of stairs, fourteen in all, to a little drawing-room, or whatever the reader chooses to call it. Wordsworth himself has described the fireplace of this room as his

Half-kitchen and half-parlour fire.

It was not fully seven feet six inches high, and, in other respects, pretty nearly of the same dimensions as the rustic hall below. There was, however, in a small recess, a library of perhaps three hundred volumes, which seemed to consecrate the room as the poet's study and composing room; and such occasionally it was. But far oftener he both studied, as I found, and composed, on the high road. I had not been two minutes at the fireside, when in came Wordsworth, returning from his friendly attentions to the travellers below, who, it seemed, had been over-persuaded by hospitable solicitations to stay for this night in Grasmere, and to make out the remaining thirteen miles of their road to Keswick on the following day. Wordsworth entered. And "*what-like*" to use a Westmoreland as well as a Scottish expression—"*what-like*" was Wordsworth? A reviewer in "Tait's Magazine", noticing some recent collection of literary portraits, gives it as his opinion that Charles Lamb's head was the finest among them. This remark may have been justified by the engraved portraits; but, certainly, the critic would have cancelled it, had he seen the original heads—at least, had he seen them in youth or in maturity; for Charles Lamb bore age with less disadvantage to the intellectual expression of his appearance than Wordsworth, in whom a sanguine complexion had, of late years, usurped upon the original bronze-tint; and this change of hue, and change in the quality of skin, had been made fourfold more conspicuous, and more unfavourable in its general effect, by the harsh contrast of grizzled hair which had displaced the original brown. No change in personal appearance ever can have been so unfortunate; for, generally speaking, whatever other disadvantages old age may bring along with it, one effect, at least in male subjects, has a compensating tendency—that it removes any tone of vigour too harsh, and mitigates the expression of power too unsubdued. But, in Wordsworth, the effect of the change has been to substitute an air of animal vigour, or, at least, hardiness, as if derived from constant exposure to the wind and weather, for the fine sombre complexion which he once wore, resembling that of a Venetian senator or a Spanish monk.

Here, however, in describing the personal appearance of Wordsworth, I go back, of course, to the point of time at which I am speaking. He was, upon the whole, not a well-made man. His legs were pointedly condemned by all female connoisseurs in legs; not that they were bad in any way which *would* force itself upon your notice—there was no absolute deformity about them; and undoubtedly they had been serviceable legs beyond the average standard of human requisition; for I calculate, upon good data, that with these identical legs

Wordsworth must have traversed a distance of 175,000 to 180,000 English miles—a mode of exertion which, to him, stood in the stead of alcohol and all other stimulants whatsoever to the animal spirits; to which, indeed, he was indebted for a life of unclouded happiness, and we for much of what is most excellent in his writings. But, useful as they have proved themselves, the Wordsworthian legs were certainly not ornamental; and it was really a pity, as I agreed with a lady in thinking, that he had not another pair for evening dress parties—when no boots lend their friendly aid to mask our imperfections from the eyes of female rigorists—those *elegantes formarum spectatrices.* A sculptor would certainly have disapproved of their contour. But the worst part of Wordsworth's person was the bust; there was a narrowness and a droop about the shoulders which became striking, and had an effect of meanness, when brought into close juxtaposition with a figure of a more statuesque build. Once on a summer evening, walking in the Vale of Langdale with Wordsworth, his sister, and Mr J——, a native Westmoreland clergyman, I remember that Miss Wordsworth was positively mortified by the peculiar illustration which settled upon this defective conformation. Mr J——, a fine towering figure, six feet high, massy and columnar in his proportions, happened to be walking, a little in advance, with Wordsworth; Miss Wordsworth and myself being in the rear; and from the nature of the conversation which then prevailed in our front rank, something or other about money, devises, buying and selling, we of the rear-guard thought it requisite to preserve this arrangement for a space of three miles or more; during which time, at intervals, Miss Wordsworth would exclaim, in a tone of vexation, "Is it possible,—can that be William? How very mean he looks!" And she did not conceal a mortification that seemed really painful, until I, for my part, could not forbear laughing outright at the serious interest which she carried into this trifle. She was, however, right, as regarded the mere visual judgment. Wordsworth's figure, with all its defects, was brought into powerful relief by one which had been cast in a more square and massy mould; and in such a case it impressed a spectator with a sense of absolute meanness, more especially when viewed from behind and not counteracted by his countenance; and yet Wordsworth was of a good height (five feet ten), and not a slender man; on the contrary, by the side of Southey, his limbs looked thick, almost in a disproportionate degree. But the total effect of Wordsworth's person was always worst in a state of motion. Meantime, his face—that was one which would have made amends for greater defects of figure. Many such, and finer, I have seen amongst the portraits of Titian, and, in a later period, amongst those of Vandyke, from the great era of Charles I, as also from the court of Elizabeth and of Charles II, but none which has more impressed me in my own time.

Wordsworth's face was, if not absolutely the indigenous face of the Lake district, at any rate a variety of that face, a modification of that original type. The head was well filled out; and there, to begin with, was a great advantage over the head of Charles Lamb, which was absolutely truncated in the posterior region—sawn off, as it were, by no timid sawyer. The forehead was not remarkably lofty—and, by the way, some artists, in their ardour for realizing their phrenological preconceptions, not suffering nature to surrender quietly and by slow degrees her real alphabet of signs and hieroglyphic characters, but forcing her language prematurely into conformity with their own crude speculations, have given to Sir Walter Scott a pile of forehead which is unpleasing and cataphysical, in fact, a caricature of anything that is ever seen in nature, and would (if real) be esteemed a deformity; in one instance—that which was introduced in some annual or other—the forehead makes about two-thirds of the entire face. Wordsworth's forehead is also liable to caricature misrepresentations in these days of phrenology: but, whatever it may appear to be in any man's fanciful portrait, the real living forehead, as I have been in the habit of seeing it for more than five-and-twenty years, is not remarkable for its height; but it *is*, perhaps, remarkable for its breadth and expansive development. Neither are the eyes of Wordsworth "large", as is erroneously stated somewhere in "Peter's Letters"; on the contrary, they are (I think) rather small; but *that* does not interfere with their effect, which at times is fine, and suitable to his intellectual character. At times, I say, for the depth and subtlety of eyes, even their colouring (as to condensation or dilation), varies exceedingly with the state of the stomach; and, if young ladies were aware of the magical transformations which can be wrought in the depth and sweetness of the eye by a few weeks' walking exercise, I fancy we should see their habits in this point altered greatly for the better. I have seen Wordsworth's eyes oftentimes affected powerfully in this respect; his eyes are not, under any circumstances, bright, lustrous, or piercing; but, after a long day's toil in walking, I have seen them assume an appearance the most solemn and spiritual that it is possible for the human eye to wear. The light which resides in them is at no time a superficial light; but, under favourable accidents, it is a light which seems to come from unfathomed depths: in fact, it is more truly entitled to be held "the light that never was on land or sea", a light radiating from some far spiritual world, than any the most idealizing that ever yet a painter's hand created. The nose, a little arched, is large; which, by the way (according to a natural phrenology, existing centuries ago amongst some of the lowest amongst the human species), has always been accounted an unequivocal expression of animal appetites organically strong. And that expressed the simple truth: Wordsworth's intellectual passions were fervent and strong: but they rested upon a basis of preternatural animal sensibility diffused through *all* the animal passions (or appetites); and something of that will be found to hold of all poets who have been great by original force and power, not (as Virgil) by means of fine management and exquisite artifice of composition applied to their conceptions.

DE QUINCEY: *Literary Reminiscences*

IV

WORDSWORTH AND BOOKS

Wordsworth lived in the open air: Southey in his library, which Coleridge used to call his wife. Southey had particularly elegant habits (Wordsworth called them finical) in the use of books. Wordsworth, on the other hand, was so negligent, and so self-indulgent in the same case, that as Southey, laughing, expressed it to me some years afterwards, when I was staying at Greta Hall on a visit—"To introduce Wordsworth into one's library, is like letting a bear into a tulip garden". What I mean by self-indulgent is this: generally it happens that new books baffle and mock one's curiosity by their uncut leaves; and the trial is pretty much the same, as when, in some town, where you are utterly unknown, you meet the postman at a distance from your inn, with some letter for yourself from a dear, dear friend in foreign regions, without money to pay the postage. How is it with you, dear reader, in such a case? Are you not tempted (*I am* grievously) to snatch the letter from his tantalizing hand, spite of the roar which you anticipate of "Stop thief!" and make off as fast as you can for some solitary street in the suburbs, where you may instantly effect an entrance upon your new estate before the purchase money is paid down? Such were Wordsworth's feelings in regard to new books; of which the first exemplification I had was early in my acquaintance with him, and on occasion of a book which (if any could) justified the too summary style of his advances in rifling its charms. On a level with the eye, when sitting at the tea-table in my little cottage at Grasmere, stood the collective works of Edmund Burke. The book was to me an eye-sore and an ear-sore for many a year, in consequence of the cacophonous title lettered by the bookseller upon the back—"Burke's Works" Wordsworth took down the volume; unfortunately it was uncut; fortunately, and by a special Providence as to him, it seemed, tea was proceeding at the time. Dry toast required butter; butter required knives; and knives then lay on the table; but sad it was for the virgin purity of Mr Burke's as yet unsunned pages, that every knife bore upon its blade testimonies of the service it had rendered. Did *that* stop Wordsworth? Did that cause him to call for another knife? Not at all; he

> Look'd at the knife that caus'd his pain:
> And look'd and sigh'd, and look'd and sigh'd again;

and then, after this momentary tribute to regret, he tore his way into the heart of the volume with this knife that left its greasy honours behind it upon every page: and are they not there to this day? This personal experience just brought me acquainted with Wordsworth's habits, and that particular, especially, with his intense impatience for one minute's delay which would have brought a remedy; and yet the reader may believe that it is no affectation in me to say, that fifty such cases could have given me but little pain, when I explain, that whatever could be made good by money at that time I did not regard. Had the book been an old black-letter book, having a value from its rarity, I should have been disturbed in an indescribable degree; but simply with reference to the utter impossibility of reproducing that mode of value. As to the Burke, it was a common book; I had bought the book, with many others, at the sale of Sir Cecil Wray's library, for about two-thirds of the selling price: I could easily replace it; and I mention the case at all only to illustrate the excess of Wordsworth's outrages on books, which made him, in Southey's eyes, a mere monster; for Southey's beautiful library was his estate; and this difference of habits would alone have sufficed to alienate him from Wordsworth. And so I argued in other cases of the same nature. Meantime, had Wordsworth done as Coleridge did, how cheerfully should I have acquiesced in his destruction (such as it was, in a pecuniary sense) of books, as the very highest obligation he could confer. Coleridge often spoiled a book; but, in the course of doing this, he enriched that book with so many and so valuable notes, tossing about him with such lavish profusion, from such a cornucopia of discursive reading, and such a fusing intellect, commentaries so many-angled and so many-coloured, that I have envied many a man whose luck has placed him in the way of such injuries; and that man must have been a churl (though, God knows! too often this churl *has* existed) who could have found in his heart to complain. But Wordsworth rarely, indeed, wrote on the margin of books; and, when he did, nothing could less illustrate his intellectual superiority. The comments were such as might have been made by anybody.

In Roderick Random, for example, I found a note upon a certain luscious description, to the effect "that such things should be left to the imagination of the reader—not expressed". In another place, that it was "improper"; and, in a third, "that the principle laid down was doubtful", or, as Sir Roger de Coverley observes, "that much might be said on both sides". All this, however, indicates nothing more than that different men require to be roused by different stimulants. Wordsworth, in his marginal notes, thought of nothing but delivering himself of a strong feeling, with which he wished to challenge the reader's sympathy. Coleridge imagined an audience before him; and, however doubtful that consummation might seem, I am satisfied that he never wrote a line for which he did not feel the momentary inspiration of sympathy and applause, under the confidence that, sooner or later, all which he had committed to the chance margins of books would converge and assemble in some common reservoir of reception. Bread scattered upon the water will be gathered after many days. This, perhaps, was the consolation that supported him; and the prospect that, for a time, his Arethusa of truth would flow underground, did not, perhaps, disturb, but rather cheered and elevated the sublime old somnambulist. Meantime, Wordsworth's habits of using books—which, I am satisfied, would, in those days, alone have kept him at a distance from most men with fine libraries—were not vulgar; not the habits of those who turn over the page by means of a wet finger, (though even this abomination I have seen perpetrated by a Cambridge tutor and fellow of a college; but then he had been bred up as a ploughman, and the son of a ploughman;) no; but his habits were more properly barbarous and licentious, and in the spirit of audacity belonging *de jure* to no man but him who could plead an income of four or five hundred thousand per annum, and to whom the Bodleian or the Vatican would be a three years' purchase. Gross, meantime, was his delusion upon this subject. Himself he regarded as the golden mean between the too little and the too much of care for books; and, as it happened that every one of his friends far exceeded him in this point, curiously felicitous was the explanation which he gave of this superfluous case, so as to bring it within the natural operation of some known fact in the man's peculiar situation.

De Quincey: *Literary Reminiscences*

V

Southey *to* Landor[1]

May 2, 1808.

I have sent you all that is written of the Curse of Kehama: you offered to print it for me; if ever I finish the poem it will be because of that offer, though without the slightest intention of accepting it. Enough is written to open the story of the poem, and serve as a specimen of its manner, though much of what is to follow would be in a wilder strain. Tell me if your ear is offended with the rhymes when they occur, or if it misses them when they fail. I wish it had never been begun, because I like it too well to throw it behind the fire, and not well enough to complete it without the "go on" of some one whose approbation is worth having.

My history as an author is not a very honorable one to the age in which we live. By giving up my whole time to worthless work in reviews, magazines, and newspapers, I could thrive, as by giving up half my time to them, I contrive to live. In the time thus employed every year I could certainly produce such a poem as Thalaba, and if I did I should starve. You have awakened in me projects which I have dismissed contentedly, and, as I thought, for ever. If you think Kehama deserves to be finished, I will borrow hours from sleep, and finish it by rising two hours before my customary time; and when it is finished I will try whether subscribers can be procured for five hundred copies, by which means I should receive the whole profit to myself. The bookseller's share is too much like the lion in the fable: 30 or 33 per cent. they first deduct as booksellers, and then half the residue as

[1] Southey was the only literary man of his own age with whom Landor was ever at all intimate. Their friendship, however, was a lifelong one.

publishers. I have no reason to complain of mine: they treat me with great respect and great liberality, but I wish to be independent of them; and this, if it could be effected, would make me so.

The will and the power to produce anything great are not often found together. I wish you would write in English, because it is a better language than Latin, and because the disuse of English as a living and literary language would be the greatest evil that could befall mankind. It would cost you little labour to write perspicuously, and thus get rid of your only fault. . . .

Literary fame is the only fame of which a wise man ought to be ambitious, because it is the only lasting and living fame. Bonaparte will be forgotten before his time in Purgatory is half over, or but just remembered like Nimrod, or other cut-throats of antiquity, who serve for us the commonplaces of declamation. If you made yourself King of Crete, you would differ from a hundred other adventurers only in chronology, and in the course of a millenium or two, nothing more would be known of your conquest than what would be found in the stereotype Gebir prefixed as an account of the author. Pour out your mind in a great poem, and you will exercise authority over the feelings and opinions of mankind as long as the language lasts in which you write. . . .

Farewell! I wish you had purchased Loweswater instead of Llantony. I wish you were married, because the proverb about a rolling stone applies to a single heart, and I wish you were as much a Quaker as I am. Christian stoicism is wholesome for all minds; were I your confessor, I should enjoin you to throw aside Rousseau, and make Epictetus your manual. Probatum est.

Yours truly,

Robert Southey

VI

COLERIDGE'S 1808 LECTURES

It was not long after this event that my own introduction to Coleridge occurred. At that time some negotiation was pending between him and the Royal Institution, which ended in their engaging him to deliver a course of lectures on Poetry and the Fine Arts during the ensuing winter. For this series (twelve or sixteen, I think) he received a sum of one hundred guineas. And, considering the slightness of the pains which he bestowed upon them, he was well remunerated. I fear that they did not increase his reputation; for never did any man treat his audience with less respect, or his task with less careful attention. I was in London for part of the time, and can report the circumstances, having made a point of attending duly at the appointed hours. Coleridge was at that time living uncomfortably enough at the "Courier" office, in the Strand. In such a situation, annoyed by the sound of feet passing his chamber-door continually to the printing-rooms of this great establishment, and with no gentle ministrations of female hands to sustain his cheerfulness, naturally enough his spirits flagged; and he took more than ordinary doses of opium. I called upon him daily, and pitied his forlorn condition. There was no bell in the room; which for many months answered the double purpose of bed-room and sitting-room. Consequently, I often saw him, picturesquely enveloped in nightcaps, surmounted by handkerchiefs indorsed upon handkerchiefs, shouting from the attics of the "Courier" office, down three or four flights of stairs, to a certain "Mrs Brainbridge", his sole attendant, whose dwelling was in the subterranean regions of the house. There did I often see the philosopher, with the most lugubrious of faces, invoking with all his might this uncouth name of "Brainbridge", each syllable of which he intonated with long-drawn emphasis, in order to overpower the hostile hubbub coming downwards from the creaking press, and the roar from the Strand, which entered at all the front windows. "Mistress Brainbridge! I say, Mistress Brainbridge!" was the perpetual cry, until I expected to hear the Strand, and distant Fleet Street, take up the echo of "Brainbridge!" Thus unhappily situated, he sank more than ever under the dominion of opium; so that, at two o'clock, when he should have been in attendance at the Royal Institution, he was too often unable to rise from bed. Then came dismissals of audience after audience, with pleas of illness; and on many of his lecture days I have seen all Albemarle Street closed by a "lock" of carriages, filled with women of distinction, until the servants of the Institution or their own footmen advanced to the carriage-doors with the intelligence that Mr Coleridge had been suddenly taken ill. This plea, which at first had been received with expressions of concern, repeated too often, began to rouse disgust. Many in anger, and some in real uncertainty whether it would not be trouble thrown away, ceased to attend. And we that were more constant too often found reason to be disappointed with the quality of his lecture. His appearance was generally that of a person struggling with pain and overmastering illness. His lips were baked with feverish heat, and often black in colour; and, in spite of the water which he continued drinking through the whole course of his lecture, he often seemed to labour under an almost paralytic inability to raise the upper jaw from the lower. In such a state, it is clear that nothing could save the lecture itself from reflecting his own feebleness and exhaustion, except the advantage of having been pre-composed in some happier mood. But that never happened: most unfortunately he relied upon his extempore ability to carry him through. Now, had he been in spirits, or had he gathered animation, and kindled by his own motion, no written lecture could have been more effectual than one of his unpremeditated colloquial harangues. But either he was depressed originally below the point from which any re-ascent was possible, or else this re-action was intercepted by continual disgust from looking back upon his own ill-success; for, assuredly, he never once recovered that free and eloquent movement of thought which he could command at any time in a private company. The passages he read, moreover, in illustrating his doctrines, were generally unhappily chosen, because chosen at haphazard, from the difficulty of finding at a moment's summons those passages which his purpose required. Nor do I remember any that produced much effect, except two or three, which I myself put ready marked into his hands, among the Metrical Romances edited by Ritson.

DE QUINCEY: *Literary Reminiscences*

VII

COLERIDGE AMONG THE LAKES

At the Lakes, and summoned abroad by scenery so exquisite—living, too, in the bosom of a family endeared to him by long friendship and by sympathy the closest with all his propensities and tastes—Coleridge (it may be thought) could not sequester himself so profoundly as at the "Courier" Office within his own shell, or shut himself out so completely from that large dominion of eye and ear amongst the hills, the fields, and the woods, which once he had exercised so delightfully to himself, and with a participation so immortal, through his exquisite poems, to all generations. He was not now reduced to depend upon "Mrs Brainbridge"——(Mistress Brain—Brain—Brainbridge, I say—— Oh heavens! *is* there, *can* there, *was* there, *will* there ever at any future period be, an undeniable use in saying and in pressing upon the attention of the Strand and Fleet Street at their earliest convenience the painful subject of Mistress Brain—Brain—Brainbridge, I say—— Do you hear, Mrs Brain—Brain—Brainbridge——? Brain or Bain, it matters little—Bran or Brain, it's all one, I conceive): here, on the contrary, he looked out from his study windows upon the sublime hills of *Seat Sandal* and *Arthur's Chair*, and upon pastoral cottages at their feet; and all around him he heard hourly the murmurings of happy life, the sound of female voices, and the innocent laughter of children. But apparently he was not happy; opium, was it, or what was it, that poisoned all natural pleasure at its sources? He burrowed continually deeper into scholastic subtleties and metaphysical abstractions; and, like that class described by Seneca in the luxurious Rome of *his* days, he lived chiefly by candlelight. At two or four o'clock in the afternoon he would make his first appearance. Through the silence of the night, when all other lights had disappeared in the quiet cottages of Grasmere, *his* lamp might be seen invariably by the belated traveller, as he descended the long steep from Dunmailraise; and at seven or eight o'clock in the morning, when man was going forth to his labour, this insulated son of reverie was retiring to bed.

DE QUINCEY: *Literary Reminiscences*

VIII

GRETA HALL

The house itself, Greta Hall, stood upon a little eminence overhanging the river Greta. There was nothing remarkable in its internal arrangements: in all respects, it was a very plain unadorned family dwelling; large enough, by a little contrivance, to accommodate two or, in some sense, three families, viz. Mr Southey, and *his* family; Mr Coleridge, and *his*; together with Mrs Lovell, who, when her son was with her, might be said to compose a third. Mrs Coleridge, Mrs Southey, and Mrs Lovell were sisters; all having come originally from Bristol; and, as the different sets of children in this one house had each three several aunts, all the ladies, by turns, assuming that relation twice over, it was one of Southey's many amusing jests, to call the hill on which Greta Hall was placed, the *ant-hill*. Mrs Lovell was the widow of Mr Robert Lovell, who had published a volume of poems, in conjunction with Southey, somewhere about the year 1797, under the signatures of Bion and Moschus. This lady, having one only son, did not require any large suite of rooms; and the less so, as her son quitted her, at an early age, to pursue a professional education. The house had therefore been divided (not by absolute partition, into two distinct apartments, but by an amicable distribution of rooms) between the two families of Mr Coleridge and Mr Southey; Mr Coleridge had a separate study, which was distinguished by nothing except by an organ amongst its furniture, and by a magnificent view from its window, (or windows,) if that could be considered a distinction, in a situation whose local necessities presented you with magnificent objects in whatever direction you might happen to turn your eyes. In the morning, the two families might live apart; but they met at dinner, and in a common drawing-room; and Southey's library, in both senses of the word, was placed at the service of all the ladies alike. However, they did not intrude upon him, except in cases where they wished for a larger reception room, or a more interesting place for suggesting the topics of conversation. Interesting this room was, indeed, and in a degree not often rivalled. The library—the collection of books, I mean, which formed the most conspicuous part of its furniture within—was in all senses a good one. The books were chiefly English, Spanish, and Portuguese; well selected, being the great cardinal classics of the three literatures; fine copies, and decorated externally with a reasonable elegance, so as to make them in harmony with the other embellishments of the room. This effect was aided by the horizontal arrangement upon brackets, of many rare manuscripts—Spanish or Portuguese. Made thus gay within, this room stood in little need of attractions from without. Yet, even upon the gloomiest day of winter, the landscape from the different windows was too permanently commanding in its grandeur, too essentially independent of the seasons or the pomp of woods, to fail in fascinating the gaze of the coldest and dullest of spectators. The lake of Derwent Water in one direction, with its lovely islands—a lake about ten miles in circuit, and shaped pretty much like a boy's kite; the lake of Bassinthwaite in another; the mountains of Newlands arranging themselves like pavilions; the gorgeous confusion of Borrowdale just revealing its sublime chaos through the narrow vista of its gorge; all these objects lay in different angles to the front; whilst the sullen rear, not fully visible on this side of the house, was closed for many a league by the vast and towering masses of Skiddaw and Blencathara—mountains which are rather to be considered as frontier barriers, and chains of hilly ground, cutting the county of Cumberland into great chambers and different climates, than as insulated eminences; so vast is the area which they occupy; though there *are* also such separate and insulated heights, and nearly amongst the highest in the country. Southey's lot had therefore fallen, locally considered, into a goodly heritage. This grand panorama of mountain scenery, so varied, so expansive, and yet having the delightful feeling about it of a deep seclusion and dell-like sequestration from the world—a feeling which, in the midst of so expansive an area, spread out below his windows, could not have been sustained by any barriers less elevated than Glaramara, Skiddaw, or (which could be also descried) "the mighty Helvellyn and Catchedicam"; this congregation of hill and lake, so wide, and yet so prison-like, in its separation from all beyond it, lay for ever under the eyes of Southey. His position locally and, in some respects, intellectually reminded one of Gibbon: but with great advantage in the comparison to Southey. The little town of Keswick and its adjacent lake bore something of the same relation to mighty London that Geneva and its lake may be thought to bear towards brilliant Paris. Southey, like Gibbon, was a miscellaneous scholar; he, like Gibbon, of vast historical research; he, like Gibbon, signally industrious, and patient, and elaborate in collecting the materials for his historical works. Like Gibbon, he had dedicated a life of competent ease, in a pecuniary sense, to literature; like Gibbon, he had gathered to the shores of a beautiful lake, remote from great capitals, a large, or, at least, sufficient library; (in each case, I believe, the library ranged, as to numerical amount, between seven and ten thousand;) and, like Gibbon, he was the most accomplished litterateur amongst the erudite scholars of his time, and the most of an erudite scholar amongst the accomplished litterateurs. After all these points of agreement known, it remains as a pure advantage on the side of Southey—a mere *lucro ponatur*—that he was a poet; and, by all men's confession, a respectable poet, brilliant in his descriptive powers, and fascinating in his narration, however much he might want of

> The vision and the faculty divine.

It is remarkable amongst the series of parallelisms that have been or might be pursued between two men, both had the honour of retreating from a parliamentary life; Gibbon, after some silent and inert experience of that warfare; Southey, with a prudent foresight of the ruin to his health and literary usefulness, won from the experience of his nearest friends.

DE QUINCEY: *Literary Reminiscences*

BYRON IN 1809

The first time I saw Lord Byron, he was rehearsing the part of Leander, under the auspices of Mr Jackson, the prize-fighter. It was in the river Thames, before his first visit to Greece. There used to be a bathing-machine stationed on the eastern side of Westminster Bridge; and I had been bathing, and was standing on this machine adjusting my clothes, when I noticed a respectable-looking manly person, who was eyeing something at a distance. This was Mr Jackson waiting for his pupil. The latter was swimming with somebody for a wager. I forgot what his tutor said of him; but he spoke in terms of praise. I saw nothing in Lord Byron at that time, but a young man who, like myself, had written a bad volume of poems; and though I had a sympathy with him on this account, and more respect for his rank than I was willing to suppose, my sympathy was not an agreeable one; so, contenting myself with seeing his lordship's head bob up and down in the water, like a buoy, I came away.

Lord Byron, when he afterwards came to see me in prison, was pleased to regret that I had not stayed. He told me, that the sight of my volume at Harrow had been one of his incentives to write verses, and that he had had the same passion for friendship which I had displayed in it. To my astonishment he quoted some of the lines, and would not hear me speak ill of them. His harbinger in the visit was Moore. Moore told me, that, besides liking my politics, his lordship liked the *Feast of the Poets*, and would be glad to make my acquaintance. I said I felt myself highly flattered, and should be proud to entertain his lordship as well as a poor patriot could. He was accordingly invited to dinner. His friend only stipulated that there should be "fish and vegetables for the noble bard"; his lordship at that time being anti-carnivorous in his eating. He came, and we passed a very pleasant afternoon, talking of books, and school, and of their friend and brother poet the late Rev. Mr Bowles, whose sonnets were among the early inspirations of Coleridge.

LEIGH HUNT'S *Autobiography*

LITERARY LONDON

I

LAMB *to* COLERIDGE

Monday, *October* 30, 1809.

Dear Coleridge,—I have but this moment received your letter, dated the 9th instant, having just come off a journey from Wiltshire, where I have been with Mary on a visit to Hazlitt. The journey has been of infinite service to her. We have had nothing but sunshiny days, and daily walks from eight to twenty miles a-day; have seen Wilton, Salisbury, Stonehenge, &c. Her illness lasted but six weeks; it left her weak, but the country has made us whole. We came back to our Hogarth Room. I have made several acquisitions since you saw them,—and found Nos. 8, 9, 10 of the *Friend*. The account of Luther in the Warteburg is as fine as any thing I ever read. God forbid that a man who has such things to say should be silenced for want of £100. This Custom-and-Duty age would have made the Preacher on the Mount take out a licence, and St Paul's Epistles would not have been missible without a stamp. O that you may find means to go on! But alas! where is Sir G. Beaumont?—Sotheby? What is become of the rich Auditors in Albemarle Street? Your letter has saddened me.

I am so tired with my journey, being up all night, that I have neither things nor words in my power. I believe I expressed my admiration of the pamphlet[1]. Its power over

[1] Wordsworth's *Convention of Cintra.*

me was like that which Milton's pamphlets must have had on his contemporaries, who were tuned to them. What a piece of prose! Do you hear if it is read at all? I am out of the world of readers. I hate all that do read, for they read nothing but reviews and new books. I gather myself up unto the old things.

I have put up shelves. You never saw a bookcase in more true harmony with the contents than what I've nailed up in a room, which, though new, has more aptitudes for growing old than you shall often see—as one sometimes gets a friend in the middle of life, who becomes an old friend in a short time. My rooms are luxurious; one is for prints and one for books; a Summer and a Winter parlour. When shall I ever see you in them?

C. L.

II

Somewhere in this period it was, by the way, that I had an opportunity of introducing to his knowledge my brother, "poor Pink". Lamb liked him; and the more so from an accident which occurred at the very second interview that he and Pink ever had. It was in Bond Street, at an exhibition of two large and splendid pictures by Salvator Rosa,—one representing a forest scene and a forest recluse (of what character in Salvator's intention may be doubted, but in the little printed account of the paintings he was described as Diogenes). These pictures were, I should think, twelve feet high at the least, consequently upon a large scale; and the tone of colouring was peculiarly sombre, or rather cold; and it tended even to the monotonous. One almost uniform cheerless tint of yellowish green, with some little perhaps of a warmish umber, overspread the distances; and the foreground showed little else than a heavy dull-toned black. Pink, who knew as little of painting as the *bow'sons* of his various ships, had, however, a profound sensibility to some of its effects; and, if he ever ran up hastily and fearfully to London from Portsmouth, it was sure to be at the time when the annual exhibition of the

Academy was open. No exhibition was ever missed by him, whether of a public or comparatively private nature. In particular, he had attended, with infinite delight, the exhibition (in Newman Street, I think) of Mr West's pictures. *Death and his Pale Horse* prodigiously attracted him; and others, from the freshness and gorgeousness of their colouring, had absolutely fascinated his eye. It may be imagined, therefore, with what disgust he viewed two subjects, from which the vast name of the painter had led him to expect so much, but which from the low style of the colouring yielded him so little. There might be forty people in the room at the time my brother and I were there. We had stood for ten or fifteen minutes, examining the pictures, when at length I noticed Charles Lamb, and, at a little distance, his sister. If a creditor had wished to seize upon either, no surer place in London (no, not Drury Lane, or Covent Garden) for finding them than an exhibition from the works of the old masters. And, moreover, as, amongst certain classes of birds, if you have one you are sure of the other, so, with respect to the Lambs (unless in those dreary seasons when the "*dual* unity", as it is most affectingly termed by Wordsworth, had been for a time sundered into a widowed desolation by the periodic affliction), seeing or hearing the brother, you knew that the sister could not be far off. If she *were*, you sighed, knew what that meant, and asked no questions.

Lamb, upon seeing us, advanced to shake hands; but he paused one moment to await the critical dogma which he perceived to be at that time issuing from Pink's lips. That it was vituperation in a high degree, anybody near us might hear; and some actually turned round in fright upon catching these profane words: "D—— the fellow! I could do better myself". Wherewith, perhaps unconsciously, but perhaps also by way of enforcing his thought, Pink (who had brought home from his long sea life a detestable practice of chewing tobacco) ejaculated a quid of some coarse quality, that lighted upon the frame of the great master's picture, and, for aught I know, may be sticking there yet. Lamb could not have approved such a judgment, nor perhaps the immeasurable presumption that might seem to have accompanied such a judgment from most men, or from an artist; but he knew that Pink was a mere sailor, knowing nothing historically of art, nor much of the pretensions of the mighty artists. Or, had it been otherwise, at all events, he admired and loved, beyond all other qualities whatsoever, a hearty, cordial sincerity. Honest homely obstinacy, not to be enslaved by a great name—though that, again, may, by possibility, become in process of time itself an affectation—Lamb almost reverenced; and therefore it need not surprise anybody that, in the midst of his loud, unrepressed laughter, he came up to my brother, and offered his hand, with an air of friendliness that flattered Pink, and a little misled him: for, that evening, on dining with Pink, he said to me—"That Lamb's a sensible fellow. You see how evidently he approved of what I remarked about that old humbugging rascal, Salvator Rosa". Lamb, in this point, had a feature of character in common with Sir Walter Scott (at least I suppose it to have been a feature of Sir Walter's mind, upon the information of Professor Wilson): that, if a man had, or if he supposed him to have, a strongly marked combination or tendency of feelings, of opinions, of likings, or of dislikings—what in fact, we call a *character*—no matter whether it were built upon prejudices the most extravagant, or ignorance the most profound, provided only it were sincere, and not mere lawless audacity, but were self-consistent, and had *unity* as respected itself—in that extent he was sure to manifest liking and respect for the man. And hence it was that Lamb liked Pink much more for this Gothic and outrageous sentence upon Salvator Rosa than he would have liked him for the very best, profoundest, or most comprehensive critique upon that artist that could have been delivered. Pink, on the other hand, liked Lamb greatly, and used, in all his letters, to request that I would present his best regards to that Charles Lamb, "who wouldn't be humbugged by the old rascal in Bond Street".

DE QUINCEY: *Literary Reminiscences*

III

1810.

Nov. 14th.—Saw Coleridge for the first time in private, at Charles Lamb's. A short interview, which allowed of little opportunity for the display of his peculiar powers. He related to us that Jeffrey, the editor of the *Edinburgh Review*, had lately called on him, and assured him that he was a great admirer of Wordsworth's poetry, that the Lyrical Ballads were always on his table, and that Wordsworth had been attacked in the *Review* simply because the errors of men of genius ought to be exposed. Towards me, Coleridge added, Jeffrey was even flattering. He was like a schoolboy, who having tried his man and been thrashed, becomes contentedly a fag.

Nov. 15th.—A very delightful evening at Charles Lamb's; Coleridge, Morgan, M. Burney, etc. there. Coleridge very eloquent on German metaphysics and poetry, Wordsworth, and Spanish politics.

Of Wordsworth he spoke with great warmth of praise, but objected to some of his poems. Wishing to avoid an undue regard to the high and genteel in society, Wordsworth had attached himself unreasonably to the low, so that he himself erred at last. He should have recollected that verse being the language of passion, and passion dictating energetic expressions, it became him to make his subjects and style accord. One asks why tales so simple were not in prose. With "malice prepense" he fixes on objects of reflection, which do not naturally excite it. Coleridge censured the disproportion in the machinery of the poem on the Gipsies. Had the whole world been standing idle, more powerful arguments to expose evil could not have been brought forward. Of Kant he spoke in terms of high admiration. . . . He made an elaborate distinction between fancy and imagination. The excess of fancy is delirium, of imagination mania. Fancy is the arbitrary bringing together of things that lie remote, and forming them into a unity. The materials lie ready for the fancy, which acts by a sort of juxtaposition. On the other hand the imagination under excitement generates and produces a form of its own.

The "seas of milk and ships of amber" he quoted as fanciful delirium. He related as a sort of disease of imagination, what had occurred to himself. He had been watching intently the motions of a kite among the mountains of Westmoreland, when on a sudden he saw two kites in an opposite direction. This delusion lasted some time. At last he discovered that the two kites were the fluttering branches of a tree beyond a wall.

HENRY CRABB ROBINSON'S *Diary*

IV

1811.

July 24th.—Late at C. Lamb's. Found a large party there. Southey had been with Blake, and admired both his designs and his poetic talents. At the same time he held him to be a decided madman. Blake, he said, spoke of his visions with the diffidence which is usual with such people, and did not seem to expect that he should be believed. He showed Southey a perfectly mad poem, called "Jerusalem". Oxford Street is in Jerusalem.

December 5th.—Accompanied Mrs Rutt to Coleridge's lecture. In this he surpassed himself in talking in a very interesting way, without speaking at all on the subject announced. According to advertisement, he was to lecture on "Romeo and Juliet" and Shakespeare's female characters. Instead of this he began with a defence of school-flogging, in preference at least to Lancaster's mode of punishing, without pretending to find the least connection between that topic and poetry. Afterwards he remarked on the character of the age of Elizabeth and James I as compared with that of Charles I; distinguished not very clearly between wit and fancy; referred to the different languages of Europe; attacked the fashionable notion concerning poetic diction; ridiculed the tautology of Johnson's line, "If observation, with extensive view", etc.; and warmly defended Shakespeare against the charge of impurity. While Coleridge was commenting on Lancaster's mode of punishing boys, Lamb whispered, "It is a pity he did not leave this till he got to 'Henry VI', for then he might say he could not help taking part against the Lancastrians". Afterwards, when Coleridge was running from topic to topic, Lamb said, "This is not much amiss. He promised a lecture on the Nurse in 'Romeo and Juliet', and in its place he has given one in the *manner* of the Nurse".

HENRY CRABB ROBINSON'S *Diary*

V

1812.

January 14*th.*—Heard Hazlitt's first lecture on the "History of English Philosophy". He seems to have no conception of the difference between a lecture and a book. What he said was sensible and excellent, but he delivered himself in a low monotonous voice, with his eyes fixed on his MS., not once daring to look at his audience; and he read so rapidly that no one could possibly give to the matter the attention it required.

January 15*th.*—Tea with the Lambs. An evening at cards. Hazlitt there, much depressed. He seemed disposed to give up the lectures altogether. The cause of his reading so rapidly was, that he was told to limit himself to an hour, and what he had prepared would have taken three hours, if it had been read slowly.

January 16*th.*—At Coleridge's lecture. He reviewed Johnson's "Preface", and vindicated warmly Milton's moral and political character, but I think with less than his usual ability. He excited a hiss once by calling Johnson a *fellow*, for which he happily apologized by observing that it is in the nature of evil to beget evil, and that we are thus apt to fall into the fault we censure. He remarked on Milton's minor poems, and the nature of blank verse. The latter half of the lecture was very good.

January 20*th.*—In the evening at Coleridge's lecture. Conclusion of Milton. Not one of the happiest of Coleridge's efforts. Rogers was there, and with him was Lord Byron. He was wrapped up, but I recognised his club foot, and, indeed, his countenance and general appearance.

January 21*st.*—Hazlitt's second lecture. His delivery vastly improved, and I hope he will now get on. He read at

LIBRARY ST. MARY'S COLLEGE

Basil Montagu's last night half his first lecture. He was to read the whole, but abruptly broke off, and could not be persuaded to read the remainder. Lamb and other friends were there.

HENRY CRABB ROBINSON'S *Diary*

VI

AN EVENING AT LAMB'S

Come like shadows—so depart.

B——[1] it was, I think, who suggested this subject, as well as the defence of Guy Faux, which I urged him to execute. As, however, he would undertake neither, I suppose I must do both—a task for which he would have been much fitter, no less from the temerity than the felicity of his pen—

> Never so sure our rapture to create
> As when it touch'd the brink of all we hate.

Compared with him I shall, I fear, make but a common-place piece of business of it; but I should be loth the idea was entirely lost, and besides I may avail myself of some hints of his in the progress of it. I am sometimes, I suspect, a better reporter of the ideas of other people than expounder of my own. I pursue the one too far into paradox or mysticism; the others I am not bound to follow farther than I like, or than seems fair and reasonable.

On the question being started, A——[2] said, "I suppose the two first persons you would choose to see would be the two greatest names in English literature, Sir Isaac Newton and Mr Locke?" In this A——, as usual, reckoned without his host. Every one burst out a laughing at the expression of B——'s face, in which impatience was restrained by courtesy. "Yes, the greatest names," he stammered out hastily, "but they were not persons—not persons." "Not persons?" said A——, looking wise and foolish at the same time, afraid his triumph might be premature. "That is", rejoined B——,

[1] Lamb. [2] William Ayrton.

"not characters, you know. By Mr Locke and Sir Isaac Newton, you mean the Essay on the Human Understanding, and the *Principia*, which we have to this day. Beyond their contents there is nothing personally interesting in the men. But what we want to see any one *bodily* for, is when there is something peculiar, striking in the individuals, more than we can learn from their writings, and yet are curious to know. I dare say Locke and Newton were very like Kneller's portraits of them. But who could paint Shakspeare?" "Ay," retorted A——, "there it is; then I suppose you would prefer seeing him and Milton instead?" "No," said B——, "neither. I have seen so much of Shakspeare on the stage and on bookstalls, in frontispieces and on mantle-pieces, that I am quite tired of the everlasting repetition: and as to Milton's face, the impressions that have come down to us of it I do not like; it is too starched and puritanical; and I should be afraid of losing some of the manna of his poetry in the leaven of his countenance and the precisian's band and gown."—"I shall guess no more", said A——. "Who is it, then, you would like to see 'in his habit as he lived', if you had your choice of the whole range of English literature?" B—— then named Sir Thomas Brown and Fulke Greville, the friend of Sir Philip Sidney, as the two worthies whom he should feel the greatest pleasure to encounter on the floor of his apartment in their night-gown and slippers, and to exchange friendly greeting with them. At this A—— laughed outright, and conceived B—— was jesting with him; but as no one followed his example, he thought there might be something in it, and waited for an explanation in a state of whimsical suspense. B—— then (as well as I can remember a conversation that passed twenty years ago—how time slips!) went on as follows. "The reason why I pitch upon these two authors is, that their writings are riddles, and they themselves the most mysterious of personages. They resemble the soothsayers of old, who dealt in dark hints and doubtful oracles; and I should like to ask them the meaning of what no mortal but themselves, I should suppose, can fathom. There is Dr Johnson, I have no curiosity, no strange uncertainty about him:

he and Boswell together have pretty well let me into the secret of what passed through his mind. He and other writers like him are sufficiently explicit: my friends, whose repose I should be tempted to disturb, (were it in my power) are implicit, inextricable, inscrutable.

And call up him who left half-told
The story of Cambuscan bold.

"When I look at that obscure but gorgeous prose-composition (the *Urn-burial*) I seem to myself to look into a deep abyss, at the bottom of which are hid pearls and rich treasure; or it is like a stately labyrinth of doubt and withering speculation, and I would invoke the spirit of the author to lead me through it. Besides, who would not be curious to see the lineaments of a man who, having himself been twice married, wished that mankind were propagated like trees! As to Fulke Greville, he is like nothing but one of his own 'Prologues spoken by the ghost of an old king of Ormus', a truly formidable and inviting personage: his style is apocalyptical, cabalistical, a knot worthy of such an apparition to untie; and for the unravelling a passage or two, I would stand the brunt of an encounter with so portentous a commentator!" "I am afraid in that case", said A——, "that if the mystery were once cleared up, the merit might be lost"; and turning to me, whispered a friendly apprehension, that while B—— continued to admire these old crabbed authors, he would never become a popular writer. Dr Donne was mentioned as a writer of the same period, with a very interesting countenance, whose history was singular, and whose meaning was often quite as *uncomeatable*, without a personal citation from the dead, as that of any of his contemporaries. The volume was produced; and while some one was expatiating on the exquisite simplicity and beauty of the portrait prefixed to the old edition, A—— got hold of the poetry, and exclaiming "What have we here?" read the following:

Here lies a She-Sun and a He-Moon here,
She gives the best light to his sphere,
Or each is both and all, and so
They unto one another nothing owe.

There was no resisting this, till B——, seizing the volume, turned to the beautiful "Lines to his Mistress", dissuading her from accompanying him abroad, and read them with suffused features and a faltering tongue.

Some one then inquired of B—— if we could not see from the window the Temple-walk in which Chaucer used to take his exercise; and on his name being put to the vote, I was pleased to find that there was a general sensation in his favour in all but A——, who said something about the ruggedness of the metre, and even objected to the quaintness of the orthography. I was vexed at this superficial gloss, pertinaciously reducing every thing to its own trite level, and asked "if he did not think it would be worth while to scan the eye that had first greeted the Muse in that dim twilight and early dawn of English literature; to see the head, round which the visions of fancy must have played like gleams of inspiration or a sudden glory; to watch those lips that 'lisped in numbers, for the numbers came'—as by a miracle, or as if the dumb should speak? Nor was it alone that he had been the first to tune his native tongue (however imperfectly to modern ears); but he was himself a noble, manly character, standing before his age and striving to advance it; a pleasant humourist withal, who has not only handed down to us the living manners of his time, but had, no doubt, store of curious and quaint devices, and would make as hearty a companion as Mine Host of Tabard. His interview with Petrarch is fraught with interest. Yet I would rather have seen Chaucer in company with the author of the Decameron, and have heard them exchange their best stories together, the Squire's Tale against the Story of the Falcon, the Wife of Bath's Prologue against the Adventures of Friar Albert. How fine to see the high mysterious brow which learning then wore, relieved by the gay, familiar tone of men of the world, and by the courtesies of genius. Surely, the thoughts and feelings which passed through the minds of these great revivers of learning, these Cadmuses who sowed the teeth of letters, must have stamped an expression on their features, as different from the moderns as their books, and well worth the perusal".

"Dante", I continued, "is as interesting a person as his own Ugolino, one whose lineaments curiosity would as eagerly devour in order to penetrate his spirit, and the only one of the Italian poets I should care much to see. There is a fine portrait of Ariosto by no less a hand than Titian's; light, Moorish, spirited, but not answering our idea. The same artist's large colossal profile of Peter Aretine is the only likeness of the kind that has the effect of conversing with 'the mighty dead', and this is truly spectral, ghastly, necromantic." B—— put it to me if I should like to see Spenser as well as Chaucer; and I answered without hesitation, "No; for that his beauties were ideal, visionary, not palpable or personal, and therefore connected with less curiosity about the man. His poetry was the essence of romance, a very halo round the bright orb of fancy; and the bringing in the individual might dissolve the charm. No tones of voice could come up to the mellifluous cadence of his verse; no form but of a winged angel could vie with the airy shapes he has described. He was (to our apprehensions) rather 'a creature of the element, that lived in the rainbow and played in the plighted clouds', than an ordinary mortal. Or if he did appear, I should wish it to be as a mere vision, like one of his own pageants, and that he should pass by unquestioned like a dream or sound—

——*That* was Arion crown'd:
So went he playing on the wat'ry plain!"

Captain C.[1] muttered something about Columbus, and M. C.[2] hinted at the Wandering Jew; but the last was set aside as spurious, and the first made over to the New World.

"I should like", said Miss D——,[3] "to have seen Pope talking with Patty Blount; and I *have* seen Goldsmith." Every one turned round to look at Miss D——, as if by so doing they too could get a sight of Goldsmith.

"Where", asked a harsh croaking voice, "was Dr Johnson in the years 1745–6? He did not write any thing that we know of, nor is there any account of him in Boswell during

[1] Captain Burney. [2] Martin Burney.
[3] Mrs Reynolds.

those two years. Was he in Scotland with the Pretender? He seems to have passed through the scenes in the Highlands in company with Boswell many years after 'with lack-lustre eye', yet as if they were familiar to him, or associated in his mind with interests that he durst not explain. If so, it would be an additional reason for my liking him; and I would give something to have seen him seated in the tent with the youthful Majesty of Britain, and penning the Proclamation to all true subjects and adherents of the legitimate Government."

"I thought", said A——, turning short round upon B——, "that you of the Lake School did not like Pope?" "Not like Pope! My dear sir, you must be under a mistake—I can read him over and over for ever!" "Why certainly, the 'Essay on Man' must be allowed to be a master-piece." "It may be so, but I seldom look into it." "Oh! then it's his Satires you admire?" "No, not his Satires, but his friendly Epistles and his compliments." "Compliments! I did not know he ever made any." "The finest", said B——, "that were ever paid by the wit of man. Each of them is worth an estate for life—nay, is an immortality. There is that superb one to Lord Cornbury:

> Despise low joys, low gains;
> Disdain whatever Cornbury disdains;
> Be virtuous, and be happy for your pains.

Was there ever more artful insinuation of idolatrous praise? And then that noble apotheosis of his friend Lord Mansfield (however little deserved), when, speaking of the House of Lords, he adds—

> Conspicuous scene! another yet is nigh,
> (More silent far) where kings and poets lie;
> Where Murray (long enough his country's pride)
> Shall be no more than Tully or than Hyde!

And with what a fine turn of indignant flattery he addresses Lord Bolingbroke—

> Why rail they then, if but one wreath of mine,
> Oh! all accomplish'd St John, deck thy shrine?"

"Or turn", continued B——, with a slight hectic on his cheek and his eye glistening, "to his list of early friends:

> But why then publish? Granville the polite,
> And knowing Walsh, would tell me I could write;
> Well-natured Garth inflamed with early praise,
> And Congreve loved and Swift endured my lays:
> The courtly Talbot, Somers, Sheffield read,
> Ev'n mitred Rochester would nod the head;
> And St John's self (great Dryden's friend before)
> Received with open arms one poet more.
> Happy my studies, if by these approved!
> Happier their author, if by these beloved!
> From these the world will judge of men and books,
> Not from the Burnets, Oldmixons, and Cooks."

Here his voice totally failed him, and throwing down the book, he said, "Do you think I would not wish to have been friends with such a man as this?"

"What say you to Dryden?" "He rather made a show of himself, and courted popularity in that lowest temple of Fame, a coffee-house, so as in some measure to vulgarize one's idea of him. Pope, on the contrary, reached the very *beau ideal* of what a poet's life should be; and his fame while living seemed to be an emanation from that which was to circle his name after death. He was so far enviable (and one would feel proud to have witnessed the rare spectacle in him) that he was almost the only poet and man of genius who met with his reward on this side of the tomb, who realized in friends, fortune, the esteem of the world, the most sanguine hopes of a youthful ambition, and who found that sort of patronage from the great during his lifetime which they would be thought anxious to bestow upon him after his death. Read Gay's verses to him on his supposed return from Greece, after his translation of Homer was finished, and say if you would not gladly join the bright procession that welcomed him home, or see it once more land at Whitehall-stairs." "Still", said Miss D——, "I would rather have seen him talking with Patty Blount, or riding by in a coronet-coach with Lady Mary Wortley Montagu!"

E——[1], who was deep in a game of piquet at the other end of the room, whispered to M. C. to ask if Junius would not be a fit person to invoke from the dead. "Yes," said B——, "provided he would agree to lay aside his mask."

We were now at a stand for a short time, when Fielding was mentioned as a candidate: only one, however, seconded the proposition. "Richardson?" "By all means, but only to look at him through the glass-door of his back-shop, hard at work upon one of his novels (the most extraordinary contrast that ever was presented between an author and his works), but not to let him come behind his counter lest he should want you to turn customer, nor to go upstairs with him, lest he should offer to read the first manuscript of Sir Charles Grandison, which was originally written in eight and twenty volumes octavo, or get out the letters of his female correspondents, to prove that Joseph Andrews was low."

There was but one statesman in the whole of English history that any one expressed the least desire to see—Oliver Cromwell, with his fine, frank, rough, pimply face, and wily policy;—and one enthusiast, John Bunyan, the immortal author of the Pilgrim's Progress. It seemed that if he came into the room, dreams would follow him, and that each person would nod under his golden cloud, "nigh-sphered in Heaven", a canopy as strange and stately as any in Homer.

Of all persons near our own time, Garrick's name was received with the greatest enthusiasm, who was proposed by J. F.——[2] He presently superseded both Hogarth and Handel, who had been talked of, but then it was on condition that he should act in tragedy and comedy, in the play and the farce, Lear and Wildair and Abel Drugger. What a *sight for sore eyes* that would be! Who would not part with a year's income at least, almost with a year of his natural life, to be present at it? Besides, as he could not act alone, and recitations are unsatisfactory things, what a troop he must bring with him—the silver-tongued Barry, and Quin, and Shuter and Weston, and Mrs Clive and Mrs Pritchard, of whom I have heard my father speak as so great a favourite when he was

[1] Colonel Phillips. [2] Barron Field.

young! This would indeed be a revival of the dead, the restoring of art; and so much the more desirable, as such is the lurking scepticism mingled with our overstrained admiration of past excellence, that though we have the speeches of Burke, the portraits of Reynolds, the writings of Goldsmith, and the conversation of Johnson, to show what people could do at that period, and to confirm the universal testimony to the merits of Garrick; yet, as it was before our time, we have our misgivings, as if he was probably after all little better than a Bartlemy-fair actor, dressed out to play Macbeth in a scarlet coat and laced cocked-hat. For one, I should like to have seen and heard with my own eyes and ears. Certainly, by all accounts, if any one was ever moved by the true histrionic *æstus*, it was Garrick. When he followed the Ghost in Hamlet, he did not drop the sword, as most actors do behind the scenes, but kept the point raised the whole way round, so fully was he possessed with the idea, or so anxious not to lose sight of his part for a moment. Once at a splendid dinner-party at Lord ——'s, they suddenly missed Garrick, and could not imagine what was become of him, till they were drawn to the window by the convulsive screams and peals of laughter of a young negro boy, who was rolling on the ground in an ecstasy of delight to see Garrick mimicking a turkey-cock in the court-yard, with his coat-tail stuck out behind, and in a seeming flutter of feathered rage and pride. Of our party only two persons present had seen the British Roscius; and they seemed as willing as the rest to renew their acquaintance with their old favourite.

We were interrupted in the hey-day and mid-career of this fanciful speculation, by a grumbler in a corner, who declared it was a shame to make all this rout about a mere player and farce-writer, to the neglect and exclusion of the fine old dramatists, the contemporaries and rivals of Shakespeare. B—— said he had anticipated this objection when he had named the author of Mustapha and Alaham; and out of caprice insisted upon keeping him to represent the set, in preference to the wild hair-brained enthusiast Kit Marlowe; to the sexton of St Ann's, Webster, with his melancholy yew-trees and death's-heads; to Deckar, who was but a garrulous proser; to the voluminous Heywood; and even to Beaumont and Fletcher, whom we might offend by complimenting the wrong author on their joint productions. Lord Brook, on the contrary, stood quite by himself, or in Cowley's words, was "a vast species alone". Some one hinted at the circumstance of his being a lord, which rather startled B——, but he said a *ghost* would perhaps dispense with strict etiquette, on being regularly addressed by his title. Ben Jonson divided our suffrages pretty equally. Some were afraid he would begin to traduce Shakespeare, who was not present to defend himself. "If he grows disagreeable," it was whispered aloud, "there is G——[1] can match him." At length his romantic visit to Drummond of Hawthornden was mentioned, and turned the scale in his favour.

B—— inquired if there was any one that was hanged that I would choose to mention? And I answered, Eugene Aram. The name of the "Admirable Crichton" was suddenly started as a splendid example of *waste* talents, so different from the generality of his countrymen. This choice was mightily approved by a North-Briton present, who declared himself descended from that prodigy of learning and accomplishment, and said he had family-plate in his possession as vouchers for the fact, with the initials A. C.—*Admirable Crichton*! H——[2] laughed or rather roared as heartily at this as I should think he has done for many years.

The last-named Mitre-courtier[3] then wished to know whether there were any metaphysicians to whom one might be tempted to apply the wizard spell? I replied, there were only six in modern times deserving the name—Hobbes, Berkeley, Butler, Hartley, Hume, Leibnitz; and perhaps Jonathan Edwards, a Massachusets man. As to the French, who talked fluently of having *created* this science, there was not a title in any of their writings, that was not to be found literally in the authors I had mentioned. [Horne Tooke, who might have a claim to come in under the head of Grammar,

[1] William Godwin. [2] Leigh Hunt.

[3] B—— at this time occupied chambers in Mitre Court, Fleet Street. [Hazlitt.]

was still living.] None of these names seemed to excite much interest, and I did not plead for the re-appearance of those who might be thought best fitted by the abstracted nature of their studies for their present spiritual and disembodied state, and who, even while on this living stage, were nearly divested of common flesh and blood. As A—— with an uneasy fidgetty face was about to put some question about Mr Locke and Dugald Stewart, he was prevented by M. C. who observed, "If J—— was here, he would undoubtedly be for having up those profound and redoubted scholiasts, Thomas Aquinas and Duns Scotus". I said this might be fair enough in him who had read or fancied he had read the original works, but I did not see how we could have any right to call up these authors to give an account of themselves in person, till we had looked into their writings.

"But shall we have nothing to say", interrogated G. J——, "to the Legend of Good Women?" "Name, name, Mr J——," cried H—— in a boisterous tone of friendly exultation, "name as many as you please, without reserve or fear of molestation!" J—— was perplexed between so many amiable recollections, that the name of the lady of his choice expired in a pensive whiff of his pipe; and B—— impatiently declared for the Duchess of Newcastle. Mrs Hutchinson was no sooner mentioned, than she carried the day from the Duchess. We were the less solicitous on this subject of filling up the posthumous lists of Good Women, as there was already one in the room as good, as sensible, and in all respects as exemplary, as the best of them could be for their lives! "I should like vastly to have seen Ninon de l'Enclos", said that incomparable person; and this immediately put us in mind that we had neglected to pay honour due to our friends on the other side of the Channel: Voltaire, the patriarch of levity, and Rousseau, the father of sentiment, Montaigne and Rabelais (great in wisdom and in wit), Molière and that illustrious group that are collected round him (in the print of that subject) to hear him read his comedy of the Tartuffe at the house of Ninon; Racine, La Fontaine, Rochefoucault, St Evremont, &c.

"There is one person", said a shrill, querulous voice, "I would rather see than all these—Don Quixote!"

"Come, come!" said H——; "I thought we should have no heroes, real or fabulous. What say you, Mr B——? Are you for eking out your shadowy list with such names as Alexander, Julius Cæsar, Tamerlane, or Ghengis Khan?" "Excuse me," said B——, "on the subject of characters in active life, plotters and disturbers of the world, I have a crotchet of my own, which I beg leave to reserve." "No, no! come, out with your worthies!" "What do you think of Guy Faux and Judas Iscariot?" H—— turned an eye upon him like a wild Indian, but cordial and full of smothered glee. "Your most exquisite reason!" was echoed on all sides; and A—— thought that B—— had now fairly entangled himself. "Why, I cannot but think", retorted he of the wistful countenance, "that Guy Faux, that poor fluttering annual scare-crow of straw and rags, is an ill-used gentleman. I would give something to see him sitting pale and emaciated, surrounded by his matches and his barrels of gunpowder, and expecting the moment that was to transport him to Paradise for his heroic self-devotion; but if I say any more, there is that fellow G—— will make something of it. And as to Judas Iscariot, my reason is different. I would fain see the face of him, who, having dipped his hand in the same dish with the Son of Man, could afterwards betray him. I have no conception of such a thing; nor have I ever seen any picture (not even Leonardo's very fine one) that gave me the least idea of it." "You have said enough, Mr B——, to justify your choice."

"Oh! ever right, Menenius,—ever right!"

"There is only one other person I can ever think of after this", continued H——; but without mentioning a name that once put on a semblance of mortality. "If Shakespeare was to come into the room, we should all rise up to meet him; but if that person was to come into it, we should all fall down and try to kiss the hem of his garment!"

As a lady present seemed now to get uneasy at the turn the conversation had taken, we rose up to go. The morning broke with that dim, dubious light by which Giotto, Cimabue, and Ghirlandaio must have seen to paint their earliest works; and we parted to meet again and renew similar topics at night, the next night, and the night after that, till that night overspread Europe which saw no dawn. The same event, in truth, broke up our little Congress that broke up the great one. But that was to meet again: our deliberations have never been resumed.

HAZLITT: *Of Persons One Would Wish to Have Seen*

VII

COLERIDGE *to* SOUTHEY

71, Berners Street, Tuesday, *February* 8, 1813.

My dear Southey,

It is seldom that a man can with *literal truth* apologise for delay in writing; but for the last three weeks I have had more upon my hands and spirits than my health was equal to.

The first copy I can procure of the second edition (of the play[1]) I will do my best to get franked to you. You will, I hope, think it much improved as a poem. Dr Bell, who is all kindness and goodness, came to me in no small bustle this morning in consequence of "a censure passed on the 'Remorse' by a man of great talents, both in prose and verse, who was impartial, and thought highly of the work on the whole". What was it, think you? There were many unequal lines in the Play, but which he did not choose to specify. Dr Bell would not mention the critic's name, but was very earnest with me to procure some indifferent person of good sense to read it over, by way of spectacles to an author's own dim judgment. Soon after he left me I discovered that the critic was Gifford, who had said good-naturedly that I ought to be whipt for leaving so many weak and slovenly lines in so fine a poem. What the lines were *he* would not say and *I* do not care. Inequalities have every poem, even an Epic—much more a Dramatic Poem must have and ought to have. The

[1] Coleridge's tragedy, *Remorse*, was his one genuinely popular success.

question is, are they in their own place *dissonances*? If so I am the last man to stickle for them, who am nicknamed in the Green Room the "anomalous author", from my utter indifference or prompt facility in sanctioning every omission that was suggested. The paragraph in the *Quarterly Review* respecting me, as ridiculed in "Rejected Addresses", was surely unworthy of a man of sense like Gifford. What reason could *he* have to suppose me a man so childishly irritable as to be provoked by a trifle so contemptible? If he had, how could he think it a parody at all? But the noise which the "Rejected Addresses" made, the notice taken of Smith the author by Lord Holland, Byron, etc., give a melancholy confirmation of my assertion in the "Friend" that "we worship the vilest reptile if only the brainless head be expiated by the sting of personal malignity in the tail". I wish I could procure for you the *Examiner* and Drakard's London Paper. They are forced to affect admiration for the Tragedy, but yet abuse me they must, and so comes the old infamous *crambe bis millies cocta* of the "sentimentalities, puerilities, whinings, and meannesses, both of style and thought", in my former writings, but without (which is worth notice both in these gentlemen and in all our former Zoili), without one single quotation or reference in proof or exemplification. No wonder! for excepting the "Three Graves" which was announced as not meant for poetry, and the poem on the Tethered Ass, with the motto *Sermoni propriora,* and which, like your "Dancing Bear", might be called a ludicro-splenetic copy of verses, with the diction purposely appropriate, they might (as at the first appearance of my poems they did) find, indeed, all the opposite vices. But if it had not been for the *Preface* to W.'s *Lyrical Ballads,* they would never themselves have dreamt of affected simplicity and meanness of thought and diction. This slang has gone on for fourteen years against us, and really deserves to be exposed....

The House was crowded again last night, and the Manager told me that they lost £200 by suspending it on the Saturday night that Jack Bannister came out.

THE LAUREATESHIP

To Robert Southey, Esq., Keswick

Abbotsford, *September* 4, 1813.

My dear Southey—On my return here I found, to my no small surprise, a letter tendering me the laurel vacant by the death of the poetical Pye. I have declined the appointment, as being incompetent to the task of annual commemoration; but chiefly as being provided for in my professional department, and unwilling to incur the censure of engrossing the emolument attached to one of the few appointments which seems proper to be filled by a man of literature who has no other views in life. Will you forgive me, my dear friend, if I own I had you in my recollection? I have given Croker the hint, and otherwise endeavoured to throw the office into your option. I am uncertain if you will like it, for the laurel has certainly been tarnished by some of its wearers, and, as at present managed, its duties are inconvenient and somewhat liable to ridicule. But the latter matter might be amended, as I think the Regent's good sense would lead him to lay aside these annual commemorations; and as to the former point it has been worn by Dryden of old, and by Warton in modern days. If you quote my own refusal against me, I reply—first, I have been luckier than you in holding two offices not usually conjoined; secondly, I did not refuse it from any foolish prejudice against the situation, otherwise how durst I mention it to you, my elder brother in the muse?—but from a sort of internal hope that they would give it to you, upon whom it would be so much more worthily conferred. For I am not such an ass as not to know that you are my better in poetry, though I have had, probably but for a time, the tide of popularity in my favour. I have not time to add ten thousand other reasons, but I only wished to tell you how the matter was, and to beg you to think before you reject the offer which I flatter myself will be made to you. If I had not been, like Dogberry, a fellow with two gowns already, I should have jumped at it like a cock at a gooseberry.—Ever yours most truly,

Walter Scott

LEIGH HUNT IN PRISON

On February 3, 1813, Leigh Hunt and his brother John were sentenced to two years' imprisonment for a criminal libel of the Prince Regent, which had appeared in their weekly paper, the *Examiner*. Commenting on the extravagant eulogies showered on the Regent, Hunt had pointed out, among other things, "that this 'Mecaenas of the age' patronised not a single deserving writer!...that this 'Conqueror of Hearts' was the disappointer of hopes!—that this 'Exciter of desire' (bravo! Messieurs of the *Post*)—this 'Adonis in loveliness' was a corpulent man of fifty!"

I

I now applied to the magistrates for permission to have my wife and children constantly with me, which was granted. Not so my request to move into the gaoler's house. Mr Holme Sumner, on occasion of a petition from a subsequent prisoner, told the House of Commons that my room had a view over the Surrey hills, and that I was very well content with it. I could not feel obliged to him for this postliminous piece of enjoyment, especially when I remembered that he had done all in his power to prevent my removal out of the room, precisely (as it appeared to us) because it looked upon nothing but the felons, and because I was *not* contented. In fact, you could not see out of the windows at all, without getting on a chair; and then, all that you saw was the miserable men whose chains had been clanking from daylight. The perpetual sound of these chains wore upon my spirits in a manner to which my state of health allowed me reasonably to object. The yard, also, in which I took exercise, was very small. The gaoler proposed that I should be allowed to occupy apartments in his house, and walk occasionally in the prison garden; adding, that I should certainly die if I did not; and his opinion was seconded by that of the medical man. Mine host was sincere in this, if in nothing else. Telling us, one day, how warmly he had put it to the magistrates, and how he insisted that I should not survive, he turned round upon me, and, to the doctor's astonishment, added, "Nor, Mister, will you".

The doctor then proposed that I should be removed into the prison infirmary; and this proposal was granted. Infirmary had, I confess, an awkward sound, even to my ears. I fancied a room shared with other sick persons, not the best fitted for companions; but the good-natured doctor (his name was Dixon) undeceived me. The infirmary was divided into four wards, with as many small rooms attached to them. The two upper wards were occupied, but the two on the floor had never been used: and one of these, not very providently (for I had not yet learned to think of money), I turned into a noble room. I papered the walls with a trellis of roses; I had the ceiling coloured with clouds and sky; the barred windows I screened with Venetian blinds; and when my bookcases were set up with their busts, and flowers and a pianoforte made their appearance, perhaps there was not a handsomer room on that side the water. I took a pleasure, when a stranger knocked at the door, to see him come in and stare about him. The surprise on issuing from the Borough, and passing through the avenues of a gaol, was dramatic. Charles Lamb declared there was no other such room, except in a fairy tale.

But I possessed another surprise; which was a garden. There was a little yard outside the room, railed off from another belonging to the neighbouring ward. This yard I shut in with green palings, adorned it with a trellis, bordered it with a thick bed of earth from a nursery, and even contrived to have a grass-plot. The earth I filled with flowers and young trees. There was an apple-tree, from which we managed to get a pudding the second year. As to my flowers, they were allowed to be perfect. Thomas Moore, who came to see me with Lord Byron, told me he had seen no such heart's-ease. I bought the *Parnaso Italiano* while in prison, and used often to think of a passage in it, while looking at this miniature piece of horticulture:

Mio picciol orto,
A me sei vigna, e campo, e selva, e prato. BALDI.

My little garden,
To me thou'rt vineyard, field, and meadow, and wood.

Here I wrote and read in fine weather, sometimes under an awning. In autumn, my trellises were hung with scarlet-runners, which added to the flowery investment. I used to shut my eyes in my arm-chair, and affect to think myself hundreds of miles off.

But my triumph was in issuing forth of a morning. A wicket out of the garden led into the large one belonging to the prison. The latter was only for vegetables; but it contained a cherry-tree, which I saw twice in blossom. I parcelled out the ground in my imagination into favourite districts. I made a point of dressing myself as if for a long walk; and then, putting on my gloves, and taking my book under my arm, stepped forth, requesting my wife not to wait dinner if I was too late. My eldest little boy, to whom Lamb addressed some charming verses on the occasion, was my constant companion, and we used to play all sorts of juvenile games together. It was, probably, in dreaming of one of these games (but the words had a more touching effect on my ear) that he exclaimed one night in his sleep, "No: I'm not lost; I'm found". Neither he nor I were very strong at that time; but I have lived to see him a man of eight and forty; and wherever he is found, a generous hand and a great understanding will be found together.

I entered prison the 3rd of February, 1813, and removed to my new apartments the 16th of March, happy to get out of the noise of the chains. When I sat amidst my books, and saw the imaginary sky overhead, and my paper roses about me, I drank in the quiet at my ears, as if they were thirsty.

My friends were allowed to be with me till ten o'clock at night, when the under-turnkey, a young man with his lantern, and much ambitious gentility of deportment, came to see them out. I believe we scattered an urbanity about the prison, till then unknown. Even William Hazlitt, who there first did me the honour of a visit, would stand interchanging amenities at the threshold, which I had great difficulty in making him pass. I know not which kept his hat off with the greater pertinacity of deference, I to the diffident cutter-up of Tory dukes and kings, or he to the amazing prisoner and invalid who issued out of a bower of roses. There came my old friends and school-fellows, Pitman, whose wit and animal spirits have still kept him alive; Mitchell, now no more, who translated Aristophanes; and Barnes, gone too, who always reminded me of Fielding. It was he that introduced me to the late Mr Thomas Alsager, the kindest of neighbours, a man of business, who contrived to be a scholar and a musician. Alsager loved his leisure, and yet would start up at a moment's notice to do the least of a prisoner's biddings.

My now old friend, Cowden Clarke, with his ever young and wise heart, was good enough to be his own introducer, paving his way, like a proper visitor of prisons, with baskets of fruit.

The Lambs came to comfort me in all weathers, hail or sunshine, in daylight and in darkness, even in the dreadful frost and snow of the beginning of 1814.

To evils I have owed some of my greatest blessings. It was imprisonment that brought me acquainted with my friend of friends, Shelley. I had seen little of him before; but he wrote to me, making me a princely offer, which at that time I stood in no need of.

LEIGH HUNT'S *Autobiography*

II

Wednesday, *December* 1, 1813.

To-day responded to La Baronne de Staël Holstein, and sent to Leigh Hunt (an acquisition to my acquaintance—through Moore—of last summer) a copy of the two Turkish tales. Hunt is an extraordinary character, and not exactly of the present age. He reminds me more of the Pym and Hampden times—much talent, great independence of spirit, and an austere, yet not repulsive, aspect. If he goes on *qualis ab incepto*, I know few men who will deserve more praise or obtain it. I must go and see him again;—the rapid succession of adventure, since last summer, added to some serious uneasiness and business, have interrupted our acquaintance; but he is a man worth knowing; and though, for his own sake, I wish him out of prison, I like to study character in such situations. He has been unshaken, and will continue so. I don't think him deeply versed in life;—he is a bigot of virtue (not religion) and enamoured of the beauty of that "empty name", as the last breath of Brutus pronounced, and every day proves it. He is, perhaps, a little opinionated, as all men who are the *centre* of *circles*, wide or narrow—the Sir Oracles, in whose name two or three are gathered—must be, and as even Johnson was; but, withal, a valuable man, and less vain than success and even the consciousness of preferring "the right to the expedient" might excuse.

BYRON: *Journal*

THE EXCURSION

I

LAMB *to* WORDSWORTH

August 14, 1814.

Dear Wordsworth,—I cannot tell you how pleased I was at the receipt of the great armful of poetry which you have sent me; and to get it before the rest of the world too! I have gone quite through with it, and was thinking to have accomplished that pleasure a second time before I wrote to thank you, but M. Burney came in the night (while we were out) and made holy theft of it, but we expect restitution in a day or two. It is the noblest conversational poem I ever read—a day in Heaven. The part (or rather main body) which has left the sweetest odour on my memory (a bad term for the remains of an impression so recent) is the Tales of the Churchyard;—the only girl among seven brethren, born out of due time, and not duly taken away again,—the deaf man and the blind man;—the Jacobite and the Hanoverian, whom antipathies reconcile; the Scarron-entry of the rusticating parson upon his solitude; —these were all new to me too. My having known the story of Margaret (at the beginning), a very old acquaintance, even as long back as when I saw you first at Stowey, did not make her reappearance less fresh. I don't know what to pick out of this best of books upon the best subjects for partial naming. That gorgeous sunset is famous; I think it must have been the identical one we saw on Salisbury Plain five years ago, that drew Phillips from the card-table, where he had sat from rise of that luminary to its unequalled set; but neither he nor I had gifted eyes to see those symbols of common things glorified, such as the prophets saw them in that sunset—the wheel, the potter's clay, the wash-pot, the wine-press, the almond-tree rod, the baskets of figs, the fourfold visaged head, the throne, and Him that sat thereon.

One feeling I was particularly struck with, as what I recognised so very lately at Harrow Church on entering in it after a hot and secular day's pleasure, the instantaneous coolness and calming, almost transforming properties of a country church just entered; a certain fragrance which it has, either from its holiness, or being kept shut all the week, or the air that is let in being pure country, exactly what you have reduced into words; but I am feeling that which I cannot express. Reading your lines about it fixed me for a time, a monument in Harrow Church. Do you know it? with its fine long spire, white as washed marble, to be seen, by vantage of its high site, as far as Salisbury spire itself almost.

I shall select a day or two, very shortly, when I am coolest in brain, to have a steady second reading, which I feel will lead to many more, for it will be a stock book with me while eyes or spectacles shall be lent me. There is a great deal of noble matter about mountain scenery, yet not so much as to overpower and discountenance a poor Londoner or south-countryman entirely, though Mary seems to have felt it occasionally a little too powerfully, for it was her remark during reading it, that by your system it was doubtful whether a liver in towns had a soul to be saved. She almost trembled for that invisible part of us in her.

Save for a late excursion to Harrow, and a day or two on the banks of the Thames this Summer, rural images were fast fading from my mind, and by the wise provision of the Regent, all that was countryfy'd in the Parks is all but obliterated. The very colour of green is vanished; the whole surface of

Hyde Park is dry crumbling sand (*Arabia Arenosa*), not a vestige or hint of grass ever having grown there. Booths and drinking-places go all round it for a mile and half, I am confident—I might say two miles in circuit. The stench in liquors, *bad* tobacco, dirty people and provisions, conquers the air, and we are stifled and suffocated in Hyde Park.

Order after order has been issued by Lord Sidmouth in the name of the Regent (acting in behalf of his Royal father) for the dispersion of the varlets, but in vain. The *vis unita* of all the publicans in London, Westminster, Marylebone, and miles round, is too powerful a force to put down. The Regent has raised a phantom which he cannot lay. There they'll stay probably for ever. The whole beauty of the place is gone—that lake-look of the Serpentine—it has got foolish ships upon it; but something whispers to have confidence in Nature and its revival—

> At the coming of the *milder day*,
> These monuments shall all be overgrown.

Meantime I confess to have smoked one delicious pipe in one of the cleanliest and goodliest of the booths; a tent rather—

> Oh call it not a booth!

erected by the public spirit of Watson, who keeps the Adam and Eve at Pancras, (the ale-houses have all emigrated, with their train of bottles, mugs, corkscrews, waiters, into Hyde Park—whole ale-houses, with all their ale!) in company with some of the Guards that had been in France, and a fine French girl, habited like a princess of banditti, which one of the dogs had transported from the Garonne to the Serpentine. The unusual scene in Hyde Park, by candle-light, in open air—good tobacco, bottled stout,—made it look like an interval in a campaign, a repose after battle. I almost fancied scars smarting, and was ready to club a story with my comrades of some of my lying deeds. After all, the fireworks were splendid; the rockets in clusters, in trees and all shapes, spreading about like young stars in the making, floundering about in space (like unbroke horses), till some of Newton's calculations should fix them; but then they went out. Any one who could see 'em, and the still finer showers of gloomy rain-fire that fell sulkily and angrily from 'em, and could go to bed without dreaming of the last day, must be as hardened an atheist as....

The conclusion of this epistle getting gloomy, I have chosen this part to desire *our* kindest loves to Mrs Wordsworth and to Dorothea. Will none of you ever be in London again?

Again let me thank you for your present, and assure you that fireworks and triumphs have not distracted me from receiving a calm and noble enjoyment from it, (which I trust I shall often,) and I sincerely congratulate you on its appearance.

With kindest remembrances to you and your household, we remain, yours sincerely,

C. Lamb and sister

II

Lamb *to* Wordsworth

December, 1814.

Dear Wordsworth—I told you my Review[1] was a very imperfect one. But what you will see in the *Quarterly* is a spurious one, which Mr Baviad Gifford has palmed upon it for mine. I never felt more vexed in my life than when I read it. I cannot give you an idea of what he has done to it, out of spite at me, because he once suffered me to be called a lunatic in his Review. The *language* he has altered throughout. Whatever inadequateness it had to its subject, it was, in point of composition, the prettiest piece of prose I ever writ: and so my sister (to whom alone I read the MS.) said. That charm, if it had any, is all gone: more than a third of the substance is cut away, and that not all from one place, but *passim*, so as to make utter nonsense. Every warm expression is changed for a nasty cold one.

I have not the cursed alteration by me; I shall never look at it again; but for a specimen, I remember I had said the poet of the *Excursion* "walks through common forests as through some Dodona or enchanted wood, and every casual bird that

[1] Lamb's review of *The Excursion* appeared in *The Quarterly Review* for October, 1814.

flits upon the boughs, like that miraculous one in Tasso, but in language more piercing than any articulate sounds, reveals to him far higher love-lays". It is now (besides half-a-dozen alterations in the same half-dozen lines) "but in language more *intelligent* reveals to him";—that is one I remember.

But that would have been little, putting his damn'd shoemaker phraseology (for he was a shoemaker) instead of mine, which has been tinctured with better authors than his ignorance can comprehend;—for I reckon myself a dab at *prose*;—verse I leave to my betters: God help them, if they are to be so reviewed by friend and foe as you have been this quarter! I have read "It won't do". But worse than altering words: he has kept a few members only of the part I had done best, which was to explain all I could of your "Scheme of Harmonies", as I had ventured to call it, between the external universe and what within us answers to it. To do this I had accumulated a good many short passages, rising in length to the end, weaving in the extracts as if they came in as a part of the text naturally, not obtruding them as specimens. Of this part a little is left, but so as, without conjuration, no man could tell what I was driving at. A proof of it you may see (though not judge of the whole of the injustice) by these words. I had spoken something about "natural methodism"; and after follows, "and *therefore* the tale of Margaret should have been postponed" (I forget my words, or his words); now the reasons for postponing it are as deducible from what goes before as they are from the 104th Psalm. The passage whence I deduced it has vanished, but clapping a colon before a *therefore* is always reason enough for Mr Baviad Gifford to allow to a reviewer that is not himself. I assure you my complaints are well founded. I know how sore a word altered makes one; but, indeed, of this review the whole complexion is gone. I regret only that I did not keep a copy. I am sure you would have been pleased with it, because I have been feeding my fancy for some months with the notion of pleasing you. Its imperfection or inadequateness in size and method I knew; but for the *writing part* of it I was fully satisfied; I hoped it would make more than atonement. Ten or twelve distinct passages come to my mind, which are gone; and what is left is, of course, the worse for their having been there; the eyes are pulled out, and the bleeding sockets are left.

I read it at Arch's shop with my face burning with vexation secretly, with just such a feeling as if it had been a review written against myself, making false quotations from me. But I am ashamed to say so much about a short piece. How are *you* served! and the labours of years turned into contempt by scoundrels!

But I could not but protest against your taking that thing as mine. Every *pretty* expression, (I know there were many,) every warm expression, (there was nothing else,) is vulgarised and frozen. But if they catch me in their camps again, let them spitchcock me! They had a right to do it, as no name appears to it; and Mr Shoemaker Gifford, I suppose, never waived a right he had since he commenced author. God confound him and all caitiffs!

C. L.

LAMB AT HOME

1814.

November 17th.—After nine I went to Charles Lamb's, whose parties are now only once a month. I played a couple of rubbers pleasantly, and afterwards chatted with Hazlitt till one o'clock. He is become an Edinburgh Reviewer through the recommendation of Lady Macintosh, who had sent to the *Champion* office to know the author of the articles on Institutions. Hazlitt sent those and other writings to Jeffrey, and has been in a very flattering manner enrolled in the corps. This has put him in good spirits, and he now again hopes that his talents will be appreciated, and become a subsistence to him.

November 21st.—In the evening I stepped over to Lamb, and sat with him from ten to eleven. He was very chatty and pleasant. Pictures and poetry were the subjects of our talk. He thinks no description in "The Excursion" so good as the history of the country parson who had been a courtier. In this I agree with him. But he dislikes "The Magdalen", which he says would be as good in prose; in which I do *not* agree with him.

December 20th.—Late in the evening Lamb called, to ask me to sit with him while he smoked his pipe. I called on him late last night, and he seemed absurdly grateful for the visit. He wanted society, being alone. I abstained from inquiring after his sister, and trust he will appreciate the motive.

HENRY CRABB ROBINSON'S *Diary*

WORDSWORTH IN LONDON

1815.

May 7th.—On returning from a walk to Shooter's Hill, I found a card from Wordsworth, and running to Lamb's I found Mr and Mrs Wordsworth there. After sitting half an hour with them, I accompanied them to their lodgings near Cavendish Square. Mrs Wordsworth appears to be a mild and amiable woman, not so lively or animated as Miss Wordsworth but, like her, devoted to the poet.

May 9th.—Took tea with the Lambs. Mr and Mrs Wordsworth were there. We had a long chat, of which, however, I can relate but little. Wordsworth, in answer to the common reproach that his sensibility is excited by objects which produce no effect on others, admits the fact, and is proud of it. He says that he cannot be accused of being insensible to the real concerns of life. He does not waste his feelings on unworthy objects, for he is alive to the actual interests of society. I think the justification is complete. If Wordsworth expected immediate popularity, he would betray an ignorance of public taste impossible in a man of observation....

Wordsworth particularly recommended to me among his Poems of Imagination "Yew Trees", and a description of Night. These he says are among the best for the imaginative power displayed in them. I have since read them. They are fine, but I believe I do not understand in what their excellence consists. The poet himself, as Hazlitt has well observed, has a pride in deriving no aid from his subject. It is the mere power which he is conscious of exerting in which he delights, not the production of a work in which men rejoice on account of the sympathies and sensibilities it excites in them. Hence he does

LIBRARY ST. MARY'S COLLEGE

not much esteem his "Laodamia", as it belongs to the inferior class of poems founded on the affections. In this, as in other peculiarities of Wordsworth, there is a German bent in his mind.

June 17th.—I went late to Lamb's. His party were there, and a numerous and odd set they were—for the greater part interesting and amusing people—George Dyer, Captain and Martin Burney, Ayrton, Phillips, Hazlitt and wife, Alsager, Barron Field, Coulson, John Collier, Talfourd, White, Lloyd, and Basil Montagu. The latter I had never before been in company with; his feeling face and gentle tones are very interesting. Wordsworth says of him that he is a "philanthropized courtier".

June 18th.—Breakfasted at Wordsworth's. Wordsworth was not at home, but I stayed chatting with the ladies till he returned; and several persons dropping in, I was kept there till two o'clock, and was much amused. Scott, editor of the *Champion*, and Haydon, the painter, stayed a considerable time. Scott is a little swarthy man.... Haydon has an animated countenance, but did not say much. Both he and Scott seemed to entertain a high reverence for the poet.

HENRY CRABB ROBINSON'S *Diary*

BYRON IN LONDON

I

It was in the spring of 1815 that, chancing to be in London, I had the advantage of a personal introduction to Lord Byron. Report had prepared me to meet a man of peculiar habits and a quick temper, and I had some doubts whether we were likely to suit each other in society. I was most agreeably disappointed in this respect. I found Lord Byron in the highest degree courteous, and even kind. We met for an hour or two almost daily, in Mr Murray's drawing-room, and found a great deal to say to each other. We also met frequently in parties and evening society, so that for about two months I had the advantage of a considerable intimacy with this distinguished individual. Our sentiments agreed a good deal, except upon the subjects of religion and politics, upon neither of which

I was inclined to believe that Lord Byron entertained very fixed opinions. I remember saying to him, that I really thought that if he lived a few years he would alter his sentiments. He answered, rather sharply—"I suppose you are one of those who prophesy I shall turn Methodist". I replied—"No; I don't expect your conversion to be of such an ordinary kind. I would rather look to see you retreat upon the Catholic faith, and distinguish yourself by the austerity of your penances". He smiled gravely, and seemed to allow I might be right. On politics, he used sometimes to express a high strain of what is now called Liberalism; but it appeared to me that the pleasure it afforded him, as a vehicle for displaying his wit and satire against individuals in office, was at the bottom of this habit of thinking, rather than any real conviction of the political principles on which he talked. He was certainly proud of his rank and ancient family, and, in that respect, as much an aristocrat as was consistent with good sense and good breeding. Some disgusts, how adopted I know not, seemed to me to have given this peculiar and (as it appeared to me) contradictory cast of mind; but, at heart, I would have termed Byron a patrician on principle.

Lord Byron's reading did not seem to me to have been very extensive, either in poetry or history. Having the advantage of him in that respect, and possessing a good competent share of such reading as is little read, I was sometimes able to put under his eyes objects which had for him the interest of novelty. I remember particularly repeating to him the fine poem of Hardyknute, an imitation of the old Scottish ballad, with which he was so much affected, that some one who was in the same apartment asked me what I could possibly have been telling Byron by which he was so much agitated.

Like the old heroes in Homer, we exchanged gifts. I gave Byron a beautiful dagger mounted with gold, which had been the property of the redoubted Elfi Bey. But I was to play the part of Diomed in *The Iliad*, for Byron sent me, some time after, a large sepulchral vase of silver. It was full of dead men's bones, and had inscriptions on two sides of the base. One ran thus: "The bones contained in this urn were found in certain ancient sepulchres within the long walls of Athens, in the month of February, 1811". The other face bears the lines of Juvenal—"*Expende—quot libras in duce summo invenies?—Mors sola fatetur quantula sint hominum corpuscula*". To these I have added a third inscription, in these words—"The gift of Lord Byron to Walter Scott". There was a letter with this vase, more valuable to me than the gift itself, from the kindness with which the donor expressed himself towards me. I left it naturally in the urn with the bones; but it is now missing. As the theft was not of a nature to be practised by a mere domestic, I am compelled to suspect the inhospitality of some individual of higher station, most gratuitously exercised certainly, since, after what I have here said, no one will probably choose to boast of possessing this literary curiosity. We had a good deal of laughing, I remember, on what the public might be supposed to think, or say, concerning the gloomy and ominous nature of our mutual gifts. He was often melancholy—almost gloomy. When I observed him in this humour, I used either to wait till it went off of its own accord, or till some natural and easy mode occurred of leading him into conversation, when the shadows almost always left his countenance, like the mist rising from a landscape. In conversation, he was very animated.

I met him very frequently in society; our mutual acquaintances doing me the honour to think that he liked to meet with me. Some very agreeable parties I can recollect,—particularly one at Sir George Beaumont's, where the amiable landlord had assembled some persons distinguished for talent. Of these I need only mention the late Sir Humphry Davy, whose talents for literature were as remarkable as his empire over science. Mr Richard Sharp and Mr Rogers were also present.

I think I also remarked in Byron's temper starts of suspicion, when he seemed to pause and consider whether there had not been a secret, and perhaps offensive, meaning in something casually said to him. In this case, I also judged it best to let his mind, like a troubled spring, work itself clear, which it did in a minute or two. I was considerably older, you will recollect, than my noble friend, and had no reason to fear his misconstruing my sentiments towards him, nor had I ever the slightest reason to doubt that they were kindly returned on his part. If I had occasion to be mortified by the display of genius which threw into the shade such pretensions as I was then supposed to possess, I might console myself that, in my own case, the materials of mental happiness had been mingled in a greater proportion.

I rummage my brains in vain for what often rushes into my head unbidden,—little traits and sayings which recall his looks, manner, tone, and gestures; and I have always continued to think that a crisis of life was arrived in which a new career of fame was opened to him, and that had he been permitted to start upon it, he would have obliterated the memory of such parts of his life as friends would wish to forget.

Contributed by SCOTT to MOORE'S *Life of Byron*

II

BYRON *to* COLERIDGE

Scott had become acquainted with the MS. version of *Christabel* as early as 1803, and it had influenced his metrical tales from *The Lay of the Last Minstrel* onwards. Byron, on meeting Coleridge and hearing *Christabel* read, was equally impressed by it and used all his influence to secure its publication. Coleridge had evidently accused Scott of plagiarism from the poem.

October 27, 1815.

Dear Sir,

I have the *Christabelle* safe, and am glad to see it in such progress; surely a little effort would complete the poem. On your question with W. Scott, I know not how to speak; he is a friend of mine, and, though I cannot contradict your statement, I must look to the most favourable part of it. All I have ever seen of him has been frank, fair, and warm in regard towards you, and when he repeated this very production it was with such mention as it deserves, and *that* could not be faint praise.

But I am partly in the same scrape myself, as you will see by the enclosed extract from an unpublished poem, which I assure you was written before (not seeing your *Christabelle*, for that you know I never did till this day) but before I heard Mr S. repeat it, which he did in June last, and this thing was begun in January and more than half written before the Summer. The coincidence is only in this particular passage, and, if you will allow me, in publishing it (which I shall perhaps do *quietly* in Murray's collected Edition of my rhymes—though not *separately*), I will give the extract from you, and state that the original thought and expression have been many years in the *Christabelle*. The stories, scenes, etc., are in general quite different; mine is the siege of Corinth in 1715, when the Turks retook the Morea from the Venetians. The Ground is quite familiar to me, for I have passed the Isthmus *six*, I think—*eight*, times in my way to and fro. The hero is a renegade, and, the night before the storm of the City, he is supposed to have an apparition, or wraith of his mistress, to warn him of his destiny, as he sits among the ruins of an old temple.

I write to you in the greatest hurry. I know not what you may think of this. If you like, I will cut out the passage, and do as well as I can without,—or what you please.

Ever yours,

Byron

P.S. Pray write soon; I will answer the other points of your letter immediately.

III

BYRON *to* LEIGH HUNT

13, Terrace, Piccadilly, *September–October* 30, 1815.

My Dear Hunt,

Many thanks for your books, of which you already know my opinion. Their external splendour should not disturb you as inappropriate—they have still more within than without. I take leave to differ with you on Wordsworth, as freely as I once agreed with you; at that time I gave him credit for a promise, which is unfulfilled. I still think his capacity warrants all you say of *it* only, but that his performances since

Lyrical Ballads are miserably inadequate to the ability which lurks within him: there is undoubtedly much natural talent spilt over the *Excursion*; but it is rain upon rocks—where it stands and stagnates, or rain upon sands—where it falls without fertilising. Who can understand him? Let those who do, make him intelligible. Jacob Behmen, Swedenborg, and Joanna Southcote, are mere types of this arch-apostle of mystery and mysticism. But I have done,—no, I have not done, for I have two petty, and perhaps unworthy objections in small matters to make to him, which, with his pretensions to accurate observation, and fury against Pope's false translation of "the Moonlight scene in Homer", I wonder he should have fallen into;—these be they:—He says of Greece in the body of his book—that it is a land of

> *Rivers*, *fertile plains*, and *sounding* shores,
> Under a cope of *variegated* sky.

The rivers are dry half the year, the plains are barren, and the shores *still* and *tideless* as the Mediterranean can make them; the sky is anything but variegated, being for months and months but "darkly, deeply, beautifully blue". The next is in his notes, where he talks of our "Monuments crowded together in the busy, etc., of a large town", as compared with the "still seclusion of a Turkish cemetery in some *remote* place". This is pure stuff; for *one* monument in our churchyards there are *ten* in the Turkish, and so crowded, that you cannot walk between them; that is, divided merely by a path or road; and as to "*remote* places", men never take the trouble in a barbarous country, to carry their dead very far; they must have lived near to where they were buried. There are no cemeteries in "remote places", except such as have the cypress and the tombstone still left, where the olive and the habitation of the living have perished.

These things I was struck with, as coming peculiarly in my own way; and in both of these he is wrong; yet I should have noticed neither, but for his attack on Pope for a like blunder, and a peevish affectation about him of despising a popularity which he will never obtain. I write in great haste, and, I doubt, *not* much to the purpose; but you have it hot and hot, just as it comes, and so let it go. By-the-way, both he and you go too far against Pope's "So when the moon", etc.; it is no translation, I know; but it is not such false description as asserted. I have read it on the spot; there is a burst, and a lightness, and a glow about the night in the Troad, which makes the "planets vivid", and the "pole glowing". The moon is—at least the sky is, clearness itself; and I know no more appropriate expression for the expansion of such a heaven—o'er the scene—the plain—the sky—Ida—the Hellespont—Simois—Scamander—and the Isles—than that of a "flood of glory". I am getting horribly lengthy, and must stop: to the whole of your letter "I say ditto to Mr Burke", as the Bristol candidate cried by way of electioneering harangue. You need not speak of morbid feelings and vexations to me; I have plenty; but I must blame partly the times, and chiefly myself: but let us forget them. *I* shall be very apt to do so when I see you next. Will you come to the theatre and see our new management? You shall cut it up to your heart's content, root and branch, afterwards, if you like; but come and see it! If not, I must come and see you.

Ever yours, very truly and affectionately,

Byron

P.S. Not a word from Moore for these two months. Pray let me have the rest of *Rimini*. You have two excellent points in that poem—originality and Italianism. I will back you as a bard against half the fellows on whom you have thrown away much good criticism and eulogy; but don't let your bookseller publish in *quarto*; it is the worst size possible for circulation. I say this on bibliopolical authority.

Again, yours ever,

B.

COLERIDGE AND LADY HAMILTON

Coleridge, during this part of his London life, I saw constantly—generally once a day, during my own stay in London; and sometimes we were jointly engaged to dinner parties. In particular, I remember one party at which we met Lady Hamilton—Lord Nelson's Lady Hamilton—the beautiful, the accomplished, the enchantress! Coleridge admired her, as who would not have done, prodigiously; and she, in her turn, was fascinated with Coleridge. He was unusually effective in his display; and she, by way of expressing her acknowledgments appropriately, performed a scene in Lady Macbeth—how splendidly, I cannot better express, than by saying that all of us who then witnessed her performance, were familiar with Mrs Siddons's matchless execution of that scene; and yet, with such a model filling our imaginations, we could not but acknowledge the possibility of another, and a different perfection, without a trace of imitation, equally original, and equally astonishing. The word "magnificent" is, in this day, most lavishly abused: daily I hear or read in the newspapers of magnificent objects, as though scattered more thickly than blackberries; but for my part I have seen few objects really deserving that epithet. Lady Hamilton was one of them. She had Medea's beauty—and Medea's power of enchantment.

DE QUINCEY'S *Literary Reminiscences*

LAMB TO WORDSWORTH

Accountant's Office, *April* 26, 1816.

Dear W.,—I have just finished the pleasing task of correcting the revise of the poems and letter.[1] I hope they will come out faultless. One blunder I saw and shuddered at. The hallucinating rascal had printed *battered* for *battened*, this last

[1] Wordsworth's *Thanksgiving Ode, with other short Pieces* and *A Letter to a Friend of Burns.*

not conveying any distinct sense to his gaping soul. The Reader (as they call 'em) had discovered it, and given it the marginal brand, but the substitutory *n* had not yet appeared. I accompanied his notice with a most pathetic address to the printer not to neglect the correction. I know how such a blunder would "batter at your peace". With regard to the works, the Letter I read with unabated satisfaction. Such a thing was wanted; called for. The parallel of Cotton with Burns I heartily approve. Izaak Walton hallows any page in which his reverend name appears. "Duty archly bending to purposes of general benevolence" is exquisite. The poems I endeavoured not to understand, but to read them with my eye alone, and I think I succeeded. (Some people will do that when they come out, you'll say.) As if I were to luxuriate to-morrow at some picture gallery I was never at before, and going by to-day by chance, found the door open, and had but five minutes to look about me, peeped in; just such a *chastised* peep I took with my mind at the lines my luxuriating eye was coursing over unrestrained, not to anticipate another day's fuller satisfaction. Coleridge is printing "Christabel", by Lord Byron's recommendation to Murray, with what he calls a vision, "Kubla Khan", which said vision he repeats so enchantingly that it irradiates and brings heaven and elysian bowers into my parlour while he sings or says it; but there is an observation, "Never tell thy dreams", and I am almost afraid that "Kubla Khan" is an owl that won't bear day-light. I fear lest it should be discovered by the lantern of typography and clear reducting to letters no better than nonsense or no sense. When I was young I used to chant with ecstasy "MILD ARCADIANS EVER BLOOMING", till somebody told me it was meant to be nonsense. Even yet I have a lingering attachment to it, and I think it better than "Windsor Forest", "Dying Christian's Address", &c. Coleridge has sent his tragedy to Drury Lane Theatre. It cannot be acted this season; and by their manner of receiving, I hope he will be able to alter it to make them accept it for next. He is, at present, under the medical care of a Mr Gilman (Killman?), a Highgate apothecary, where he plays at leaving off laud—m. I think his essentials not touched: he is very bad; but then he wonderfully picks up another day, and his face, when he repeats his verses, hath its ancient glory; an archangel a little damaged. Will Miss H. pardon our not replying at length to her kind letter? We are not quiet enough; Morgan is with us every day, going betwixt Highgate and the Temple. Coleridge is absent but four miles, and the neighbourhood of such a man is as exciting as the presence of fifty ordinary persons. 'Tis enough to be within the whiff and wind of his genius for us not to possess our souls in quiet. If I lived with him or the Author of the *Excursion*, I should, in a very little time, lose my own identity, and be dragged along in the current of other people's thoughts, hampered in a net. How cool I sit in this office, with no possible interruption further than what I may term *material*! There is not as much metaphysics in thirty-six of the people here as there is in the first page of Locke's "Treatise on the Human Understanding", or as much poetry as in any ten lines of the "Pleasures of Hope", or more natural "Beggar's Petition". I never entangle myself in any of their speculations. Interruptions, if I try to write a letter even, I have dreadful. Just now, within four lines, I was called off for ten minutes to consult dusty old books for the settlement of obsolete errors. I hold you a guinea you don't find the chasm where I left off, so excellently the wounded sense closed again and was healed.

N.B. Nothing said above to the contrary, but that I hold the personal presence of the two mentioned potent spirits at a rate as high as any; but I pay dearer. What amuses others robs me of myself: my mind is positively discharged into their greater currents, but flows with a willing violence. As to your question about work; it is far less oppressive to me than it was, from circumstances. It takes all the golden part of the day away, a solid lump, from ten to four; but it does not kill my peace as before. Some day or other I shall be in a taking again. My head aches, and you have had enough. God bless you!

C. Lamb

BYRON AND SHELLEY IN SWITZERLAND

At the end of May, 1816, Byron, who had just left England under a cloud, owing to the separation from his wife, met Shelley, who was a guest in the same hotel at Geneva. Shelley had also left his wife, and had gone abroad with Mary Godwin and their infant son; they were accompanied by her step-sister, Clare Clairmont. Soon afterwards the two poets were occupying neighbouring houses on the other side of the lake.

Shelley described the voyage he made round Lake Geneva in Byron's company in a long letter to his friend Thomas Love Peacock, the novelist, and it was printed soon afterwards as part of a slim volume called *A History of a Six Weeks' Tour.*

To T. P. Esq.

Montalegre, near Coligni, Geneva, *July* 12, 1816.

It is nearly a fortnight since I have returned from Vevai. This journey has been on every account delightful, but most especially, because then I first knew the divine beauty of Rousseau's imagination, as it exhibits itself in *Julie.* It is inconceivable what an enchantment the scene itself lends to those delineations, from which its own most touching charm arises. But I will give you an abstract of our voyage, which lasted eight days, and if you have a map of Switzerland, you can follow me. We left Montalegre at half-past two on the 23rd of June. The lake was calm, and after three hours of rowing we arrived at Hermance, a beautiful little village, containing a ruined tower, built, the villagers say, by Julius Caesar....

Leaving Hermance, we arrived at sunset at the village of Nerni. After looking at our lodgings, which were gloomy and dirty, we walked out by the side of the lake. It was beautiful to see the vast expanse of these purple and misty waters broken by the craggy islets near to its slant and "beached margin". There were many fish sporting in the lake, and multitudes were collected close to the rocks to catch the flies which inhabited them....

On returning to our inn, we found that the servant had arranged our rooms, and deprived them of the greater portion of their former disconsolate appearance. They reminded my companion of Greece: it was five years, he said, since he had slept in such beds. The influence of the recollections excited by this circumstance on our conversation gradually faded, and I retired to rest with no unpleasant sensations, thinking of our journey to-morrow, and of the pleasure of recounting the little adventures of it when we return.

The next morning we passed Yvoire, a scattered village with an ancient castle, whose houses are interspersed with trees, and which stands at a little distance from Nerni, on the promontory which bounds a deep bay, some miles in extent. So soon as we arrived at this promontory, the lake began to assume an aspect of wilder magnificence. The mountains of Savoy, whose summits were bright with snow, descended in broken slopes to the lake: on high, the rocks were dark with pine-forests, which become deeper and more immense, until the ice and snow mingle with the points of naked rock that pierce the blue air; but below, groves of walnut, chestnut, and oak, with openings of lawny fields, attested the milder climate.

As soon as we had passed the opposite promontory, we saw the river Drance, which descends from between a chasm in the mountains, and makes a plain near the lake, intersected by its divided streams. Thousands of *besolets*, beautiful water-birds, like sea-gulls, but smaller, with purple on their backs, take their station on the shallows, where its waters mingle with the lake. As we approached Evian, the mountains descended more precipitously to the lake, and masses of intermingled wood and rock overhung its shining spire.

We arrived at this town about seven o'clock, after a day which involved more rapid changes of atmosphere than I ever recollect to have observed before. The morning was cold and wet; then an easterly wind, the clouds hard and high; then thunder showers, and wind shifting to every quarter; then a warm blast from the south, and summer clouds hanging over the peaks, with bright blue sky between. About half an hour after we had arrived at Evian, a few flashes of lightning came from a dark cloud, directly overhead, and continued after the cloud had dispersed. "Diespiter, per pura tonantes egit equos": a phenomenon which certainly had no influence on me, corresponding with that which it produced on Horace....

We left Evian on the following morning, with a wind of such violence as to permit but one sail to be carried. The waves also were exceedingly high, and our boat so heavily laden, that there appeared to be some danger. We arrived, however, safe at Mellerie, after passing with great speed mighty forests which overhung the lake, and lawns of exquisite verdure, and mountains with bare and icy points, which rose immediately from the summit of the rocks, whose bases were echoing to the waves....

The lake appeared somewhat calmer as we left Mellerie, sailing close to the banks, whose magnificence augmented with the turn of every promontory. But we congratulated ourselves too soon: the wind gradually increased in violence, until it blew tremendously; and as it came from the remotest extremity of the lake, produced waves of a frightful height, and covered the whole surface with a chaos of foam. One of our boatmen, who was a dreadfully stupid fellow, persisted in holding the sail at a time when the boat was on the point of being driven under water by the hurricane. On discovering his error, he let it entirely go, and the boat for a moment refused to obey the helm; in addition, the rudder was so broken as to render the management of it very difficult; one wave fell in, and then another. My companion, an excellent swimmer, took off his coat; I did the same, and we sat with our arms crossed, every instant expecting to be swamped. The sail was however again held, the boat obeyed the helm, and, still in imminent peril from the immensity of the waves, we arrived in a few minutes at a sheltered port, in the village of St Gingoux.

I felt in this near prospect of death a mixture of sensations, among which terror entered, though but subordinately. My feelings would have been less painful had I been alone; but I know that my companion would have attempted to save me, and I was overcome with humiliation, when I thought that his life might have been risked to preserve mine. When we arrived at St Gingoux, the inhabitants, who stood on the shore, unaccustomed to see a vessel as frail as ours and fearing to venture at all on such a sea, exchanged looks of wonder and congratulation with our boatmen, who, as well as ourselves, were well pleased to set foot on shore....

As my companion rises late, I had time before breakfast, on the ensuing morning, to hunt the waterfalls of the river that fall into the lake at St Gingoux. The stream is indeed, from the declivity over which it falls, only a succession of waterfalls, which roar over the rocks with a perpetual sound, and suspend their unceasing spray on the leaves and flowers that overhang and adorn its savage banks. The path that conducted along this river sometimes avoided the precipices of its shores, by leading through meadows; sometimes threaded the base of the perpendicular and caverned rocks. I gathered in these meadows a nosegay of such flowers as I never saw in England, and which I thought more beautiful for that rarity.

On my return, after breakfast, we sailed for Clarens, determining first to see the three mouths of the Rhône, and then the castle of Chillon; the day was fine, and the water calm. We passed from the blue waters of the lake over the stream of the Rhône, which is rapid even at a great distance from its confluence with the lake; the turbid waters mixed with those of the lake, but mixed with them unwillingly. (See *Nouvelle Héloise, Lettre* 17, *Part* 4.) I read *Julie* all day; an overflowing, as it now seems, surrounded by the scenes which it has so wonderfully peopled, of sublimest genius, and more than human sensibility. Mellerie, the Castle of Chillon, Clarens, the mountains of La Valais and Savoy, present themselves to the imagination as monuments of things that were once familiar, and of beings that were once dear to it. They were created indeed by one mind, but a mind so powerfully bright as to cast a shade of falsehood on the records that are called reality.

We passed on to the Castle of Chillon, and visited its dungeons and towers. These prisons are evacuated below the lake; the principal dungeon is supported by seven columns, whose branching capitals support the roof. Close to the very walls, the lake is 800 feet deep; iron rings are fastened to these columns, and on them were engraven a multitude of names, partly those of visitors, and partly doubtless of the prisoners, of whom now no memory remains, and who thus beguiled a solitude which they have long ceased to feel. One date was as ancient as 1670. At the commencement of the Reformation, and indeed long after that period, this dungeon was the receptacle of those who shook, or who denied the system of idolatry from the effects of which mankind is even now slowly emerging.

Close to this long and lofty dungeon was a narrow cell, and beyond it one larger and far more lofty and dark, supported on two unornamented arches. Across one of these arches was a beam, now black and rotten, on which prisoners were hung in secret. I never saw a monument more terrible of that cold and inhuman tyranny which it has been the delight of man to exercise over man. It was indeed one of those many tremendous fulfilments which render the "pernicies humani generis" of the great Tacitus, so solemn and irrefragible a prophecy. The gendarme, who conducted us over this castle, told us that there was an opening to the lake, by means of a secret spring, connected with which the whole dungeon might be filled with water before the prisoners could possibly escape!...

The rain detained us two days at Ouchy. We, however, visited Lausanne, and saw Gibbon's house. We were shown the decayed summer-house where he finished his History, and the old acacias on the terrace from which he saw Mont Blanc after having written the last sentence. There is something grand and even touching in the regret which he expresses at the completion of his task. It was conceived amid the ruins of the Capitol. The sudden departure of his cherished and accustomed toil must have left him, like the death of a dear friend, sad and solitary.

My companion gathered some acacia leaves to preserve in remembrance of him. I refrained from doing so, fearing to outrage the greater and more sacred name of Rousseau; the contemplation of whose imperishable creatures had left no vacancy in my heart for mortal things. Gibbon had a cold and unimpassioned spirit. I never felt more inclination to rail at the prejudices which cling to such a thing, than now that Julie and Clarens, Lausanne and the Roman empire, compelled me to a contrast between Rousseau and Gibbon.

When we returned, in the only interval of sunshine during the day, I walked on the pier which the lake was lashing with its waves. A rainbow spanned the lake, or rather rested one extremity of its arch upon the water, and the other at the foot of the mountains of Savoy. Some white houses, I know not if they were those of Mellerie, shone through the yellow fire.

On Saturday the 30th of June we quitted Ouchy, and after two days of pleasant sailing arrived on Sunday evening at Montalegre.

S.

CRABB ROBINSON AMONG THE LAKES

1816.

September 5th.—(Ambleside.) This was one of the most delightful days of my journey; but it is not easy to describe the gratification arising from the society of most excellent persons, and partly from beautiful scenery. Mr Walter expressed so strong a desire to see Wordsworth that I resolved to take him with me on a call. After breakfast we walked to Rydal, every turn presenting new beauty. The constantly changing position of the screen of hill produced a great variety of fine objects, of which the high and narrow pass to Rydal Water is the grandest. In this valley to the right stands a spacious house the seat of the Flemings, and near it in a finer situation the house of Wordsworth. We met him in the road before the house. His salutation was most cordial. Mr Walter's plans were very soon overthrown by the conversation of the poet in such a spot. He at once agreed to protract his stay among the lakes, to spend the day at

Grasmere. Torlonia was placed on a pony, which was a wild mountaineer, and, though it could not unhorse him, ran away with him twice. From a hillock Wordsworth pointed out several houses in Grasmere in which he had lived.

During the day I took an opportunity of calling on De Quincey, my Temple-hall acquaintance. He has been very much an invalid, and his appearance bespoke ill-health.

Our evening was spent at Wordsworth's. Mr Tillbrook of Cambridge, formerly Thomas Clarkson's tutor, was there. The conversation was general, but highly interesting. The evening was very fine, and we for the first time perceived all the beauties (glories they might be called) of Rydal Mount. It is so situated as to afford from the windows of both sitting-rooms a direct view of the valley, with the head of Windermere at its extremity, and from a terrace in the garden a view on to Rydal Water, and the winding of the valley in that direction. These views are of a very different character, and may be regarded as supplementing each other.

The house, too, is convenient and large enough for a family man. And it was a serious gratification to behold so great and so good a man as Wordsworth in the bosom of his family enjoying those comforts which are apparent to the eye. He has two sons and a daughter surviving. They appear to be amiable children. And, adding to these external blessings the *mind* of the man, he may justly be considered as one of the most enviable of mankind. The injustice of the public towards him, in regard to the appreciation of his works, he is sensible of. But he is aware that though the great body of readers—the admirers of Lord Byron, for instance—cannot and ought not to be his admirers too, still he is not without his fame. And he has that expectation of posthumous renown which has cheered many a poet, who has had less legitimate claims to it, and whose expectations to it have not been disappointed.

Mr Walter sang some Scotch airs to Mr Tillbrook's flute, and we did not leave Rydal Mount till late. My companions declare that it will be to them a memorable evening.

Just as we were going to bed De Quincey called on me.

He was in much better spirits than when I saw him in the morning, and expressed a wish to walk with me about the neighbourhood.

September 9th.—(Keswick.) We were gratified by receiving an invitation to take tea with the Poet Laureate. This was given to our whole party, and our dinner was, in consequence, shortened. I had a small room on a second floor, from the windows of which I had a glimpse only of the fine mountain scenery, and could see a single house only amid gardens out of the town. The mountain was Skiddaw. The house was Southey's.

The laureate lives in a large house in a nurseryman's grounds. It enjoys a panoramic view of the mountains; and as Southey spends so much of his time within doors, this lovely and extensive view supplies the place of travelling beyond his own premises.

September 24th.—(Ambleside.) I called on Wordsworth, who offered to accompany me up Nab Scar, the lofty rocky fell immediately behind and hanging over his house. The ascent was laborious, but the view from the summit was more interesting than any I had before enjoyed from a mountain on this journey. I beheld Rydal Water from the brow of the mountain, and afterwards, under a favourable sun, though the air was far from clear, I saw Windermere, with little interruption, from the foot to the head, Esthwaite Lake, Blelham Tarn, a part of Coniston Lake, a very extensive coast with the estuary near Lancaster, etc., etc. These pleasing objects compensated for the loss of the nobler views from Helvellyn, which I might have had, had I not engaged to dine with De Quincey to-day.

Wordsworth conducted me over the fell, and left me, near De Quincey's house, a little after one. He was in bed, but rose on my arrival. I was gratified by the sight of a large collection of books, which I lounged over. De Quincey, about two, set out on a short excursion with me, which I did not so much enjoy as he seemed to expect. We crossed the sweet vale of Grasmere, and ascended the fell on the opposite corner of the valley to Easdale Tarn. The charm of this spot is the solemnity of the seclusion in which it lies. There is a semicircle of lofty and grey rocks, which are wild and rugged, but promote the repose suggested by the motionless water.

We returned to dinner at half-past four, and in an hour De Quincey accompanied me on the mountain road to Rydal Mount, and left me at the gate of Wordsworth's garden-terrace.

I took tea with Mr and Mrs Wordsworth, and Miss Hutchinson, and had four hours of conversation as varied and delightful as I ever enjoyed; but the detail ought not to be introduced into a narrative like this.

Wordsworth accompanied me to the road, and I parted from him under the impressions of thankfulness for personal attentions, in addition to the high reverence I had felt before for his character. I found De Quincey up, and chatted with him till half-past twelve.

September 25th.—This was a day of unexpected enjoyment. I lounged over books till past ten, when De Quincey came down to breakfast. It was not till past twelve we commenced our walk, which had been marked out by Wordsworth. We first passed Grasmere Church, and then, going along the opposite side of the lake, crossed by a mountain road into the vale of Great Langdale. The characteristic repose of Grasmere was fully enjoyed by me.

HENRY CRABB ROBINSON'S *Diary*

SHELLEY IN ENGLAND

Shelley had returned to England from Switzerland bringing with him the manuscript of the third canto of *Childe Harold*. He lived for a while at Bath, and then moved to Marlow to be near his friend Peacock. It was here that his friendship with Leigh Hunt ripened into the closest intimacy. It was also during this period that his first wife died and he was married to Mary Godwin. He left England again early in 1818, not long after the Court of Chancery had deprived him of the custody of the two children by his first marriage.

I

Bath, *September* 29, 1816.

My dear Lord Byron,

You have heard from Kinnaird the arrangement which has been made about "Childe Harold". You are to receive 2000 guineas. There was no objection made on Murray's [part], though there was a trifling mistake arising from his believing that he could get it for 1200, which was no sooner made than obviated. I hope soon to inform you that I have received the first proof. I saw Kinnaird, and had a long conversation with him. He informed me that Lady Byron was now in perfect health—that she was living with your sister....

You are now in Italy—you have, perhaps, forgotten all that my unwelcome anxiety reminds you of. You contemplate objects that elevate, inspire, tranquillise. You communicate the feelings, which arise out of that contemplation, to mankind; perhaps to the men of distant ages. Is there nothing in the hope of being the parent of greatness, and of goodness, which is destined, perhaps, to expand indefinitely? Is there nothing in making yourself a fountain from which the thoughts of other men shall draw strength and beauty, to excite the ambition of a mind that can despise all other ambition? You have already given evidence of very uncommon powers. Having produced thus much, with effort, as you are aware, very disproportionate to the result; what are you not further capable of effecting? What would the human race have been if Homer, or Shakespeare, had never written? or if any false modesty, or mistake of their own powers, had withheld them from consummating those unequalled achievements of mind by which we are so deeply benefited? I do not compare you with these. I do not know how great an intellectual compass you are destined to fill. I only know that your powers are astonishingly great, and that they ought to be exerted to their full extent.

It is not that I should counsel you to aspire to fame. The motive to your labours ought to be more pure, and simple. You ought to desire no more than to express your own thoughts; to address yourself to the sympathy of those who might think with you. Fame will follow those whom it is unworthy to lead. I would not that you should immediately apply yourself to the composition of an Epic Poem; or to whatever other work you should collect all your being to consummate. I would not that the natural train of your progress should be interrupted; or any step of it anticipated. I delight in much of what you have already done. I hope for much more, in the same careless spirit of ardent sentiment. I hope for no more than that you should, from some moment when the clearness of your own mind makes evident to you the "truth of things", feel that you are chosen out from all other men to some greater enterprise of thought; and that all your studies should, from that moment, tend towards that enterprise alone: that your affections, that all worldly hopes this world may have left you, should link themselves to this design. *What* it should be, I am not qualified to say. In a more presumptuous mood, I recommended the Revolution of France as a theme involving pictures of all that is best qualified to interest and instruct mankind. But it is inconsistent with the spirit in which you ought to devote yourself to so great a destiny, that you should make use of any understanding but your own—much less mine.

Shall we see you in the spring? How do your affairs go on? May I hear from you respecting these? Though anxious to know how your estates go on, I have not called on Hanson, overcome by the fear of the awkwardness of such a visit. We are now all at Bath, well and content. Clare is writing to you at this instant. Mary is reading over the fire; our cat and kitten are sleeping under the sofa; and little Willy is just gone to sleep. We are looking out for a house in some lone place; and one chief pleasure which we shall expect then, will be a visit from you. You will destroy all our rural arrangements if you fail in this promise. You will do more. You will strike a link out of the chain of life which, esteeming you, and cherishing your society as we do, we cannot easily spare Adieu.

Your sincere friend,

P. B. Shelley

II

SHELLEY

To return to Hampstead.—Shelley often came there to see me, sometimes to stop for several days. He delighted in the natural broken ground, and in the fresh air of the place, especially when the wind set in from the north-west, which used to give him an intoxication of animal spirits. Here also he swam his paper boats on the ponds, and delighted to play with my children, particularly with my eldest boy, the seriousness of whose imagination, and his susceptibility of a "grim" impression (a favourite epithet of Shelley's), highly interested him. He would play at "frightful creatures" with him, from which the other would snatch "a fearful joy", only begging him occasionally "not to do the horn", which was a way that Shelley had of screwing up his hair in front, to imitate a weapon of that sort. This was the boy (now the man of forty-eight, and himself a fine writer) to whom Lamb took such a liking on similar accounts, and addressed some charming verses as his "favourite child". I have already mentioned him during my imprisonment.

As an instance of Shelley's playfulness when he was in good spirits, he was once going to town with me in the Hampstead stage, when our only companion was an old lady, who sat silent and still after the English fashion. Shelley was fond of quoting a passage from *Richard the Second*, in the commencement of which the king, in the indulgence of his misery, exclaims—

> For Heaven's sake! let us sit upon the ground,
> And tell sad stories of the death of kings.

Shelley, who had been moved into the ebullition by something objectionable which he thought he saw in the face of our companion, startled her into a look of the most ludicrous astonishment, by suddenly calling this passage to mind, and, in his enthusiastic tone of voice, addressing me by name with the first two lines. "Hunt!" he exclaimed,—

> For Heaven's sake! let us sit upon the ground,
> And tell sad stories of the death of kings.

The old lady looked on the coach-floor, as if expecting to see us take our seats accordingly.

But here follows a graver and more characteristic anecdote. Shelley was not only anxious for the good of mankind in general. We have seen what he proposed on the subject of Reform in Parliament, and he was always very desirous of the national welfare. It was a moot point when he entered your room, whether he would begin with some half-pleasant, half-pensive joke, or quote something Greek, or ask some question about public affairs. He once came upon me at Hampstead, when I had not seen him for some time; and after grasping my hands with both his, in his usual fervent manner, he sat down, and looked at me very earnestly, with a deep, though not melancholy, interest in his face. We were sitting with our knees to the fire, to which we had been getting nearer and nearer, in the comfort of finding ourselves together. The pleasure of seeing him was my only feeling at the moment; and the air of domesticity about us was so complete, that I thought he was going to speak of some family matter, either his or my own, when he asked me, at the close of an intensity of pause, what was "the amount of the national debt".

I used to rally him on the apparent inconsequentiality of his manner upon those occasions, and he was always ready to carry on the jest, because he said that my laughter did not hinder my being in earnest.

But here follows a crowning anecdote, with which I shall close my recollections of him at this period. We shall meet him again in Italy, and there, alas! I shall have to relate events graver still.

I was returning home one night to Hampstead after the opera. As I approached the door, I heard strange and alarming shrieks, mixed with the voice of a man. The next day it was reported by the gossips that Mr Shelley, no Christian (for it was he who was there), had brought some "very strange female" into the house, no better, of course, than she ought to be. The real Christian had puzzled them. Shelley, in coming to our house that night, had found a woman lying near the top of the hill, in fits. It was a fierce winter night, with snow upon the ground; and winter loses nothing of its fierceness at Hampstead. My friend, always the promptest as well as most pitying on these occasions, knocked at the first houses he could reach, in order to have the woman taken in. The invariable answer was, that they could not do it. He asked for an outhouse to put her in, while he went for a doctor. Impossible! In vain he assured them she was no impostor. They would not dispute the point with him; but doors were closed, and windows were shut down. Had he lit upon worthy Mr Park, the philologist, that gentleman would assuredly have come, in spite of his Calvinism. But he lived too far off. Had he lit upon my friend Armitage Brown, who lived on another side of the Heath; or on his friend and neighbour Dilke; they would either of them have jumped up from amidst their books or their bed-clothes, and have gone out with him. But the paucity of Christians is astonishing, considering the number of them. Time flies; the poor woman is in convulsions; her son, a young man, lamenting over her. At last my friend sees a carriage driving up to a house at a little distance. The knock is given; the warm door opens; servants and lights pour forth. Now, thought he, is the time. He puts on his best address, which anybody might recognize for that of the highest gentleman as well as of an interesting individual, and plants himself in the way of an elderly person, who is stepping out of the carriage with his family. He tells his story. They only press on the faster. "Will you go and see her?" "No, sir; there's no necessity for that sort of thing, depend on it. Impostors swarm everywhere: the thing cannot be done; sir, your conduct is extraordinary." "Sir," cried Shelley, assuming a very different manner, and forcing the flourishing householder to stop out of astonishment, "I am sorry to say that *your* conduct is *not* extraordinary; and if my own seems to amaze you, I will tell you something which may amaze you a little more, and I hope will frighten you. It is such men as you who madden the spirits and the patience of the poor and wretched; and if ever a convulsion comes in this country (which is very probable), recollect what I tell you:—you will have your house, that you refuse to put the miserable woman into, burnt over your head." "God bless me, sir! Dear me, sir!" exclaimed the poor, frightened man, and fluttered into his mansion. The woman was then brought to our house, which was at some distance, and down a bleak path (it was in the Vale of Health); and Shelley and her son were obliged to hold her till the doctor could arrive. It appeared that she had been attending this son in London, on a criminal charge made against him, the agitation of which had thrown her into the fits on her return. The doctor said that she would have perished, had she lain there a short time longer. The next day my friend sent mother and son comfortably home to Hendon, where they were known, and whence they returned him thanks full of gratitude.

LEIGH HUNT'S *Autobiography*

III

KEATS

And now to speak of Keats, who was introduced to me by his schoolmaster's son, Charles Cowden Clarke, a man of a most genial nature and corresponding poetical taste, admirably well qualified to nourish the genius of his pupil.

I had not known the young poet long, when Shelley and he

became acquainted under my roof. Keats did not take to Shelley as kindly as Shelley did to him. Shelley's only thoughts of his new acquaintance were such as regarded his bad health, with which he sympathized, and his poetry, of which he has left such a monument of his admiration in *Adonais*. Keats, being a little too sensitive on the score of his origin, felt inclined to see in every man of birth a sort of natural enemy. Their styles in writing also were very different; and Keats, notwithstanding his unbounded sympathies with ordinary flesh and blood, and even the transcendental cosmopolitics of *Hyperion*, was so far inferior in universality to his great acquaintance, that he could not accompany him in his daedal rounds with nature, and his Archimedean endeavours to move the globe with his own hands. I am bound to state thus much; because, hopeless of recovering his health, under circumstances that made the feeling extremely bitter, an irritable morbidity appears even to have driven his suspicions to excess; and this not only with regard to the acquaintance whom he might reasonably suppose to have had some advantages over him, but to myself, who had none; for I learned the other day, with extreme pain, such as I am sure so kind and reflecting a man as Mr Monckton Milnes would not have inflicted on me could he have foreseen it, that Keats at one period of his intercourse with us suspected both Shelley and myself of a wish to see him undervalued! Such are the tricks which constant infelicity can play with the most noble natures. For Shelley, let *Adonais* answer. For myself, let every word answer which I uttered about him, living and dead, and such as I now proceed to repeat. I might as well have been told that I wished to see the flowers or the stars undervalued, or my own heart that loved him.

In everything but this reserve, which was to a certain extent encouraged by my own incuriousness (for I have no reserve myself with those whom I love)—in every other respect but this, Keats and I might have been taken for friends of the old stamp, between whom there was no such thing even as obligation, except the pleasure of it. I could not love him as deeply as I did Shelley. That was impossible.

But my affection was only second to the one which I entertained for that heart of hearts. Keats, like Shelley himself, enjoyed the usual privilege of greatness with all whom he knew, rendering it delightful to be obliged by him, and an equal, but not greater, delight to oblige. It was a pleasure to his friends to have him in their houses, and he did not grudge it. When *Endymion* was published, he was living at Hampstead with his friend, Charles Armitage Brown, who attended him most affectionately through a severe illness, and with whom, to their great mutual enjoyment, he had taken a journey into Scotland. The lakes and mountains of the north delighted him exceedingly. He beheld them with an epic eye. Afterwards, he went into the south, and luxuriated in the Isle of Wight. On Brown's leaving home a second time, to visit the same quarter, Keats, who was too ill to accompany him, came to reside with me, when his last and best volume of poems appeared, containing *Lamia*, *Isabella*, the *Eve of St Agnes*, and the noble fragment of *Hyperion*. I remember Lamb's delight and admiration on reading this book; how pleased he was with the designation of Mercury as "the star of Lethe" (rising, as it were, and glittering as he came upon that pale region); and the fine daring anticipation in that passage of the second poem—

> So the two brothers and *their murdered man*
> Rode past fair Florence.

So also the description, at once delicate and gorgeous, of Agnes praying beneath the painted window. The public are now well acquainted with those and other passages, for which Persian kings would have filled a poet's mouth with gold. I remember Keats reading to me with great relish and particularity, conscious of what he had set forth, the lines describing the supper, and ending with the words,

> Lucent syrops tinct with cinnamon.

Mr Wordsworth would have said that the vowels were not varied enough; but Keats knew where his vowels were *not* to be varied.

LEIGH HUNT'S *Autobiography*

IV

Shelley *to* Byron

Marlow, *July* 9, 1817.

My dear Lord Byron,

I called on Rogers the other day on some affairs relating to Hunt, and heard some news of you, viz. that you had been to Rome, and that you had returned to Venice. I had already acquired the preceding piece of information from the Coliseum scene in "Manfred". How is it that I have not heard from you? At first I drew from your silence a favourable augury of your early return. This is in a degree confirmed by the circumstance of Newstead being advertised for sale. I shall be among the first to greet you on your return....

I suppose you know that the tyranny, civil and religious, under which this country groans, has visited me somewhat severely. I neither like it the worse nor the better for this. It was always the object of my unbounded abhorrence. But it may become necessary that I should quit the country. It is possible that the interference exercised by Chancery in the instance of my other two children might be attempted to be extended to William. Should this be the case, I shall depart.

I have read "Manfred" with the greatest admiration. The same freedom from common rules that marked the 3rd Canto and "Chillon" is visible here; and it was that which all your earlier productions, except "Lara", wanted. But it made me dreadfully melancholy, and I fear other friends in England too. Why do you indulge this despondency? "Manfred", as far as I learn, is immensely popular; it is characterised as a very daring production.

Hunt has been with me here, and we have often spoken of you. Hunt is an excellent man, and has a great regard for you.

How is your health—and—the resolutions on which it depends? I am anxious to know whether you are free from the disorder by which you were threatened. I have lately had a kind of relapse of my constitutional disease, and if the Chancellor should threaten to invade my domestic circle, I shall seek Italy; as a refuge at once from the stupid tyranny of these laws and my disorder . . .

Ever sincerely yours,
P. B. Shelley

BYRON ON HIS CONTEMPORARIES

BYRON *to* JOHN MURRAY

September 15, 1817.

Dear Sir,

I enclose a sheet for correction, if ever you get to another edition. You will observe that the blunder in printing makes it appear as if the Château was *over* St Gingo, instead of being on the opposite shore of the Lake, over Clarens. So, separate the paragraphs, otherwise my *to*pography will seem as inaccurate as your *ty*pography on this occasion.[1]

The other day I wrote to convey my proposition with regard to the 4th and concluding canto. I have gone over it and extended it to one hundred and fifty stanzas, which is almost as long as the first two were originally, and longer by itself than any of the smaller poems except *The Corsair*. Mr Hobhouse has made some very valuable and interesting notes of considerable length, and you may be sure I will do for the text all that I can do to finish with decency. I look upon *Childe Harold* as my best; and as I begun, I think of concluding it. But I make no resolutions on that head, as I broke my former intention with regard to *The Corsair*. However, I fear that I shall never do better; and yet, not being thirty years of age, for some moons to come, one ought to be progressive as far as Intellect goes for many a good year. But I have had a devilish deal of wear and tear of mind and body in my time, besides having published too often and much already. God grant me some judgment! to do what may be most fitting in that and every thing else, for I doubt my own exceedingly.

[1] The reference is to Byron's note on *Childe Harold*, canto 3, st. xcix.

I have read *Lallah Rookh*, but not with sufficient attention yet, for I ride about, and lounge, and ponder, and—two or three other things; so that my reading is very desultory, and not so attentive as it used to be. I am very glad to hear of its popularity, for Moore is a very noble fellow in all respects, and will enjoy it without any of the bad feeling that success—good or evil—sometimes engenders in the men of rhyme. Of the poem itself, I will tell you my opinion when I have mastered it: I say of the *poem*, for I don't like the *prose* at all—at all; and in the mean time, the "Fire worshippers" is the best, and the "Veiled Prophet" the worst, of the volume.

With regard to poetry in general, I am convinced, the more I think of it, that he and *all* of us—Scott, Southey, Wordsworth, Moore, Campbell, I,—are all in the wrong, one as much as another; that we are upon a wrong revolutionary poetical system, or systems, not worth a damn in itself, and from which none but Rogers and Crabbe are free; and that the present and next generations will finally be of this opinion. I am the more confirmed in this by having lately gone over some of our classics, particularly *Pope*, whom I tried in this way,—I took Moore's poems and my own and some others, and went over them side by side with Pope's, and I was really astonished (I ought not to have been so) and mortified at the ineffable distance in point of sense, harmony, effect, and even *Imagination*, passion, and *Invention*, between the little Queen Anne's man, and of us of the Lower Empire. Depend upon it, it is all Horace then, and Claudian now, among us; and if I had to begin again, I would model myself accordingly. Crabbe's the man, but he has got a coarse and impracticable subject, and Rogers, the Grandfather of living Poetry, is retired upon half-pay, (I don't mean as a Banker),—

> Since pretty Miss Jaqueline,
> With her nose aquiline,

and has done enough, unless he were to do as he did formerly.

DEDICATORY SONNET TO LEIGH HUNT[1]

Glory and loveliness have pass'd away;
For if we wander out in early morn,
No wreathed incense do we see upborne
Into the east, to meet the smiling day:
No crowd of nymphs soft voic'd and young and gay,
In woven baskets bringing ears of corn,
Roses, and pinks, and violets, to adorn
The shrine of Flora in her early May.
But there are left delights as high as these,
And I shall ever bless my destiny,
That in a time, when under pleasant trees
Pan is no longer sought, I feel a free,
A leafy luxury, seeing I could please
With these poor offerings, a man like thee.

KEATS: *Poems*, 1817

LONDON 1817–18

I

1817.

December 27th.—I called on Lamb, and met Wordsworth with him; I afterwards returned to Lamb's. Dined at Monkhouse's. The party was small—Mr and Mrs Wordsworth and Miss Hutchinson, Coleridge and his son Hartley, and Mr Tillbrook. After dinner Charles Lamb joined the party.

Among the light conversation, Tillbrook related that Southey had received a letter from a person requesting him to make an acrostic on the name of a young lady in Essex. The writer was paying his addresses to this young lady, but had a rival who beat him in writing verses. Southey did not send the verses, and distributed in buying blankets for some poor women of Keswick the money sent in payment.

[1] Prefixed to Keats's first volume.

December 30th.—I dined with the Colliers, and spent the evening at Lamb's. I found a large party collected round the two poets, but Coleridge had the larger number. There was, however, scarcely any conversation beyond a whisper. Coleridge was philosophising in his rambling way to Monkhouse, who listened attentively—to Manning, who sometimes smiled, as if he thought Coleridge had no right to metaphysicize on chemistry without any knowledge of the subject—to Martin Burney, who was eager to interpose—and Alsager, who was content to be a listener; while Wordsworth was for a great part of the time engaged *tête-à-tête* with Talfourd. I could catch scarcely anything of the conversation. I chatted with the ladies. Miss Lamb had gone through the fatigue of a dinner-party very well, and Charles was in good spirits.

HENRY CRABB ROBINSON'S *Diary*

II

In December Wordsworth was in town, and as Keats wished to know him I made up a party to dinner of Charles Lamb, Wordsworth, Keats and Monkhouse, his friend, and a very pleasant party we had.

I wrote to Lamb, and told him the address was "22, Lisson Grove, North, at Rossi's, half way up, right hand corner". I received his characteristic reply.

My dear Haydon,

I will come with pleasure to 22 Lisson Grove, North, at Rossi's, half way up, right hand side, if I can find it.

Yours,
C. Lamb.

20. Russel Court,
Covent Garden East,
half way up, next the corner,
left hand side.

On December 28th the immortal dinner came off in my painting-room, with Jerusalem towering up behind us as a background. Wordsworth was a fine cue, and we had a glorious set-to,—on Homer, Shakespeare, Milton and Virgil.

Lamb got exceedingly merry and exquisitely witty; and his fun in the midst of Wordsworth's solemn intonations of oratory was like the sarcasm and wit of the fool in the intervals of Lear's passion. He made a speech and voted me absent, and made them drink my health. "Now," said Lamb, "you old lake poet, you rascally poet, why do you call Voltaire dull?" We all defended Wordsworth, and affirmed there was a state of mind when Voltaire would be dull. "Well," said Lamb, "here's Voltaire—the Messiah of the French nation, and a very proper one too."

He then, in a strain of humour beyond description, abused me for putting Newton's head into my picture,—"a fellow", said he, "who believed nothing unless it was as clear as the three sides of a triangle". And then he and Keats agreed he had destroyed all the poetry of the rainbow by reducing it to the prismatic colours. It was impossible to resist him, and we all drank, "Newton's health, and confusion to mathematics". It was delightful to see the good humour of Wordsworth in giving in to all our frolics without affectation and laughing as heartily as the best of us.

By this time other friends joined, amongst them poor Ritchie who was going to penetrate by Fezzan to Timbuctoo. I introduced him to all as "a gentleman going to Africa". Lamb seemed to take no notice; but all of a sudden he roared out, "Which is the gentleman we are going to lose?" We then drank the victim's health, in which Ritchie joined.

In the morning of this delightful day, a gentleman, a perfect stranger, had called on me. He said he knew my friends, had an enthusiasm for Wordsworth and begged I would procure him the happiness of an introduction. He told me he was a comptroller of stamps, and often had correspondence with the poet. I thought it a liberty; but still, as he seemed a gentleman, I told him he might come.

When we retired to tea we found the comptroller. In introducing him to Wordsworth I forgot to say who he was. After a little time the comptroller looked down, looked up and said to Wordsworth, "Don't you think, sir, Milton was a great genius?" Keats looked at me, Wordsworth looked at the comptroller. Lamb who was dozing at the fire turned round and said, "Pray, sir, did you say Milton was a great genius?" "No, sir; I asked Mr Wordsworth if he were not." "Oh," said Lamb, "then you are a silly fellow." "Charles! my dear Charles!" said Wordsworth; but Lamb, perfectly innocent of the confusion he had created, was off again by the fire.

After an awful pause the comptroller said, "Don't you think Newton a great genius?" I could not stand it any longer. Keats put his head into my books. Ritchie squeezed in a laugh. Wordsworth seemed asking himself, "Who is this?" Lamb got up, and taking a candle, said, "Sir, will you allow me to look at your phrenological development?" He then turned his back upon the poor man, and at every question of the comptroller he chaunted—

> Diddle diddle dumpling, my son John
> Went to bed with his breeches on.

The man in office, finding Wordsworth did not know who he was, said in a spasmodic and half-chuckling anticipation of assured victory, "I have had the honour of some correspondence with you, Mr Wordsworth". "With me, sir?" said Wordsworth, "not that I remember." "Don't you, sir? I am a comptroller of stamps." There was a dead silence;—the comptroller evidently thinking that was enough. While we were waiting for Wordsworth's reply, Lamb sung out

> Hey diddle diddle,
> The cat and the fiddle.

"My dear Charles!" said Wordsworth,—

> Diddle diddle dumpling, my son John,

chaunted Lamb, and then rising, exclaimed, "Do let me have another look at that gentleman's organs". Keats and I hurried Lamb into the painting-room, shut the door and gave way to inexhaustible laughter. Monkhouse followed and tried to get Lamb away. We went back but the comptroller was irreconcilable. We soothed and smiled and asked him to supper. He stayed though his dignity was sorely affected.

However, being a good-natured man, we parted all in good humour, and no ill effects followed.

All the while, until Monkhouse succeeded, we could hear Lamb struggling in the painting-room and calling at intervals, "Who is that fellow? Allow me to see his organs once more".

It was indeed an immortal evening. Wordsworth's fine intonation as he quoted Milton and Virgil, Keats' eager inspired look, Lamb's quaint sparkle of lambent humour, so speeded the stream of conversation, that in my life I never passed a more delightful time. All our fun was within bounds. Not a word passed that an apostle might not have listened to. It was a night worthy of the Elizabethan age, and my solemn Jerusalem flashing up by the flame of the fire, with Christ hanging over us like a vision, all made up a picture which will long glow upon—

> that inward eye
> Which is the bliss of solitude.

Keats made Ritchie promise he would carry his *Endymion* to the great desert of Sahara and fling it in the midst.

Poor Ritchie went to Africa, and died, as Lamb foresaw, in 1819. Keats died in 1821, at Rome. C. Lamb is gone, joking to the last. Monkhouse is dead, and Wordsworth and I are the only two now living (1841) of that glorious party.

HAYDON: *Autobiography*

III

GOSSIP FROM KEATS'S LETTERS

Your friendship for me is now getting into its teens—and I feel the past. Also every day older I get—the greater is my idea of your achievements in Art: and I am convinced that there are three things to rejoice at in this Age—The Excursion, Your Pictures, and Hazlitt's depth of Taste.

To B. R. Haydon, *January* 10, 1818

I was thinking what hindered me from writing so long, for I have so many things to say to you, and know not where to begin. It shall be upon a thing most interesting to you, my

Poem.[1] Well! I have given the first Book to Taylor; he seemed more than satisfied with it, and to my surprise proposed publishing it in Quarto if Haydon would make a drawing of some event therein, for a Frontispiece. I called on Haydon, he said he would do anything I liked, but said he would rather paint a finished picture, from it, which he seems eager to do; this in a year or two will be a glorious thing for us; and it will be, for Haydon is struck with the 1st Book. I left Haydon and the next day received a letter from him, proposing to make, as he says, with all his might, a finished chalk sketch of my head, to be engraved in the first style and put at the head of my Poem, saying at the same time he had never done the thing for any human being, and that it must have considerable effect as he will put his name to it. I begin to-day to copy my 2nd Book—"thus far into the bowels of the Land". You shall hear whether it will be Quarto or non Quarto, picture or non picture. Leigh Hunt I showed my 1st Book to—he allows it not much merit as a whole; says it is unnatural and made ten objections to it in the mere skimming over. He says the conversation is unnatural and too high-flown for Brother and Sister—says it should be simple, forgetting do you mind that they are both overshadowed by a supernatural Power, and of force could not speak like Francesca in the Rimini. He must first prove that Caliban's poetry is unnatural.—This with me completely overturns his objections—the fact is he and Shelley are hurt, and perhaps justly, at my not having showed them the affair officiously and from several hints I have had they appear much disposed to dissect and anatomise any trip or slip I may have made.—But who's afraid? Ay! Tom! Demme if I am. I went last Tuesday, an hour too late, to Hazlitt's Lecture on poetry, got there just as they were coming out, when all these pounced upon me—Hazlitt, John Hunt and Son, Wells, Bewick, all the Landseers, Bob Harris, aye and more—I know not whether Wordsworth has left town—But Sunday I dined with Hazlitt and Haydon.

To George and Thomas Keats, *January* 23, 1818

[1] *Endymion.*

I sat down to read King Lear yesterday, and felt the greatness of the thing up to the writing of a Sonnet preparatory thereto—in my next you shall have it.—There were some miserable reports of Rice's health—I went, and lo! Master Jemmy had been to the play the night before, and was out at the time—he always comes on his Legs like a Cat. I have seen a good deal of Wordsworth. Hazlitt is lecturing on Poetry at the Surrey Institution—I shall be there next Tuesday.

To Benjamin Bailey, *January* 23, 1818

I shall visit you as soon as I have copied my poem all out, I am now much beforehand with the printer, they have done none yet, and I am half afraid they will let half the season by before the printing. I am determined they shall not trouble me when I have copied it all.—Horace Smith has lent me his manuscript called "Nehemiah Muggs, an exposure of the Methodists"—perhaps I may send you a few extracts.—Hazlitt's last lecture was on Thomson, Cowper, and Crabbe, he praised Thomson and Cowper, but he gave Crabbe an unmerciful licking.—Mr Robinson a great friend of Coleridge's called on me. . . . What think you—am I to be crowned in the Capitol, am I to be made a Mandarin—No! I am to be invited, Mrs Hunt tells me, to a party at Ollier's, to keep Shakespeare's birthday—Shakespeare would stare to see me there. The Wednesday before last Shelley, Hunt and I wrote each a Sonnet on the River Nile, some day you shall read them all. I saw a sheet of 'Endymion', and have all reason to suppose they will soon get it done, there shall be nothing wanting on my part. I have been writing at intervals many songs and Sonnets, and I long to be at Teignmouth, to read them over to you: however I think I had better wait till this Book is off my mind.

To George and Thomas Keats, *February* 14, 1818

The thrushes are singing now as if they would speak to the winds, because their big brother Jack, the Spring, was not far off. I am reading Voltaire and Gibbon, although I wrote to

Reynolds the other day to prove reading of no use; I have not seen Hunt since, I am a good deal with Dilke and Brown, we are very thick; they are very kind to me, they are well. I don't think I could stop in Hampstead but for their neighbourhood. I hear Hazlitt's lectures regularly, his last was on Gray, Collins, Young, etc., and he gave a very fine piece of discriminating Criticism on Swift, Voltaire, and Rabelais. I was very disappointed with his treatment of Chatterton. I generally meet with many I know there. Lord Byron's 4th Canto is expected out, and I heard somewhere, that Walter Scott has a new Poem in readiness. I am sorry that Wordsworth has left a bad impression wherever he visited in town by his egotism, Vanity, and bigotry. Yet he is a great poet if not a philosopher. I have not yet read Shelley's Poem,[1] I do not suppose you have it yet, at the Teignmouth libraries.

To George and Thomas Keats, *February* 21, 1818

IV

1818.

January 27th.—I went to the Surrey Institution, where I heard Hazlitt lecture on Shakespeare and Milton. He delighted me much by the talent he displayed; but his bitterness of spirit broke out in a passage in which he reproached modern poets for their vanity and incapacity of admiring and loving anything but themselves. He was applauded at this part of his lecture, but I know not whether he was generally understood.

From hence I called at Collier's, and taking Mrs Collier with me, I went to a lecture by Coleridge in Fleur-de-Lis Court, Fleet Street. I was gratified unexpectedly by finding a large and respectable audience, generally of superior-looking persons, in physiognomy rather than dress. Coleridge treated of the origin of poetry and of Oriental works; but he had little animation, and an exceedingly bad cold rendered his voice scarcely audible.

February 17th.—I took tea at home, and Hamond calling, I accompanied him to Hazlitt's lecture. He spoke of the writers in the reign of Queen Anne, and was bitter, sprightly,

[1] *The Revolt of Islam.*

and full of political and personal allusions. In treating of Prior he quoted his unseemly verses against Blackmore to a congregation of saints. He drew an ingenious but not very intelligible parallel between Swift, Rabelais, and Voltaire, and even eulogised the modern infidel. So indiscreet and reckless is the man!

I then went alone to Coleridge's lecture. He spoke of Ben Jonson, Beaumont and Fletcher, etc., and further convinced me that he is as much confined within his circle of favourite ideas as any man, and that his speculations have ceased to be living thoughts, in which he is making progress. They are closed, I believe, and he has not the faculty of giving them consistency and effect.

February 24th.—I dined and took tea at Collier's, and then heard part of a lecture by Hazlitt at the Surrey Institution. He was so contemptuous towards Wordsworth, speaking of his letter about Burns, that I lost my temper. He imputed to Wordsworth the desire of representing himself as a superior man.

February 27th.—I took tea with Gurney, and invited Mrs Gurney to accompany me to Coleridge's lecture. It was on Dante and Milton—one of his very best. He digressed less than usual, and really gave information and ideas about the poets he professed to criticise. I returned to Gurney's, and heard Mr Gurney read Mrs Fry's examination before the committee of the House of Commons about Newgate—a very curious examination, and very promising as to the future improvements in prison discipline.

April 8th.—(At C. Lamb's.) There was a large party—the greater part of those who are usually there, but also Leigh Hunt and his wife. He has improved in manliness and healthfulness since I saw him last, some years ago. There was a high glee about him, which evinced high spirits, if not perfect health, and I envied his vivacity. He imitated Hazlitt capitally; Wordsworth not so well. Talfourd was there. He does not appreciate Wordsworth's fine lines on "Scorners". Hunt did not sympathise with Talfourd, but opposed him playfully, and that I liked him for.

HENRY CRABB ROBINSON'S *Diary*

V

HAZLITT ON COLERIDGE

I may say of him here, that he is the only person I ever knew who answered to the idea of a man of genius. He is the only person from whom I ever learnt any thing. There is only one thing he could learn from me in return, but *that* he has not. He was the first poet I ever knew. His genius at that time had angelic wings, and fed on manna. He talked on for ever; and you wished him to talk on for ever. His thoughts did not seem to come with labour and effort; but as if borne on the gusts of genius, and as if the wings of his imagination lifted him from off his feet. His voice rolled on the ear like the pealing organ, and its sound alone was the music of thought. His mind was clothed with wings; and raised on them, he lifted philosophy to heaven. In his descriptions, you then saw the progress of human happiness and liberty in bright and never-ending succession, like the steps of Jacob's ladder, with airy shapes ascending and descending, and with the voice of God at the top of the ladder. And shall I, who heard him then, listen to him now? Not I!... That spell is broke; that time is gone for ever, that voice is no more: but still the recollection comes rushing by with thoughts of long-past years, and rings in my ears with never-dying sound.

HAZLITT: *Lectures on the English Poets*

VI

LAMB *to* MRS WORDSWORTH

East-India House, *February* 18, 1818.

My dear Mrs Wordsworth,—I have repeatedly taken pen in hand to answer your kind letter. My sister should more properly have done it, but she having failed, I consider myself answerable for her debts. I am now trying to do it in the midst of commercial noises, and with a quill which seems more ready to glide into arithmetical figures and names of gourds, cassia, cardamoms, aloes, ginger, or tea, than into kindly

LIBRARY ST. MARY'S COLLEGE

responses and friendly recollections. The reason why I cannot write letters at home, is, that I am never alone. Plato's—(I write to W. W. now)—Plato's double-animal parted never longed more to be reciprocally re-united in the system of its first creation than I sometimes do to be but for a moment single and separate. Except my morning's walk to the office, which is like treading on sands of gold for that reason, I am never so. I cannot walk home from office but some officious friend offers his unwelcome courtesies to accompany me. All the morning I am pestered. I could sit and gravely cast up sums in great books, or compare sum with sum, and write "paid" against this, and "unpaid" against t'other, and yet reserve in some corner of my mind "some darling thoughts all my own",—faint memory of some passage in a book, or the tone of an absent friend's voice—a snatch of Miss Burrell's singing, or a gleam of Fanny Kelly's divine plain face. The two operations might be going on at the same time without thwarting, as the sun's two motions, (earth's I mean,) or as I sometimes turn round till I am giddy, in my back parlour, while my sister is walking longitudinally in the front; or as the shoulder of veal twists round with the spit, while the smoke wreathes up the chimney. But there are a set of amateurs of the Belles Lettres—the gay science—who come to me as a sort of rendezvous, putting questions of criticism, of British Institutions, Lalla Rookhs, &c.—what Coleridge said at the lecture last night—who have the form of reading men, but, for any possible use reading can be to them, but to talk of, might as well have been Ante-Cadmeans born, or have lain sucking out the sense of an Egyptian hieroglyph as long as the pyramids will last, before they should find it. These pests worrit me at business, and in all its intervals, perplexing my accounts, poisoning my little salutary warming-time at the fire, puzzling my paragraphs if I take a newspaper, cramming in between my own free thoughts and a column of figures, which had come to an amicable compromise but for them. Their noise ended, one of them, as I said, accompanies me home, lest I should be solitary for a moment; he at length takes his welcome leave at the door; up I go, mutton on table, hungry as hunter, hope to forget my cares, and bury them in the agreeable abstraction of mastication; knock at the door, in comes Mr Hazlitt, or Mr Martin Burney, or Morgan Demi-gorgon, or my brother, or somebody, to prevent my eating alone—a process absolutely necessary to my poor wretched digestion. O the pleasure of eating alone!—eating my dinner alone! let me think of it. But in they come, and make it absolutely necessary that I should open a bottle of orange; for my meat turns into stone when any one dines with me, if I have not wine. Wine can mollify stones; then *that* wine turns into acidity, acerbity, misanthropy, a hatred of my interrupters—(God bless 'em! I love some of 'em dearly), and with the hatred, a still greater aversion to their going away. Bad is the dead sea they bring upon me, choking and deadening, but worse is the deader dry sand they leave me on, if they go before bed-time. Come never, I would say to these spoilers of my dinner; but if you come, never go! The fact is, this interruption does not happen very often; but every time it comes by surprise, that present bane of my life, orange wine, with all its dreary stifling consequences, follows. Evening company I should always like had I any mornings, but I am saturated with human faces (*divine* forsooth!) and voices all the golden morning; and five evenings in a week would be as much as I should covet to be in company; but I assure you that is a wonderful week in which I can get two, or one to myself. I am never C. L., but always C. L. & Co. He who thought it not good for man to be alone, preserve me from the more prodigious monstrosity of being never by myself! I forget bed-time, but even there these sociable frogs clamber up to annoy me. Once a week, generally some singular evening that, being alone, I go to bed at the hour I ought always to be a-bed; just close to my bed-room window is the club-room of a public-house, where a set of singers, I take them to be chorus singers of the two theatres, (it must be *both of them*,) begin their orgies. They are a set of fellows (as I conceive) who, being limited by their talents to the burthen of the song at the play-houses, in revenge have got the common popular airs by Bishop, or some cheap composer, arranged for choruses;

that is, to be sung all in chorus. At least I never can catch any of the text of the plain song, nothing but the Babylonish choral howl at the tail on't. "That fury being quenched"—the howl I mean—a burden succeeds of shouts and clapping, and knocking of the table. At length overtasked nature drops under it, and escapes for a few hours into the society of the sweet silent creatures of dreams, which go away with mocks and mows at cockcrow. And then I think of the words Christabel's father used (bless me, I have dipt in the wrong ink!) to say every morning by way of variety when he awoke:

> Every knell, the Baron saith,
> Wakes us up to a world of death—

or something like it. All I mean by this senseless interrupted tale, is, that by my central situation I am a little over-companied. Not that I have any animosity against the good creatures that are so anxious to drive away the harpy solitude from me. I like 'em, and cards, and a cheerful glass; but I mean merely to give you an idea, between office confinement and after-office society, how little time I can call my own. I mean only to draw a picture, not to make an inference. I would not that I know of have it otherwise. I only wish sometimes I could exchange some of my faces and voices for the faces and voices which a late visitation brought most welcome, and carried away, leaving regret, but more pleasure, even a kind of gratitude, at being so often favoured with that kind northern visitation. My London faces and noises don't hear me—I mean no disrespect, or I should explain myself, that instead of their return 220 times a year, and the return of W. W., &c., seven times in 104 weeks, some more equal distribution might be found. I have scarce room to put in Mary's kind love, and my poor name, C. Lamb

W. H. goes on lecturing against W. W. and making copious use of quotations from said W. W. to give a zest to said lectures. S. T. C. is lecturing with success. I have not heard either him or H., but I dined with S. T. C. at Gilman's a Sunday or two since, and he was well and in good spirits.

I mean to hear some of the course; but lectures are not much to my taste, whatever the lecturer may be. If *read*, they are dismal flat, and you can't think why you are brought together to hear a man read his works, which you could read so much better at leisure yourself. If delivered extempore, I am always in pain, lest the gift of utterance should suddenly fail the orator in the middle, as it did me at the dinner given in honour of me at the London Tavern. "Gentlemen", said I, and there I stopped; the rest my feelings were under the necessity of supplying. Mrs Wordsworth *will* go on, kindly haunting us with visions of seeing the lakes once more, which never can be realised. Between us there is a great gulf, not of inexplicable moral antipathies and distances, I hope, as there seemed to be between me and that gentleman concerned in the Stamp Office, that I so strangely recoiled from at Haydon's. I think I had an instinct that he was the head of an office. I hate all such people—accountants' deputy accountants. The dear abstract notion of the East India Company, as long as she is unseen, is pretty, rather poetical; but as she makes herself manifest by the persons of such beasts, I loathe and detest her as the scarlet what-do-you-call-her of Babylon. I thought, after abridging us of all our red-letter days, they had done their worst; but I was deceived in the length to which heads of offices, those true liberty-haters, can go. They are the tyrants; not Ferdinand, nor Nero. By a decree passed this week, they have abridged us of the immemorially-observed custom of going at one o'clock of a Saturday, the little shadow of a holiday left us. Dear W. W., be thankful for liberty.

VII

Leigh Hunt *to* Shelley *and* Mrs Shelley

Lisson Grove North, *April* 24, 1818.

Well, dear and illustrious vagabonds, and how do you find yourselves? We are all well here, and as musical and flowery as ever, notwithstanding Marianne's[1] school two hours of a

[1] Mrs Hunt.

morning, which makes us all good boys and girls, and gets me up, and keeps all sorts of peevishness and noises down. We rejoiced at having your letters from Calais and Lyons, albeit Shelley found out the weak side of my friendship in not waking him,—which is very savage and "young-eyed" of him. "On which Shelley looked meek, and taking forth a pen", etc. We thought you would have a roguish passage. Just as your first letter came, some one had horrified us, by telling us of a carriage which was met in the sea by a person coming over. It was not a present to Amphitrite, was it, to make interest at Court? It is delightful to hear of Shelley's improving health. The nearer he gets to the sun, the better he will be, I doubt not; but don't let him be too much out in it and burn his wings. It was very good of Marina[1] to write such a circumstantial letter from Lyons, and almost as good of Shelley (there's modesty for you) to think so much of the *Nymphs*.[2] I hope to hear a thousand things of Italy, of the Alps, of Milan la Grande, Firenza la Bella, and Napoli la Gentile,—of the ladies, the country, the books, the operas, and of Raphael and Julio Romano, which reminds me there is also a place called Rome....

We go to plays, to operas, and even to concerts, not forgetting a sort of conversazione at Lamb's, with whom, and Alsager, I have renewed the intercourse, with infinite delight, which sickness interrupted. One of the best consequences of this is that Lamb's writings are being collected for publication by Ollier, and are now, indeed, going through the press. So we still have proof-sheets fluttering about us. As to myself in particular, I walk out quite a buck again, with my blue frock coat and new hat, waving my (orange) lily hands. I also go to the office on Saturdays. At present I have made myself a nook to write in of a morning in the corner of the room where Raphael stood—as thus:—I have taken this place under the print of Shakespeare, in a chair with a table before me, put his bust on it, with a rose-tree at the side towards the door, and filled the outside of the window with geranium, myrtle, daisies, heartsease, and a vase full of gay flowers; so

[1] Mary Shelley.

[2] A poem by Hunt.

that, with the new spring green in the garden, my books on the right, the picture of Jaques and the Stag under Milton, and two plaster-cast vases, which —— has just sent me, on each side of the Mercury on the piano, I have nothing but sights of beauty, genius, and morality all about me.... —— admired my bower the other evening, and shrieked at the sight of the heartsease. I overtook him the other day walking through the flowery part of Covent Garden Market, and peering with infinite complacency on each side of him. He has been to tea here several times, and the other night met Lamb and his sister. He tells me to say that he is alive, and has as many prejudices as usual. He means to write. Peacock went with us to the play just after you left us, and we also met him a few nights afterwards at the opera; but he has since been at Marlow, and we have neither seen nor heard of him. Mr Godwin, I hear, is well. I am going to send him Drake's books about Shakespeare, which Lamb tells me he wishes to see. Adieu. I leave the rest of the paper for Marianne.

SHELLEY AND BYRON

In August, 1818 Shelley visited Byron at Venice, and his *Julian and Maddalo* commemorates their meeting. Maddalo's child is Allegra, the daughter of Byron and Clare Clairmont, who had spent the first eighteen months of her life in Shelley's household, and had been brought by the Shelleys to Italy at Byron's request.

I rode one evening with Count Maddalo
Upon the bank of land which breaks the flow
Of Adria towards Venice: a bare strand
Of hillocks, heaped from ever-shifting sand,
Matted with thistles and amphibious weeds,
Such as from earth's embrace the salt ooze breeds,
Is this; an uninhabited sea-side,
Which the lone fisher, when his nets are dried,
Abandons; and no other object breaks
The waste, but one dwarf tree and some few stakes
Broken and unrepaired, and the tide makes

A narrow space of level sand thereon,
Where 'twas our wont to ride while day went down.
This ride was my delight. I love all waste
And solitary places; where we taste
The pleasure of believing what we see
Is boundless, as we wish our souls to be:
And such was this wide ocean, and this shore
More barren than its billows; and yet more
Than all, with a remembered friend I love
To ride as then I rode;—for the winds drove
The living spray along the sunny air
Into our faces; the blue heavens were bare,
Stripped to their depths by the awakening north;
And, from the waves, sound like delight broke forth
Harmonising with solitude, and sent
Into our hearts aëreal merriment.
So, as we rode, we talked; and the swift thought,
Winging itself with laughter, lingered not,
But flew from brain to brain,—such glee was ours,
Charged with light memories of remembered hours,
None slow enough for sadness: till we came
Homeward, which always makes the spirit tame.
This day had been cheerful but cold, and now
The sun was sinking, and the wind also.
Our talk grew somewhat serious, as may be
Talk interrupted with such raillery
As mocks itself, because it cannot scorn
The thoughts it would extinguish:—'twas forlorn,
Yet pleasing, such as once, so poets tell,
The devils held within the dales of Hell
Concerning God, freewill and destiny:
Of all that earth has been or yet may be,
All that vain men imagine or believe,
Or hope can paint or suffering may achieve,
We descanted, and I (for ever still
Is it not wise to make the best of ill?)
Argued against despondency, but pride
Made my companion take the darker side.

The sense that he was greater than his kind
Had struck, methinks, his eagle spirit blind
By gazing on its own exceeding light.
Meanwhile the sun paused ere it should alight,
Over the horizon of the mountains;—Oh,
How beautiful is sunset, when the glow
Of Heaven descends upon a land like thee,
Thou Paradise of exiles, Italy!
Thy mountains, seas, and vineyards, and the towers
Of cities they encircle!—it was ours
To stand on thee, beholding it: and then,
Just where we had dismounted, the Count's men
Were waiting for us with the gondola.—
As those who pause on some delightful way
Though bent on pleasant pilgrimage, we stood
Looking upon the evening, and the flood
Which lay between the city and the shore,
Paved with the image of the sky . . . the hoar
And aëry Alps towards the North appeared
Through mist, an heaven-sustaining bulwark reared
Between the East and West; and half the sky
Was roofed with clouds of rich emblazonry
Dark purple at the zenith, which still grew
Down the steep West into a wondrous hue
Brighter than burning gold, even to the rent
Where the swift sun yet paused in his descent
Among the many-folded hills: they were
Those famous Euganean hills, which bear,
As seen from Lido thro' the harbour piles,
The likeness of a clump of peakèd isles—
And then—as if the Earth and Sea had been
Dissolved into one lake of fire, were seen
Those mountains towering as from waves of flame
Around the vaporous sun, from which there came
The inmost purple spirit of light, and made
Their very peaks transparent. "Ere it fade,"
Said my companion, "I will show you soon
A better station"—so, o'er the lagune

We glided; and from that funereal bark
I leaned, and saw the city, and could mark
How from their many isles, in evening's gleam,
Its temples and its palaces did seem
Like fabrics of enchantment piled to Heaven.
I was about to speak, when—"We are even
Now at the point I meant", said Maddalo,
And bade the gondolieri cease to row.
"Look, Julian, on the west, and listen well
If you hear not a deep and heavy bell."
I looked, and saw between us and the sun
A building on an island; such a one
As age to age might add, for uses vile,
A windowless, deformed and dreary pile;
And on the top an open tower, where hung
A bell, which in the radiance swayed and swung;
We could just hear its hoarse and iron tongue:
The broad sun sunk behind it, and it tolled
In strong and black relief.—"What we behold
Shall be the madhouse and its belfry tower,"
Said Maddalo, "and ever at this hour
Those who may cross the water, hear that bell
Which calls the maniacs, each one from his cell,
To vespers."—"As much skill as need to pray
In thanks or hope for their dark lot have they
To their stern maker", I replied. "O ho!
You talk as in years past", said Maddalo.
"'Tis strange men change not. You were ever still
Among Christ's flock a perilous infidel,
A wolf for the meek lambs—if you can't swim
Beware of Providence." I looked on him,
But the gay smile had faded in his eye.
"And such",—he cried, "is our mortality,
And this must be the emblem and the sign
Of what should be eternal and divine!—
And like that black and dreary bell, the soul,
Hung in a heaven-illumined tower, must toll
Our thoughts and our desires to meet below

Round the rent heart and pray—as madmen do
For what? they know not,—till the night of death
As sunset that strange vision, severeth
Our memory from itself, and us from all
We sought and yet were baffled." I recall
The sense of what he said, although I mar
The force of his expressions. The broad star
Of day meanwhile had sunk behind the hill,
And the black bell became invisible,
And the red tower looked gray, and all between
The churches, ships and palaces were seen
Huddled in gloom;—into the purple sea
The orange hues of heaven sunk silently.
We hardly spoke, and soon the gondola
Conveyed me to my lodging by the way.
The following morn was rainy, cold and dim:
Ere Maddalo arose, I called on him,
And whilst I waited with his child I played;
A lovelier toy sweet Nature never made,
A serious, subtle, wild, yet gentle being,
Graceful without design and unforeseeing,
With eyes—Oh speak not of her eyes!—which seem
Twin mirrors of Italian Heaven, yet gleam
With such deep meaning, as we never see
But in the human countenance: with me
She was a special favourite: I had nursed
Her fine and feeble limbs when she came first
To this bleak world; and she yet seemed to know
On second sight her ancient playfellow,
Less changed than she was by six months or so;
For after her first shyness was worn out
We sate there, rolling billiard balls about,
When the Count entered. Salutations past—
"The word you spoke last night might well have cast
A darkness on my spirit—if man be
The passive thing you say, I should not see
Much harm in the religions and old saws
(Tho' I may never own such leaden laws)

Which break a teachless nature to the yoke:
Mine is another faith"—thus much I spoke
And noting he replied not, added: "See
This lovely child, blithe, innocent and free;
She spends a happy time with little care,
While we to such sick thoughts subjected are
As came on you last night—it is our will
That thus enchains us to permitted ill—
We might be otherwise—we might be all
We dream of happy, high, majestical.
Where is the love, beauty, and truth we seek
But in our mind? and if we were not weak
Should we be less in deed than in desire?"
"Ay, if we were not weak—and we aspire
How vainly to be strong!" said Maddalo:
"You talk Utopia". "It remains to know,"
I then rejoined, "and those who try may find
How strong the chains are which our spirit bind;
Brittle perchance as straw. . . . We are assured
Much may be conquered, much may be endured,
Of what degrades and crushes us. We know
That we have power over ourselves to do
And suffer—what, we know not till we try;
But something nobler than to live and die—
So taught those kings of old philosophy
Who reigned, before Religion made men blind;
And those who suffer with their suffering kind
Yet feel their faith, religion." "My dear friend,"
Said Maddalo, "my judgement will not bend
To your opinion, though I think you might
Make such a system refutation-tight
As far as words go. I knew one like you
Who to this city came some months ago,
With whom I argued in this sort, and he
Is now gone mad,—and so he answered me,—
Poor fellow! but if you would like to go
We'll visit him, and his wild talk will show
How vain are such aspiring theories."

"I hope to prove the induction otherwise,
And that a want of that true theory, still,
Which seeks a 'soul of goodness' in things ill
Or in himself or others, has thus bowed
His being—there are some by nature proud,
Who patient in all else demand but this—
To love and be beloved with gentleness;
And being scorned, what wonder if they die
Some living death? this is not destiny
But man's own wilful ill."

SHELLEY: *Julian and Maddalo*

KEATS AND COLERIDGE

[*April* 15, 1819.]

Brown is gone to bed—and I am tired of rhyming—there is a north wind blowing playing young gooseberry with the trees—I don't care so it helps even with a side wind a Letter to me—for I cannot put faith in any reports I hear of the Settlement; some are good and some bad. Last Sunday I took a Walk towards Highgate and in the lane that winds by the side of Lord Mansfield's park I met Mr Green our Demonstrator at Guy's in conversation with Coleridge—I joined them, after enquiring by a look whether it would be agreeable—I walked with him at his alderman-after-dinner pace for near two miles I suppose. In those two Miles he broached a thousand things—let me see if I can give you a list—Nightingales—Poetry—on Poetical Sensation—Metaphysics—Different genera and species of Dreams—Nightmare—a dream accompanied by a sense of touch—single and double touch—a dream related—First and second consciousness—the difference explained between will and Volition—so say metaphysicians from a want of smoking the second consciousness—Monsters—the Kraken—Mermaids—Southey believes in them—Southey's belief too much diluted—a Ghost story—Good morning—I heard his voice as he came towards me—I heard it as he moved away—

I had heard it all the interval—if it may be called so. He was civil enough to ask me to call on him at Highgate. Good-night!

Letter of Keats to George and Georgiana Keats

THE WAGGONER

I

THE DEDICATION

To Charles Lamb, Esq.

My Dear Friend,

When I sent you, a few weeks ago, the Tale of Peter Bell, you asked "why *The Waggoner* was not added?"—To say the truth,—from the higher tone of imagination, and the deeper touches of passion aimed at in the former, I apprehended this little Piece could not accompany it without disadvantage. In the year 1806, if I am not mistaken, *The Waggoner* was read to you in manuscript, and, as you have remembered it for so long a time, I am the more encouraged to hope that, since the localities on which the Poem partly depends did not prevent its being interesting to you, it may prove acceptable to others. Being therefore in some measure the cause of its present appearance, you must allow me the gratification of inscribing it to you; in acknowledgment of the pleasure I have derived from your Writings, and of the high esteem with which

I am very truly yours,
William Wordsworth

Rydal Mount, *May* 20, 1819.

II
LAMB'S REPLY

June 7, 1819.

My Dear Wordsworth,—You cannot imagine how proud we are here of the dedication. We read it twice for once that we do the poem. I mean all through; yet "Benjamin" is no common favourite; there is a spirit of beautiful tolerance in it. It is as good as it was in 1806; and it will be as good in 1829, if our dim eyes shall be awake to peruse it. Methinks there is a kind of shadowing affinity between the subject of the narrative and the subject of the dedication; but I will not enter into personal themes; else, substituting ****** for Ben, and the Honourable United Company of Merchants trading to the East Indies, for the master of the misused team, it might seem, by no far-fetched analogy, to point its dim warnings hitherward; but I reject the omen, especially as its import seems to have been diverted to another victim.

I will never write another letter with alternate inks. You cannot imagine how it cramps the flow of the style. I can conceive Pindar, (I do not mean to compare myself to *him*,) by the command of Hiero, the Sicilian tyrant, (was not he the tyrant of some place? fie on my neglect of history!) I can conceive him by command of Hiero or Perillus set down to pen an Isthmian or Nemean panegyric in lines, alternate red and black. I maintain he couldn't have done it; it would have been a strait-laced torture to his muse; he would have call'd for the bull for a relief. Neither could Lysidas, nor the Chorics (how do you like the word?) of Samson Agonistes, have been written with two inks. Your couplets, with points, epilogues to Mr H.'s, &c., might be even benefited by the twyfount, where one line (the second) is for point, and the first for rhyme. I think the alteration would assist, like a mould. I maintain it, you could not have written your stanzas on pre-existence with two inks. Try another; and Rogers, with his silver standish, having one ink only, I will bet my "Ode on Tobacco", against the "Pleasures of Memory",—and "Hope", too, shall put more fervour of enthusiasm into the same subject than you can with your two; he shall do it *stans pede in uno*, as it were.

The "Waggoner" is very ill put up in boards; at least it seems to me always to open at the dedication; but that is a mechanical fault. I re-read the "White Doe of Rylstone"; the title should be always written at length, as Mary Sabilla Novello, a very nice woman of our acquaintance, always signs hers at the bottom of the shortest note. Mary told her, if her name had been Mary Ann, she would have signed M. A. Novello, or M. only, dropping the A.; which makes me think, with some other trifles, that she understands something of human nature. My pen goes galloping on most rhapsodically, glad to have escaped the bondage of two inks.

Manning has just sent it home, and it came as fresh to me as the immortal creature it speaks of. M. sent it home with a note, having this passage in it: "I cannot help writing to you while I am reading Wordsworth's poem. I am got into the third canto, and say that it raises my opinion of him very much indeed. 'Tis broad, noble, poetical, with a masterly scanning of human actions, absolutely above common readers. What a manly (implied) interpretation of (bad) party-actions, as trampling the Bible, &c.!" and so he goes on.

I do not know which I like best,—the prologue (the latter part especially) to "P. Bell", or the epilogue to "Benjamin". Yes, I tell stories; I do know I like the last best; and the "Waggoner" altogether is a pleasanter remembrance to me than the "Itinerant". If it were not, the page before the first page would and ought to make it so. The sonnets are not all new to me; of those which are new, the ninth I like best. Thank you for that to Walton. I take it as a favour done to me, that, being so old a darling of mine, you should bear testimony to his worth in a book containing a dedic——: I cannot write the vain word at full length any longer.

If, as you say, the "Waggoner", in some sort, came at my call, oh for a potent voice to call forth the "Recluse" from his profound dormitory, where he sleeps forgetful of his foolish charge—the world!

Had I three inks, I would invoke him! Talfourd has written a most kind review of J. Woodvil, &c., in the *Champion*. He is your most zealous admirer, in solitude and in crowds.

H. Crabb Robinson gives me any dear prints that I happen to admire; and I love him for it and for other things. Alsager shall have his copy; but at present I have lent it *for a day only*, not choosing to part with my own. Mary's love. How do you all do, amanuenses both—marital and sororal?

C. Lamb

COLERIDGE

He was a mighty poet—and
  A subtle-souled psychologist;
All things he seemed to understand,
Of old or new—of sea or land—
  But his own mind—which was a mist.

This was a man who might have turned
  Hell into Heaven—and so in gladness
A Heaven unto himself have earned;
But he in shadows undiscerned
  Trusted,—and damned himself to madness.

He spoke of poetry, and how
  "Divine it was—a light—a love—
A spirit which like wind doth blow
As it listeth, to and fro;
  A dew rained down from God above;

"A power which comes and goes like dream,
  And which none can ever trace—
Heaven's light on earth—Truth's brightest beam."
And when he ceased there lay the gleam
  Of those words upon his face.

SHELLEY: *Peter Bell the Third*

THE CENCI

DEDICATION TO LEIGH HUNT, Esq.

My dear Friend—I inscribe with your name, from a distant country, and after an absence whose months have seemed years, this the latest of my literary efforts.

Those writings which I have hitherto published, have been little else than visions which impersonate my own apprehensions of the beautiful and the just. I can also perceive in them the literary defects incidental to youth and impatience; they are dreams of what ought to be, or may be. The drama which I now present to you is a sad reality. I lay aside the presumptuous attitude of an instructor, and am content to paint, with such colours as my own heart furnishes, that which has been.

Had I known a person more highly endowed than yourself with all that it becomes a man to possess, I had solicited for this work the ornament of his name. One more gentle, honourable, innocent and brave; one of more exalted toleration for all who do and think evil, and yet himself more free from evil; one who knows better how to receive, and how to confer a benefit, though he must ever confer far more than he can receive; one of simpler, and, in the highest sense of the word, of purer life and manners I never knew: and I had already been fortunate in friendships when your name was added to the list.

In that patient and irreconcilable enmity with domestic and political tyranny and imposture which the tenor of your life has illustrated, and which, had I health and talents, should illustrate mine, let us, comforting each other in our task, live and die.

All happiness attend you! Your affectionate friend,

Percy B. Shelley

Rome, *May* 29, 1819.

THE WORDSWORTHS IN TOWN

1820.

June 2nd.—At nine I went to Lamb's, where I found Mr and Mrs Wordsworth. Lamb was in a good humour. He read some recent compositions, which Wordsworth cordially praised. Wordsworth seemed to enjoy Lamb's society. Not much was said about his own new volume of poems. He himself spoke of "The Brownie's Cell" as his favourite. It appears that he had heard of a recluse living on the island when there himself, and afterwards of his being gone, no one knew whither, and that this is the fact on which the poem is founded.

June 11th.—Breakfasted with Monkhouse. Mr and Mrs Wordsworth there. He has resolved to make some concessions to public taste in "Peter Bell". Several offensive passages will be struck out, such as, "Is it a party in a parlour", etc., which I implored him to omit before the poem first appeared. Also the over-coarse expressions, "But I will bang your bones", etc. I never before saw him so ready to yield to the opinion of others. He is improved not a little by this, in my mind. We talked of Haydon. Wordsworth wants to have a large sum raised to enable Haydon to continue in his profession. He wants £2000 for his great picture.[1] The gross produce of the Exhibition is £1200.

June 24th.—After taking tea at home I called at Monkhouse's, and spent an agreeable evening. Wordsworth was very pleasant. Indeed he is uniformly so now. And there is absolutely no pretence for what was always an exaggerated charge against him, that he could talk only of his own poetry, and loves only his own works. He is more indulgent than he used to be of the works of others, even contemporaries and rivals, and is more open to arguments in favour of changes in his own poems. Lamb was in excellent spirits. Talfourd came in late, and we stayed till past twelve. Lamb was at last rather overcome, though it produced nothing but humorous expressions, of his desire to go on the Continent. I should delight to accompany him.

HENRY CRABB ROBINSON'S *Diary*

[1] Jerusalem.

SHELLEY AND KEATS

I

Pisa, *July* 27, 1820

My dear Keats,

I hear with great pain the dangerous accident that you have undergone, and Mr Gisborne who gives me the account of it, adds that you continue to wear a consumptive appearance. This consumption is a disease particularly fond of people who write such good verses as you have done, and with the assistance of an English winter it can often indulge its selection;—I do not think that young and amiable poets are at all bound to gratify its taste; they have entered into no bond with the Muses to that effect. But seriously (for I am joking on what I am very anxious about) I think you would do well to pass the winter after so tremendous an accident, in Italy, and if you think it as necessary as I do, so long as you could find Pisa or its neighbourhood agreeable to you, Mrs Shelley unites with myself in urging the request, that you would take up your residence with us. You might come by sea to Leghorn (France is not worth seeing, and the sea is particularly good for weak lungs), which is within a few miles of us. You ought, at all events, to see Italy, and your health, which I suggest as a motive, might be an excuse to you. I spare declamation about the statues, and the paintings, and the ruins—and what is a greater piece of forbearance—about the mountain streams and the fields, the colours of the sky, and the sky itself.

I have lately read your "Endymion" again and ever with a new sense of the treasures of poetry it contains, though treasures poured forth with indistinct profusion. This, people in general will not endure, and that is the cause of the comparatively few copies that have been sold. I feel persuaded that you are capable of the greatest things, so you but will.

I always tell Ollier to send you copies of my books.—"Prometheus Unbound" I imagine you will receive nearly at the same time with this letter. "The Cenci" I hope you have already received—it was studiously composed in a different style

Below the *good* how far? but far above the *great*.

In poetry I have sought to avoid system and mannerism; I wish those who excel me in genius would pursue the same plan.

Whether you remain in England, or journey to Italy,—believe that you carry with you my anxious wishes for your health, happiness and success wherever you are, or whatever you undertake, and that I am, yours sincerely,

P. B. Shelley

II

[*August*, 1820.]

My dear Shelley,

I am very much gratified that you, in a foreign country, and with a mind almost over-occupied, should write to me in the strain of the letter beside me. If I do not take advantage of your invitation, it will be prevented by a circumstance I have very much at heart to prophesy. There is no doubt that an English winter would put an end to me, and do so in a lingering, hateful manner. Therefore, I must either voyage or journey to Italy, as a soldier marches up to a battery. My nerves at present are the worst part of me, yet they feel soothed that, come what extreme may, I shall not be destined to remain in one spot long enough to take a hatred of any four particular bedposts. I am glad you take any pleasure in my poor poem, which I would willingly take the trouble to unwrite, if possible, did I care so much as I have done about reputation. I received a copy of the Cenci, as from yourself, from Hunt. There is only one part of it I am judge of—the poetry and dramatic effect, which by many spirits nowadays is considered the Mammon. A modern work, it is said, must have a purpose, which may be the God. An artist must serve Mammon; he must have "self-concentration"—selfishness, perhaps. You, I am sure, will forgive me for sincerely remarking that you might curb your magnanimity, and be more of an artist, and load every rift of your subject with ore. The thought of such discipline must fall like cold chains upon you, who perhaps never sat with your wings furled for six months together. And is not this extraordinary talk for the writer of Endymion, whose mind was like a pack of scattered cards? I am picked up and sorted to a pip. My imagination is a monastery, and I am its monk. I am in expectation of Prometheus every day. Could I have my own wish effected, you would have it still in manuscript, or be now putting an end to the second act. I remember you advising me not to publish my first blights, on Hampstead Heath. I am returning advice upon your hands. Most of the poems in the volume I send you have been written above two years, and would never have been published but for hope of gain; so you see I am inclined enough to take your advice now. I must express once more my deep sense of your kindness, adding my sincere thanks and respects for Mrs Shelley.

In the hope of soon seeing you, I remain most sincerely yours

John Keats

III

SHELLEY *to* PEACOCK

Pisa, *November* [probably 8], 1820.

My dear Peacock,

I also delayed to answer your last letter, because I was waiting for something to say: or at least something that should be likely to be interesting to you. The box containing my books, and consequently your Essay against the cultivation of poetry,[1] has not arrived; my wonder, meanwhile, in what manner you support such a heresy in this matter-of-fact and money-loving age, holds me in suspense. Thank you for your kindness in correcting "Prometheus" which I am afraid gave you a great deal of trouble. Among the modern things which have reached me is a volume of poems by Keats; in other

[1] *The Four Ages of Poetry*, to which Shelley's *Defence of Poetry* was a reply.

respects insignificant enough, but containing the fragment of a poem called "Hyperion". I dare say you have not time to read it; but it is certainly an astonishing piece of writing, and gives me a conception of Keats which I confess I had not before.

I hear from Mr Gisborne that you are surrounded with statements and accounts—a chaos of which you are the God; a sepulchre which encloses in a dormant state the chrysalis of the Pavonian Psyche. May you start into life some day, and give us another "Melincourt". Your "Melincourt" is exceedingly admired, and I think much more so than any of your other writings. There is more of the true spirit, and an object less indefinite, than in either "Headlong Hall" or Scythrop.

I am, speaking literally, infirm of purpose. I have great designs, and feeble hopes of ever accomplishing them. I read books, and, though I am ignorant enough, they seem to teach me nothing. To be sure, the reception the public have given me might go far enough to damp any man's enthusiasm. They teach you, it may be said, only what is true. Very true, I doubt not, and the more true the less agreeable. I can compare my experience in this respect to nothing but a series of wet blankets. I have been reading nothing but Greek and Spanish. Plato and Calderon have been my gods. We are in the town of Pisa. A school-fellow of mine from India is staying with me, and we are beginning Arabic together. Mary is writing a novel, illustrative of the manners of the Middle Ages in Italy, which she has raked out of fifty old books. I promise myself success from it; and certainly, if what is wholly original will succeed, I shall not be disappointed. A person will call on you with an order from me to deliver him the piano.—If it is at Marlow you can put him in the requisite train for getting it.

Adieu. *In publica commoda peccem, si longo sermone.*

Ever faithfully yours,

P. B. Shelley

LIBRARY ST. MARY'S COLLEGE

THE WORDSWORTHS IN TOWN

1820.

November 18th.—The afternoon was agreeable. I dined with the Wordsworths, and Lambs, and Mr Kenyon, at Monkhouse's. It was an agreeable company and a good dinner, though I could not help sleeping. Wordsworth and Monkhouse either followed my example, or set me one, and Lamb talked as if he were asleep. Wordsworth was in excellent mood. His improved and improving mildness and tolerance must very much conciliate all who know him.

November 20th.—I was glad to accompany the Wordsworths to the British Museum. I had to wait for them in the anteroom, and we had at last but a hurried survey of the antiquities. I did not perceive that Wordsworth much enjoyed the Elgin Marbles; but he is a still man when he does enjoy himself, and by no means ready to talk of his pleasure, except to his sister. We could hardly see the statues. The Memnon, however, seemed to interest him very much. Took tea with the Lambs. I accompanied Mrs and Miss Wordsworth home, and afterwards sat late with Wordsworth at Lamb's.

November 21st.—I went late to Lamb's, and stayed there an hour very pleasantly. The Wordsworths were there, and Dr Stoddart. The Doctor was very civil. Politics were hardly touched on, for Miss Kelly stepped in, thus drawing our attention to a far more agreeable subject. She pleased me much. She is neither young nor handsome, but very agreeable; her voice and manner those of a person who knows her own worth, but is at the same time not desirous to assume upon it. She talks like a sensible woman. Barry Cornwall, too, came in. Talfourd also there.

HENRY CRABB ROBINSON'S *Diary*

LONDON FROM ABROAD

You are now
In London, that great sea, whose ebb and flow
At once is deaf and loud, and on the shore
Vomits its wrecks, and still howls on for more.

Yet in its depth what treasures! You will see
That which was Godwin,—greater none than he
Though fallen—and fallen on evil times—to stand
Among the spirits of our age and land,
Before the dread tribunal of *to come*
The foremost,—while Rebuke cowers pale and dumb.
You will see Coleridge—he who sits obscure
In the exceeding lustre and the pure
Intense irradiation of a mind,
Which, with its own internal lightning blind,
Flags wearily through darkness and despair—
A cloud-encircled meteor of the air,
A hooded eagle among blinking owls.—
You will see Hunt—one of those happy souls
Which are the salt of the earth, and without whom
This world would smell like what it is—a tomb;
Who is, what others seem; his room no doubt
Is still adorned with many a cast from Shout,
With graceful flowers tastefully placed about;
And coronals of bay from ribbons hung,
And brighter wreaths in neat disorder flung;
The gifts of the most learned among some dozens
Of female friends, sisters-in-law, and cousins.
And there is he with his eternal puns,
Which beat the dullest brain for smiles, like duns
Thundering for money at a poet's door;
Alas! it is no use to say, "I'm poor!"
Or oft in graver mood, when he will look
Things wiser than were ever read in book,
Except in Shakespeare's wisest tenderness.—
You will see Hogg,—and I cannot express
His virtues,—though I know that they are great,
Because he locks, then barricades the gate
Within which they inhabit;—of his wit
And wisdom, you'll cry out when you are bit.
He is a pearl within an oyster shell,
One of the richest of the deep;—and there
Is English Peacock, with his mountain Fair,

Turned into a Flamingo;—that shy bird
That gleams i' the Indian air—have you not heard
When a man marries, dies, or turns Hindoo,
His best friends hear no more of him?—but you
Will see him, and will like him too, I hope,
With the milk-white Snowdonian Antelope
Matched with this cameleopard—his fine wit
Makes such a wound, the knife is lost in it;
A strain too learnèd for a shallow age,
Too wise for selfish bigots; let his page,
Which charms the chosen spirits of the time,
Fold itself up for the serener clime
Of years to come, and find its recompense
In that just expectation.—Wit and sense,
Virtue and human knowledge; all that might
Make this dull world a business of delight,
Are all combined in Horace Smith.—And these,
With some exceptions, which I need not tease
Your patience by descanting on,—are all
You and I know in London.

SHELLEY: *Letter to Maria Gisborne*

ON THE CONVERSATION OF AUTHORS

When a set of adepts, of *illuminati*, get about a question, it is worth while to hear them talk. They may snarl and quarrel over it, like dogs; but they pick it bare to the bone, they masticate it thoroughly.

This was the case formerly at L——'s—where we used to have many lively skirmishes at their Thursday evening parties. I doubt whether the Small-coal man's musical parties could exceed them. Oh! for the pen of John Buncle to consecrate a *petit souvenir* to their memory!—There was L—— himself, the most delightful, the most provoking, the most witty and sensible of men. He always made the best pun, and the best remark in the course of the evening. His serious conversation, like his serious writing, is his best. No one ever stammered out such fine, piquant, deep, eloquent things in half a dozen half sentences as he does. His jests scald like tears: and he probes a question with a play upon words. What a keen, laughing, hair-brained vein of home-felt truth! What choice venom! How often did we cut into the haunch of letters, while we discussed the haunch of mutton on the table! How we skimmed the cream of criticism! How we got into the heart of controversy! How we picked out the marrow of authors! "And, in our flowing cups, many a good name and true was freshly remembered." Recollect (most sage and critical reader) that in all this I was but a guest! Need I go over the names? They were but the old everlasting set—Milton and Shakespeare, Pope and Dryden, Steele and Addison, Swift and Gay, Fielding, Smollet, Sterne, Richardson, Hogarth's prints, Claude's landscapes, the Cartoons at Hampton-court, and all those things, that, having once been, must ever be. The Scotch Novels had not then been heard of: so we said nothing about them. In general, we were hard upon the moderns. The author of the Rambler was only tolerated in Boswell's Life of him; and it was as much as any one could do to edge in a word for Junius. L—— could not bear Gil Blas. This was a fault. I remember the greatest triumph I ever had was in persuading him, after some years' difficulty, that Fielding was better than Smollet. On one occasion, he was for making out a list of persons famous in history that one would wish to see again—at the head of whom were Pontius Pilate, Sir Thomas Browne, and Dr Faustus—but we black-balled most of his list! But with what a gusto would he describe his favourite authors, Donne, or Sir Philip Sidney, and call their most crabbed passages *delicious*! He tried them on his palate as epicures taste olives, and his observations had a smack in them, like a roughness on the tongue. With what discrimination he hinted a defect in what he admired most—as in saying that the display of the sumptuous banquet in Paradise Regained was not in true keeping, as the simplest fare was all that was necessary to tempt the extremity of hunger—and stating that Adam and Eve in Paradise Lost were too much like married people. He has furnished many a text for C—— to preach upon. There was no fuss or cant about him: nor were his sweets or his sours ever diluted with one particle of affectation. I cannot say that the party at L——'s were all of one description. There were honorary members, lay-brothers. Wit and good fellowship was the motto inscribed over the door. When a stranger came in, it was not asked, "Has he written any thing?"—we were above that pedantry; but we waited to see what he could do. If he could take a hand at piquet, he was welcome to sit down. If a person liked any thing, if he took snuff heartily, it was sufficient. He would understand, by analogy, the pungency of other things, besides Irish blackguard, or Scotch rappee. A character was good any where, in a room or on paper. But we abhorred insipidity, affectation, and fine gentlemen. There was one of our party who never failed to mark "two for his Nob" at cribbage, and he was thought no mean person. This was Ned P——, and a better fellow in his way breathes not. There was ——, who asserted some incredible matter of fact as a likely paradox, and settled all controversies by an *ipse dixit*, a *fiat* of his will, hammering out many a hard theory on the anvil of his brain—the Baron Munchausen of politics and practical philosophy:—there was Captain ——, who had you at an advantage by never understanding you:—there was Jem White, the author of Falstaff's Letters, who the other day left this dull world to go in search of more kindred spirits, "turning like the latter end of a lover's lute":—there was A——, who sometimes dropped in, the Will Honeycomb of our set—and Mrs R——, who, being of a quiet turn, loved to hear a noisy debate. An utterly uninformed person might have supposed this a scene of vulgar confusion and uproar. While the most critical question was pending, while the most difficult problem in philosophy was solving, P—— cried out, "That's game", and M. B. muttered a quotation over the last remains of a veal-pie at a side-table. Once, and only once, the literary interest overcame the general. For C—— was riding the high German horse, and demonstrating the Categories of the Transcendental philosophy to the author of the Road to Ruin; who insisted on his knowledge of German, and German metaphysics, having read the *Critique of Pure Reason* in the original. "My dear Mr Holcroft," said C——, in a tone of infinitely provoking conciliation, "you really put me in mind of a sweet pretty German girl, about fifteen, that I met with in the Hartz forest in Germany—and who one day, as I was reading the Limits of the Knowable and the Unknowable, the profoundest of all his works, with great attention, came behind my chair, and leaning over, said, What, *you* read Kant? Why, *I* that am German born, don't understand him!" This was too much to bear, and Holcroft, starting up, called out in no measured tone, "Mr C——, you are the most eloquent man I ever met with, and the most troublesome with your eloquence!" P—— held the cribbage-peg that was to mark him game, suspended in his hand; and the whist table was silent for a moment. I saw Holcroft down stairs, and, on coming to the landing-place in Mitre-court, he stopped me to observe, that "he thought Mr C—— a very clever man, with a great command of language, but that he feared he did not always affix very precise ideas to the words he used". After he was gone, we had our laugh out, and went on with the argument on the nature of Reason, the Imagination, and the Will. I wish I could find a publisher for it: it would make a supplement to the *Biographia Literaria* in a volume and a half octavo.

Those days are over! An event, the name of which I wish never to mention, broke up our party, like a bomb-shell thrown into the room: and now we seldom meet—

> Like angels' visits, short and far between.

There is no longer the same set of persons, nor of associations. L—— does not live where he did. By shifting his abode, his notions seem less fixed. He does not wear his old snuff-coloured coat and breeches. It looks like an alteration in his style. An author and a wit should have a separate costume, a particular cloth: he should present something positive and singular to the mind, like Mr Douce of the Museum. Our faith in the religion of letters will not bear to be taken to pieces, and put together again by caprice or accident. L. H—— goes there sometimes. He has a fine vinous spirit about him, and tropical blood in his veins: but he is better at his own table. He has a great flow of pleasantry and delightful animal spirits: but his hits do not tell like L——'s; you cannot repeat them the next day. He requires not only to be appreciated, but to have a select circle of admirers and devotees, to feel himself quite at home. He sits at the head of a party with great gaiety and grace; has an elegant manner and turn of features; is never at a loss—*aliquando sufflaminandus erat*—has continual sportive sallies of wit or fancy; tells a story capitally; mimics an actor, or an acquaintance, to admiration; laughs with great glee and good humour at his own or other people's jokes; understands the point of an equivoque, or an observation immediately; has a taste and knowledge of books, of music, of medals; manages an argument adroitly; is genteel and gallant, and has a set of bye-phrases and quaint allusions always at hand to produce a laugh:—if he has a fault, it is that he does not listen so well as he speaks, is impatient of interruption, and is fond of being looked up to, without considering by whom. I believe, however, he has pretty well seen the folly of this. Neither is his ready display of personal accomplishment and variety of resources an advantage to his writings. They sometimes present a desultory and slip-shod appearance, owing to this very circumstance. The same things that tell, perhaps, best, to a private circle round the fireside, are not always intelligible to the public, nor does he take pains to make them so. He is too confident and secure of his audience. That which may be entertaining enough with the assistance of a certain liveliness of manner, may read very flat on paper, because it is abstracted from all the circumstances that had set it off to advantage. A writer should recollect that he has only to trust to the immediate impression of words, like a musician who sings without the accompaniment of an instrument. There is nothing to help out, or slubber over, the defects of the voice in the one case, nor of the style in the other. The reader may, if he pleases, get a very good idea of L. H——'s conversation from a very agreeable paper he has lately published, called the

Indicator, than which nothing can be more happily conceived or executed.

Wordsworth sometimes talks like a man inspired on subjects of poetry (his own out of the question)—Coleridge well on every subject, and G—dwin on none. To finish this subject—Mrs M——'s conversation is as fine-cut as her features, and I like to sit in the room with that sort of coronet face. What she says leaves a flavour, like fine green tea. H—t's is like champaigne, and N——'s like anchovy sandwiches. H—yd—n's is like a game at trap-ball: L—'s like snap-dragon: and my own (if I do not mistake the matter) is not very much unlike a game at nine-pins!... One source of the conversation of authors, is the character of other authors, and on that they are rich indeed. What things they say! What stories they tell of one another, more particularly of their friends! If I durst only give some of these confidential communications! ... The reader may perhaps think the foregoing a specimen of them:—but indeed he is mistaken.

We hear it often said of a great author, or a great actress, that they are very stupid people in private. But he was a fool that said so. *Tell me your company, and I'll tell you your manners.* In conversation, as in other things, the action and reaction should bear a certain proportion to each other.—Authors may, in some sense, be looked upon as foreigners, who are not naturalized even in their native soil. L—— once came down into the country to see us. He was "like the most capricious poet Ovid among the Goths". The country people thought him an oddity, and did not understand his jokes. It would be strange if they had; for he did not make any, while he staid. But when we crossed the country to Oxford, then he spoke a little. He and the old colleges were hail-fellow well met; and in the quadrangles, he "walked gowned".

HAZLITT

LAMB TO HAZLITT

Dr H.—Lest you should come to-morrow, I write to say that Mary is ill again. The last thing she read was "Thursday nights",[1] which seemed to give her unmixed delight, and she was sorry for what she said to you that night. The article is a treasure to us for ever.

C. L.

COLERIDGE AS BOOK-BORROWER

To one like Elia, whose treasures are rather cased in leather covers than closed in iron coffers, there is a class of alienators more formidable than that which I have touched upon; I mean your *borrowers of books*—those mutilators of collections, spoilers of the symmetry of shelves, and creators of odd volumes. There is Comberbatch,[2] matchless in his depredations!

That foul gap in the bottom shelf facing you, like a great eye-tooth knocked out—(you are now with me in my little back study in Bloomsbury, Reader!)—with the huge Switzer-like tomes on each side (like the Guildhall giants, in their reformed posture, guardant of nothing) once held the tallest of my folios, *Opera Bonaventuræ*, choice and massy divinity, to which its two supporters (school divinity also, but of a lesser calibre,—Bellarmine, and Holy Thomas) showed but as dwarfs,—itself an Ascapart!—*that* Comberbatch abstracted upon the faith of a theory he holds, which is more easy, I confess, for me to suffer by than to refute, namely, that "the title to property in a book (my Bonaventure, for instance) is in exact ratio to the claimant's powers of understanding and appreciating the same". Should he go on acting upon this theory, which of our shelves is safe?

1 The second essay *On the Conversation of Authors*, from which the previous extract is taken. It had appeared in *The London Magazine* for September, 1820.

2 While an undergraduate, Coleridge ran away and enlisted as a private in the Dragoons under the name of Silas Tompkins Comberbatch.

The slight vacuum in the left-hand case—two shelves from the ceiling—scarcely distinguishable but by the quick eye of a loser—was whilom the commodious resting-place of Browne on Urn Burial. C. will hardly allege that he knows more about that treatise than I do, who introduced it to him, and was indeed the first (of the moderns) to discover its beauties—but so have I known a foolish lover to praise his mistress in the presence of a rival more qualified to carry her off than himself.—Just below, Dodsley's dramas want their fourth volume, where Vittoria Corombona is! The remainder nine are as distasteful as Priam's refuse sons, when the Fates *borrowed* Hector. Here stood the Anatomy of Melancholy, in sober state.—There loitered the Complete Angler; quiet as in life, by some stream side. In yonder nook, John Buncle, a widower-volume, with "eyes closed", mourns his ravished mate.

One justice I must do my friend, that if he sometimes, like the sea, sweeps away a treasure, at another time, sea-like, he throws up as rich an equivalent to match it. I have a small under-collection of this nature (my friend's gatherings in his various calls), picked up, he has forgotten at what odd places, and deposited with as little memory at mine. I take in these orphans, the twice-deserted. These proselytes of the gate are welcome as the true Hebrews. There they stand in conjunction; natives, and naturalised. The latter seem as little disposed to inquire out their true lineage as I am.—I charge no warehouse-room for these deodands, nor shall ever put myself to the ungentlemanly trouble of advertising a sale of them to pay expenses.

To lose a volume to C. carries some sense and meaning in it. You are sure that he will make one hearty meal on your viands, if he can give no account of the platter after it. But what moved thee, wayward, spiteful K.,[1] to be so importunate to carry off with thee, in spite of tears and adjurations to thee to forbear, the Letters of that princely woman, the thrice noble Margaret Newcastle—knowing at the time, and knowing that I knew also, thou most assuredly wouldst never turn over one leaf of the illustrious folio:—what but the mere spirit of

[1] Kemble, the famous actor.

contradiction, and childish love of getting the better of thy friend?—Then, worst cut of all! to transport it with thee to the Gallican land—

> Unworthy land to harbour such a sweetness,
> A virtue in which all ennobling thoughts dwelt,
> Pure thoughts, kind thoughts, high thoughts, her sex's wonder!

——hadst thou not thy play-books, and books of jests and fancies, about thee, to keep thee merry, even as thou keepest all companies with thy quips and mirthful tales? Child of the Green-room, it was unkindly done of thee. Thy wife, too, that part-French, better-part-English-woman!—that *she* could fix upon no other treatise to bear away, in kindly token of remembering us, than the works of Fulke Greville, Lord Brook—of which no Frenchman, nor woman of France, Italy, or England, was ever by nature constituted to comprehend a tittle! *Was there not Zimmerman on Solitude?*

Reader, if haply thou art blessed with a moderate collection, be shy of showing it; or if thy heart overfloweth to lend them, lend thy books; but let it be to such a one as S. T. C.—he will return them (generally anticipating the time appointed) with usury; enriched with annotations, tripling their value. I have had experience. Many are these precious MSS. of his—(in *matter* oftentimes, and almost in *quantity* not unfrequently, vying with the originals) in no very clerkly hand—legible in my Daniel; in old Burton; in Sir Thomas Browne; and those abstruser cogitations of the Greville, now, alas! wandering in Pagan lands.—I counsel thee, shut not thy heart, nor thy library, against S. T. C.

LAMB: *The Two Races of Men*

HUNT ON LAMB AND COLERIDGE

Let me console myself a little by remembering how much Hazlitt and Lamb, and others, were pleased with the *Indicator*. I speak most of them, because they talked most to me about it. Hazlitt's favourite paper (for they liked it enough to have favourite papers) was the one on *Sleep*; perhaps because there is a picture in it of a sleeping despot; though he repeated, with more enthusiasm than he was accustomed to do, the conclusion about the parent and the bride. Lamb preferred the paper on *Coaches and their Horses*, that on the *Deaths of Little Children*, and (I think) the one entitled *Thoughts and Guesses on Human Nature*. Shelley took to the story of the *Fair Revenge*; and the paper that was most liked by Keats, if I remember, was the one on a hot summer's day, entitled *A Now*. He was with me while I was writing and reading it to him, and contributed one or two of the passages. Keats first published in the *Indicator* his beautiful poem *La Belle Dame sans Mercy*, and the *Dream after reading Dante's Episode of Paulo and Francesca*. Lord Holland, I was told, had a regard for the portraits of the *Old Lady* and the *Old Gentleman* &c., which had appeared in the *Examiner*; and a late gallant captain in the navy was pleased to wonder how I became so well acquainted with seamen (in the article entitled *Seamen on Shore*). They had "sat to me" for their portraits. The common sailor was a son of my nurse at school, and the officer a connection of my own by marriage.

Let me take this opportunity of recording my recollections in general of my friend Lamb; of all the world's friend, particularly of his oldest friends, Coleridge and Southey; for I think he never modified or withheld any opinion (in private or bookwards) except in consideration of what he thought they might not like.

Charles Lamb had a head worthy of Aristotle, with as fine a heart as ever beat in human bosom, and limbs very fragile to sustain it. There was a caricature of him sold in the shops, which pretended to be a likeness. Procter went into the shop in a passion, and asked the man what he meant by putting forth such a libel. The man apologized, and said that the artist meant no offence. There never was a true portrait of Lamb. His features were strongly yet delicately cut: he had a fine eye as well as forehead; and no face carried in it greater marks of thought and feeling. It resembled that of Bacon, with less worldly vigour and more sensibility.

As his frame, so was his genius. It was as fit for thought as could be, and equally as unfit for action; and this rendered him melancholy, apprehensive, humorous, and willing to make the best of everything as it was, both from tenderness of heart and abhorrence of alteration. His understanding was too great to admit an absurdity; his frame was not strong enough to deliver it from fear. His sensibility to strong contrasts was the foundation of his humour, which was that of a wit at once melancholy and willing to be pleased. He would beard a superstition, and shudder at the old phantasm while he did it. One could have imagined him cracking a jest in the teeth of a ghost, and then melting into thin air himself, out of sympathy with the awful. His humour and his knowledge both, were those of Hamlet, of Molière, of Carlin, who shook a city with laughter, and, in order to divert his melancholy, was recommended to go and hear himself. Yet he extracted a real pleasure out of his jokes, because good-heartedness retains that privilege when it fails in everything else. I should say he condescended to be a punster, if condescension had been a word befitting wisdom like his. Being told that somebody had lampooned him, he said, "Very well, I'll Lamb-pun him". His puns were admirable, and often contained as deep things as the wisdom of some who have greater names; such a man, for instance, as Nicole, the Frenchman, who was a baby to him. Lamb would have cracked a score of jokes at Nicole, worth his whole book of sentences; pelted his head with pearls. Nicole would not have understood him, but Rochefoucault would, and Pascal too; and some of our old Englishmen would have understood him still better. He would have been worthy of hearing Shakespeare read one of his scenes to him, hot from the brain. Commonplace found a great comforter in him, as long as it was good-natured; it was to the ill-natured or the dictatorial only that he was startling. Willing to see society go on as it did, because he despaired of seeing it otherwise, but not at all agreeing in his interior with the common notions of crime and punishment, he "*dumb-founded*" a long tirade against vice one evening, by taking the pipe out of his mouth, and asking the speaker, "Whether he meant to say that a thief was not a good man?" To a person abusing Voltaire, and indiscreetly opposing his character to that of Jesus Christ, he said admirably well (though he by no means overrated Voltaire, nor wanted reverence in the other quarter), that "Voltaire was a very good Jesus Christ *for the French*". He liked to see the church-goers continue to go to church, and wrote a tale in his sister's admirable little book (*Mrs Leicester's School*) to encourage the rising generation to do so; but to a conscientious deist he had nothing to object; and if an atheist had found every other door shut against him, he would assuredly not have found his. I believe he would have had the world remain precisely as it was, provided it innovated no farther; but this spirit in him was anything but a worldly one, or for his own interest. He hardly contemplated with patience the new buildings in the Regent's Park: and, privately speaking, he had a grudge against *official* heaven-expounders, or clergymen. He would rather, however, have been with a crowd that he disliked, than felt himself alone. He said to me one day, with a face of great solemnity, "What must have been that man's feelings, who thought himself *the first deist*?" Finding no footing in certainty, he delighted to confound the borders of theoretical truth and falsehood. He was fond of telling wild stories to children, engrafted on things about them; wrote letters to people abroad, telling them that a friend of theirs [Mr Alsager, the commercial editor of the *Times*] had come out in genteel comedy; and persuaded George Dyer that *Lord Castlereagh* was the author of *Waverley*!...

He knew how many false conclusions and pretensions are made by men who profess to be guided by facts only, as if facts could not be misconceived, or figments taken for them; and therefore, one day, when somebody was speaking of a person who valued himself on being a matter-of-fact-man, "Now", said he, "I value myself on being a matter-of-lie man." This did not hinder his being a man of the greatest veracity, in the ordinary sense of the word; but "truth", he said, "was precious, and not to be wasted on everybody".

I will append to this account of Lamb, though I had not the good fortune to know much of him personally, my impression respecting his friend Coleridge.

Coleridge was as little fitted for action as Lamb, but on a

different account. His person was of a good height, but as sluggish and solid as the other's was light and fragile. He had, perhaps, suffered it to look old before its time, for want of exercise. His hair was white at fifty; and as he generally dressed in black, and had a very tranquil demeanour, his appearance was gentlemanly, and for several years before his death was reverend. Nevertheless, there was something invincibly young in the look of his face. It was round and fresh-coloured, with agreeable features, and an open, indolent, good-natured mouth. This boy-like expression was very becoming in one who dreamed and speculated as he did when he was really a boy, and who passed his life apart from the rest of the world, with a book, and his flowers. His forehead was prodigious—a great piece of placid marble; and his fine eyes, in which all the activity of his mind seemed to concentrate, moved under it with a sprightly ease, as if it was pastime to them to carry all that thought.

And it was pastime. Hazlitt said that Coleridge's genius appeared to him like a spirit, all head and wings, eternally floating about in etherealities. He gave me a different impression. I fancied him a good-natured wizard, very fond of earth, and conscious of reposing with weight enough in his easy chair, but able to conjure his etherealities about him in the twinkling of an eye. He could also change them by thousands, and dismiss them as easily when his dinner came. It was a mighty intellect put upon a sensual body; and the reason why he did little more with it than talk and dream was, that it is agreeable to such a body to do little else.

However, if the world is to remain always as it is, give me to all eternity new talk of Coleridge, and new essays of Charles Lamb. They will reconcile it beyond all others: and that is much.

Coleridge was fat, and began to lament, in very delightful verses, that he was getting infirm. There was no old age in his verses. I heard him one day, under the Grove at Highgate, repeat one of his melodious lamentations, as he walked up and down, his voice undulating in a stream of music, and his regrets of youth sparkling with visions ever young. At the same time, he did me the honour to show me that he did not think so ill of all modern liberalism as some might suppose, denouncing the pretensions of the money-getting in a style which I should hardly venture upon, and never could equal; and asking with a triumphant eloquence what chastity itself were worth, if it were a casket, not to keep love in, but hate, and strife, and worldliness? On the same occasion, he built up a metaphor out of a flower, in a style surpassing the famous passage in Milton; deducing it from its root in religious mystery, and carrying it up into the bright, consummate flower, "the bridal chamber of reproductiveness". Of all "the Muse's mysteries", he was as great a high-priest as Spenser; and Spenser himself might have gone to Highgate to hear him talk, and thank him for his *Ancient Mariner*. His voice did not always sound very sincere; but perhaps the humble and deprecating tone of it, on those occasions, was out of consideration for the infirmities of his hearers, rather than produced by his own. He recited his *Kubla Khan* one morning to Lord Byron, in his lordship's house in Piccadilly, when I happened to be in another room. I remember the other's coming away from him, highly struck with his poem, and saying how wonderfully he talked. This was the impression of everybody who heard him.

It is no secret that Coleridge lived in the Grove at Highgate with a friendly family, who had sense and kindness enough to know that they did themselves honour by looking after the comfort of such a man. His room looked upon a delicious prospect of wood and meadow, with coloured gardens under the window, like an embroidery to the mantle. I thought, when I first saw it, that he had taken up his dwelling-place like an abbot. Here he cultivated his flowers, and had a set of birds for his pensioners, who came to breakfast with him. He might have been seen taking his daily stroll up and down, with his black coat and white locks, and a book in his hand; and was a great acquaintance of the little children. His main occupation, I believe, was reading. He loved to read old folios, and to make old voyages with Purchas and Marco Polo; the seas being in good visionary condition, and the vessel well stocked with botargoes.

LEIGH HUNT'S *Autobiography*

DE QUINCEY IN LONDON

Not till 1821, and again in 1823, did I come to know Charles Lamb thoroughly. Politics, national enthusiasm, had then gone to sleep. I had come up to London in a case connected with my own private interest. In the same spirit of frankness that I have shown on other occasions in these personal sketches, I shall here not scruple to mention that certain pecuniary embarrassments had rendered it necessary that I should extricate myself by literary toils. I was ill at that time, and for years after—ill from the effects of opium upon the liver; and one primary indication of any illness felt in that organ is peculiar depression of spirits. Hence arose a singular effect of reciprocal action, in maintaining a state of dejection. From the original physical depression caused by the derangement of the liver arose a sympathetic depression of the mind, disposing me to believe that I never *could* extricate myself; and from this belief arose, by reaction, a thousand-fold increase of the physical depression. I began to view my unhappy London life—a life of literary toils, odious to my heart—as a permanent state of exile from my Westmoreland home. My three eldest children, at that time in the most interesting stages of childhood and infancy, were in Westmoreland; and so powerful was my feeling (derived merely from a deranged liver) of some long, never-ending separation from my family, that at length, in pure weakness of mind, I was obliged to relinquish my daily walks in Hyde Park and Kensington Gardens, from the misery of seeing childhood in multitudes, that too forcibly recalled my own. The Picture of Fox-ghyll, my Westmoreland abode, and the solitary fells about it, upon which those were roaming whom I could not see, was for ever before my eyes. And it must be remembered that distance—the mere amount of distance—has much to do in such a case. You are equally divided from those you love, it is very true, by one hundred miles. But that, being a space which in England we often traverse in eight or ten hours, even without the benefit of railroads, has come to seem nothing at all. Fox-ghyll, on the other hand, was two hundred and eighty miles distant; and, from the obstacles at the latter end of the journey (cross-roads and interruptions of all public communications), it seemed twice as long.

Meantime, it is very true that the labours I had to face would not, even to myself, in a state of good bodily health, have appeared alarming. *Myself*, I say—for, in any state of health, I do not write with rapidity. Under the influence of opium, however, when it reaches its maximum in diseasing the liver and deranging the digestive functions, all exertion whatever is revolting in excess; intellectual exertion, above all, is connected habitually, when performed under opium influence, with a sense of disgust the most profound for the subject (no matter what) which detains the thoughts; all that morning freshness of animal spirits which, under ordinary circumstances, consumes, as it were, and swallows up the interval between oneself and one's distant object (consumes, that is, in the same sense as Virgil describes a high-blooded horse, on the fret for starting, as traversing the ground with his eye, and devouring the distance in fancy before it is approached): all that dewy freshness is exhaled and burnt off by the parching effects of opium on the animal economy. You feel like one of Swift's *Strulbrugs*, prematurely exhausted of life; and molehills are inevitably exaggerated by the feelings into mountains. Not that it was molehills exactly which I had then to surmount—they were moderate hills; but that made it all the worse in the result, since my judgment could not altogether refuse to go along with my feelings. I was, beside, and had been for some time, engaged in the task of unthreading the labyrinth by which I had reached, unawares, my present state of slavery to opium. I was descending the mighty ladder, stretching to the clouds as it seemed, by which I had imperceptibly attained my giddy altitude—that point from which it had seemed equally impossible to go forward or backward. To wean myself from opium I had resolved inexorably; and finally I accomplished my vow. But the transition state was the worst state of all to support. All the pains of martyrdom were there: all the ravages in the economy of the great central organ, the stomach, which had been wrought by opium; the sickening disgust which attended each separate respiration; and the rooted deprivation of the appetite and the digestion—all these must be weathered for months, and without the stimulus (however false and treacherous) which, for some part of each day, the old doses of laudanum would have supplied. These doses were to be continually diminished; and, under this difficult dilemma: if, as some people advised, the diminution were made by so trifling a quantity as to be imperceptible—in that case, the duration of the process was interminable and hopeless. Thirty years would not have sufficed to carry it through. On the other hand, if twenty-five to fifty drops were withdrawn each day (that is, from one to two grains of opium) inevitably within three, four, or five days, the deduction began to tell grievously; and the effect was to restore the craving for opium more keenly than ever. There was the collision of both evils—that from the laudanum, and that from the want of laudanum. The last was a state of distress perpetually increasing; the other was one which did not sensibly diminish—no, not for a long period of months. Irregular motions, impressed by a potent agent upon the blood or other processes of life, are slow to subside; they maintain themselves long after the exciting cause has been partially or even wholly withdrawn; and, in my case, they did not perfectly subside into the motion of tranquil health for several years.

From all this it will be easy to understand the *fact*—though, after all, it is impossible, without a similar experience, to understand the *amount*—of my suffering and despondency in the daily task upon which circumstances had thrown me at this period—the task of writing and producing something for the journals *invita Minerva*. Over and above the principal operation of my suffering state, as felt in the enormous difficulty with which it loaded every act of exertion, there was another secondary effect which always followed as a reaction from the first. And that this was no accident or peculiarity attached to my individual temperament, I may presume from the circumstance that Mr Coleridge experienced the very same sensations, in the same situation, throughout his literary life, and has often noticed it to me with surprise and vexation. The sensation was that of powerful disgust with any subject with which he had occupied his thoughts, or had exerted his powers of composition for any length of time, and an equal disgust with the result of his exertions—powerful abhorrence I may call it, absolute loathing, of all that he had produced. In Mr Coleridge's case, speaking at least of the time from 1807 to 1815, this effect was a most unhappy one; as it tended to check or even to suppress his attempts at writing for the press, in a degree which cannot but have been injurious for all of us who wished to benefit by his original intellect, then in the very pomp of its vigour. This effect was, indeed, more extensive than with myself; with Coleridge, even *talking* upon a subject, and throwing out his thoughts upon it liberally and generally, was an insurmountable bar to writing upon it with effect. In the same proportion in which he had been felicitous as a talker, did he come to loathe and recoil from the subject ever afterwards; or, at least, so long as any impressions remained behind of his own display. And so far did this go—so uniformly and so notoriously to those about him—that Miss Hutchinson, a young lady in those days whom Coleridge greatly admired, and loved as a sister, submitted at times to the trouble of taking down what fell from his lips, in the hope that it might serve as materials to be worked up at some future period, when the disgust should have subsided, or perhaps, in spite of that disgust, when he should see the topics and their illustrations all collected for him, without the painful effort of recovering them by calling up loathsome trains of thought. It was even suggested, and at one time (I believe) formally proposed, by some of Coleridge's friends, that, to save from perishing the overflowing opulence of golden thoughts continually welling up and flowing to waste in the course of his ordinary conversation, some short-hand writer, having the suitable accomplishments of a learned education and habits of study, should be introduced as a domestic companion. But the scheme was dropped; perhaps from the feeling in Coleridge himself that he would not command his usual felicity, or his natural power of thought, under the consciousness of an echo sitting by his side, and repeating to the world all the half-developed thoughts or half-expressed suggestions which he might happen to throw out. In the meantime, for the want of some such attendant, certain it is that many valuable papers perished....

Reverting to my own case, which was pretty nearly the same as his, there was, however, this difference—that, at times, when I had slept at more regular hours for several nights consecutively, and had armed myself by a sudden increase of the opium for several days running, I recovered, at times, a remarkable glow of jovial spirits. In some such artificial respites it was from my usual state of distress, and purchased at a heavy price of subsequent suffering, that I wrote the greater part of the Opium Confessions in the autumn of 1821. The introductory part (*i.e.* the narrative part) written for the double purpose of creating an interest in what followed, and of making it intelligible, since, without this narration, the dreams (which were the real object of the whole work) would have had no meaning, but would have been mere incoherencies—this narrative part was written with singular rapidity. The rest might be said to have occupied an unusual length of time; since, though the mere penmanship might have been performed within moderate limits (and in fact under some pressure from the printer), the dreams had been composed slowly, and by separate efforts of thought, at wide intervals of time, according to the accidental prevalence, at any particular time, of the separate elements of such dream in my own real dream-experience. These circumstances I mention to account for my having written anything in a happy or genial state of mind, when I was in general in a state so opposite, by my own description, to everything like enjoyment. That description, as a *general* one, states most truly the unhappy condition, and the somewhat extraordinary condition of feeling, to which opium had brought me. I, like Mr Coleridge, could not endure what I had written for some time after I had written it. I also shrunk from treating any subject which I had considered; but more, I believe, as recoiling from the intricacy and the elaborateness which had been made known to me in the course of considering it, and on account of the difficulty or the toilsomeness which might be fairly presumed from the mere fact that

I *had* long considered it, or could have found it necessary to do so, than from any blind mechanical feeling inevitably associated (as in Coleridge it was) with a second survey of the same subject.

One other effect there was from the opium, and I believe it had some place in Coleridge's list of morbid affections caused by opium, and of disturbances extended even to the intellect—which was, that the judgment was for a time grievously injured, sometimes even totally abolished, as applied to anything which I had recently written. Fresh from the labour of composition, I believe, indeed, that almost every man, unless he has had a very long and close experience in the practice of writing, finds himself a little dazzled and bewildered in computing the effect, as it will appear to neutral eyes, of what he has produced. This result from the hurry and effort of composition doubtless we all experience, or at some time *have* experienced. But the incapacitation which I speak of here, as due to opium, is of another kind, and of another degree. It is mere childish helplessness, or senile paralysis, of the judgment, which distresses the man in attempting to grasp the upshot and total effect (the *tout ensemble*) of what he has himself so recently produced. There is the same imbecility in attempting to hold things steadily together, and to bring them under a comprehensive or unifying act of the judging faculty, as there is in the efforts of a drunken man to follow a chain of reasoning. Opium is said to have some *specific* effect of debilitation upon the memory; that is, not merely the general one which might be supposed to accompany its morbid effects upon the bodily system, but some other, more direct, subtle, and exclusive; and this, of whatever nature, may possibly extend to the faculty of judging.

Such, however, over and above the more known and more obvious ill effects upon the spirits and the health, were some of the stronger and more subtle effects of opium in disturbing the intellectual system, as well as the animal, the functions of the will also no less than those of the intellect, from which both Coleridge and myself were suffering at the period to which I now refer (1821–25): evils which found their fullest exemplification in the very act upon which circumstances had now thrown me as the *sine qua non* of my extrication from difficulties—viz. the act of literary composition. This necessity, the fact of its being my one sole resource for the present, and the established experience which I now had of the peculiar embarrassments and counteracting forces which I should find in opium, but still more in the train of consequences left behind by past opium—strongly co-operated with the mere physical despondency arising out of the liver. And this state of partial unhappiness, amongst other outward indications, expressed itself by one mark, which some people are apt greatly to misapprehend, as if it were some result of a sentimental turn of feeling—I mean perpetual sighs. But medical men must very well know that a certain state of the liver, *mechanically*, and without any co-operation of the will, expresses itself in sighs. I was much too firm-minded, and too reasonable, to murmur or complain. I certainly suffered deeply, as one who finds himself a banished man from all that he loves, and who had not the consolations of hope, but feared too profoundly that all my efforts—efforts poisoned so sadly by opium—might be unavailing for the end. But still I endured in silence. The mechanical sighs, however, revealed, or seemed to reveal, what was present in my thoughts. Lamb doubtless remarked them; he knew the general outline of my situation; and, after this, he set himself, with all the kindness of a brother, Miss Lamb with the kindness of a sister, to relieve my gloom by the closest attentions. They absolutely persecuted me with hospitalities; and, as it was by their fireside that I felt most cheered, and sometimes elevated into hope, it may be supposed that I did not neglect to avail myself of the golden hours thus benignantly interposed amongst my hours of solitude, despondency, and labour but partially effectual.

Thus then it arose, and at this period, that I had my first experience of Lamb's nature and peculiar powers. During one part of the time, I, whose lodgings were in York Street, Covent Garden, became near neighbours to the Lambs—who (with a view to the two great theatres, I believe) emigrated from the Temple for some months to Russell Street. With their usual delicacy, the Lambs seemed to guess that, in my frame of mind, society of a mixed character might not be acceptable to me. Accordingly, they did not ask me to their parties, unless where they happened to be small ones: but, as often as they were free of engagements themselves—come I must, to dine with them and stay as late as I would.

The very first time on which these dinner invitations began, a scene occurred with Charles Lamb which so nearly resembled the Coleridge and "Ancient Mariner" mystification of years long past that perhaps, with all my knowledge of his character, I might have supposed him angry or offended in good earnest, had I not recurred to the lesson of that early introductory visit to the Temple. Some accident, or perhaps it was Lamb himself, had introduced the subject of Hazlitt. . . . In answer to what I considered Lamb's extravagant estimate of Hazlitt, I had said that the misanthropy which gives so unpleasant a tone to that writer's works was, of itself, sufficient to disgust a reader whose feelings do not happen to flow in that channel; that it was, moreover, a crude misanthropy, not resting upon any consistent basis, representing no great principles, good or bad, but simply the peevishness of a disappointed man. I admitted that such a passion as a noble misanthropy was possible; but that there was an ignoble misanthropy; or (taking an illustration, which I knew would tell with Lamb better than all arguments) on the one hand there was the lofty, nay sublime, misanthropy of Timon, on the other hand the low, villainous misanthropy of Apemantus. Now, the cynicism of Hazlitt, as also of another writer, who, in our times, affected misanthropy, if not exactly that of Apemantus, was too much akin to it; not built on the wild indignation of a generous nature outraged in its best feelings, but in the envy of a discontented one. Lamb paused a little; but at length said that it was for the intellectual Hazlitt, not the moral Hazlitt, that he professed so much admiration. Now, as all people must admit the splendid originality of much that Hazlitt has done, here there might have been a ready means, by favour of the latitude allowed to general expressions, for one, like me, who disliked disputing, to effect a compromise with my opponent. But, unfortunately, Lamb chose to insinuate (whether sincerely and deliberately I cannot say) that Hazlitt was another Coleridge, and that, allowing for his want of poetic power, he was *non tam impar quam dispar*. This I could not stand. I, whose studies had been chiefly in the field of philosophy, could judge of *that*, if I could judge of anything; and certainly I felt entitled to say that anything which Hazlitt might have attempted in philosophy—as his "Essay on the Principles of Human Action", and his polemic "Essay against the Hartleian theory", supposing even that these were not derived entirely from Coleridge (as C. used to assert)—could, at the best, be received only as evidences of ingenuity and a natural turn for philosophizing, but, for any systematic education or regular course of reading in philosophy, these little works are satisfactory proofs that Hazlitt had them not. The very language and terminology which belong to philosophy, and are indispensable to its free motion, do not seem to have been known to him. And, whatever gleams of wandering truth might flash at times upon his mind, he was at the mercy of every random impulse; had no principles upon any subject; was eminently one-sided; and viewed all things under the angle which chance circumstances presented, never from a central station. Something of this I said, not wishing or hoping to disturb Lamb's opinion, but piqued a little by what seemed to me not so much honour done to Hazlitt as wrong done to Coleridge. Lamb felt, or counterfeited, a warmth that for the moment looked like anger. "I know not", he said, "where you have been so lucky as to find finer thinkers than Hazlitt; for my part, I know of none such. You live, I think, or have lived, in Grasmere. Well, I was once there. I was at Keswick, and all over that wild country; yet none such could I find there. But, stay, there are the caves in your neighbourhood, as well as the lakes; these we did not visit. No, Mary," turning to his sister, "you know we didn't visit the caves. So, perhaps, these great men live there. Oh! yes, doubtless, they live in the caves of Westmoreland. But you must allow for us poor Londoners. Hazlitt serves for *our* purposes. And in this poor, little inconsiderable place of London, he is one of our very prime thinkers. But certainly I ought to have made an exception on behalf of the philosophers in the caves." And thus he ran on, until it was difficult to know whether to understand him in jest or earnest.

DE QUINCEY: *London Reminiscences*

WORDSWORTH, LEIGH HUNT AND SHELLEY

I

A well-known writer says with much boldness, both in the thought and expression, that "a Lord is imprisoned in the Bastille of a *name*, and cannot enlarge himself into man"; and I have known men of genius in the same predicament. Why must a man be for ever mouthing out his own poetry, comparing himself with Milton, passage by passage, and weighing every line in a balance of posthumous fame which he holds in his own hands? It argues a want of imagination as well as common sense. Has he no ideas but what he has put into verse; or none in common with his hearers? Why should he think it the only scholar-like thing, the only "virtue extant", to see the merit of his writings, and that "men were brutes without them"? Why should he bear a grudge to all art, to all beauty, to all wisdom, that does not spring from his own brain? Or why should he fondly imagine that there is but one fine thing in the world, namely, poetry, and that he is the only poet in it? It will never do. Poetry is a very fine thing; but there are other things besides it. Everything must have its turn. Does a wise man think to enlarge his comprehension by turning his eyes only on himself, or hope to conciliate the admiration of others by scouting, proscribing, and loathing all that they delight in? He must either have a disproportionate idea of himself, or be ignorant of the world in which he lives. It is quite enough to have one class of people born to think the universe made for them!—It seems also to argue a want of repose, of confidence, and firm faith in a man's real pretensions, to be always dragging them into the foreground, as if the proverb held here—*Out of sight, out of mind.* Does he, for instance, conceive that no one would ever think of his poetry unless he forced it upon them by repeating it himself? Does he believe all competition, all allowance of another's merit, fatal to him? Must he, like Moody in *The Country Girl*, lock up the faculties of his admirers in ignorance of all other fine things, painting, music, the antique, lest they should play truant to him? Methinks such a proceeding implies no good opinion of his own genius or their good taste: it is deficient in dignity and in good taste. Surely if anyone is convinced of the reality of an acquisition, he can bear not to have it spoken of every minute. If he knows he has an undoubted superiority in any respect, he will not be uneasy because every one he meets is not in the secret, nor staggered by the report of rival excellence. One of the first mathematicians and classical scholars of the day was mentioning it as a compliment to himself that a cousin of his, a girl from school, had said to him, "You know [Manning] is a very plain good sort of a young man, but he is not anything at all out of the common". Leigh Hunt once said to me, "I wonder I never heard you speak on this subject before, which you seem to have studied a good deal". I answered, "Why, we were not reduced to that, that I know of!"...

There are persons who, without being chargeable with the vice here spoken of, yet "stand accountant for as great a sin"; though not dull and monotonous, they are vivacious mannerists in their conversation, and excessive egoists. Though they run after a thousand subjects in mere gaiety of heart, their delight still flows from one idea, namely, themselves. Open the book in what page you will, there is a frontispiece of themselves staring you in the face. They are a sort of Jacks o' the Green, with a sprig of laurel, a little tinsel, and a little smut, but still playing antics and keeping in incessant motion, to extract attention and extort your pittance of approbation. Whether they talk of the town or the country, poetry or politics, it comes to much the same thing. If they talk to you of the town, its diversions, "its palaces, its ladies, and its streets", they are the delight, the grace, the ornament of it. If they are describing the charms of the country, they give no account of any individual spot or object or source of pleasure but the circumstance of their being there. "With them conversing, we forget all place, all seasons, and their change." They perhaps pluck a leaf or a flower, patronise it, and hand it to you to admire, but select no one feature of beauty or grandeur to dispute the palm of perfection with their own persons. Their rural descriptions are mere landscape backgrounds with their own portraits in an engaging attitude in front. They are not observing or enjoying the scene, but doing the honours as masters of the ceremonies to nature, and arbiters of elegance to all humanity. If they tell a love-tale of enamoured princesses, it is plain they fancy themselves the hero of the piece. If they discuss poetry, their encomiums still turn on something genial and unsophisticated, meaning their own style. If they enter into politics, it is understood that a hint from them to the potentates of Europe is sufficient. In short, as a lover (talk of what you will) brings in his mistress at every turn, so these persons contrive to divert your attention to the same darling object—they are, in fact, in love with themselves, and, like lovers, should be left to keep their own company.

HAZLITT: *On People with one Idea*

II

The author of the *Prometheus Unbound* has a fire in his eye, a fever in his blood, a maggot in his brain, a hectic flutter in his speech, which mark out the philosophic fanatic. He is sanguine-complexioned and shrill-voiced. As is often observable in the case of religious enthusiasts, there is a slenderness of constitutional *stamina*, which renders the flesh no match for the spirit. His bending, flexible form appears to take no strong hold of things, does not grapple with the world about him, but slides from it like a river—

And in its liquid texture mortal wound
Receives no more than can the fluid air.

The shock of accident, the weight of authority make no impression on his opinions, which retire like a feather, or rise from the encounter unhurt through their own buoyancy. He is clogged by no dull system of realities, no earth-bound feelings, no rooted prejudices, by nothing that belongs to the mighty trunk and hard husk of habit, but is drawn up by irresistible levity to the regions of mere speculation and fancy, to the spheres of air and fire, where the delighted spirit floats in "seas of pearl and clouds of amber". There is no *caput mortuum* of worn-out, threadbare experience to serve as ballast to his mind; it is all volatile intellectual salt of tartar, that refuses to combine its evanescent, inflammable essence with anything solid or anything lasting. Bubbles are to him the only reality—touch them, and they vanish. Curiosity is the only proper category of his mind, and though a man in knowledge, he is a child in feeling. Hence he puts everything into a metaphysical crucible to judge of it himself and exhibit it to others as a subject of interesting experiment, without first making it over to the ordeal of his common sense or trying it on his heart. This faculty of speculating at random on all questions may in its overgrown and uninformed state do much mischief without intending it, like an overgrown child with the power of a man. Mr Shelley has been accused of vanity—I think he is chargeable with extreme levity; but this levity is so great that I do not believe he is sensible of its consequences. He strives to overturn all established creeds and systems; but this is in him a defect of constitution. He runs before the most extravagant opinions; but this is because he is held back by none of the merely mechanical checks of sympathy and habit. He tampers with all sorts of obnoxious subjects; but it is less because he is gratified with the rankness of the taint than captivated with the intellectual phosphoric light they emit. It would seem that he wished not so much to convince or inform as to shock the public by the tenor of his productions; but I suspect he is more intent upon startling himself with his electrical experiments in morals and philosophy; and though they may scorch other people, they are to him harmless amusements, but coruscations of an Aurora Borealis, that "play round the head, but do not reach the heart". Still I could wish that he would put a stop to the incessant, alarming whirl of his voltaic battery. With his zeal, his talent, and his fancy, he would do more good and less harm if he took less pleasure in feeling his heart flutter in unison with the panic-struck apprehensions of his readers.[1]

HAZLITT: *On Paradox and Common-Place*

SCOTT

January 5, 1821.

Rose late—dull and drooping—the weather dripping and dense. Snow on the ground, and sirocco above in the sky, like yesterday. Roads up to the horse's belly, so that riding (at least for pleasure) is not very feasible. Added a postscript to my letter to Murray. Read the conclusion, for the fiftieth time (I have read all W. Scott's novels at least fifty times), of the third series of *Tales of my Landlord*—grand work—Scotch Fielding, as well as great English poet—wonderful man! I long to get drunk with him.

BYRON: *Ravenna Journal*

THE DEATH OF KEATS

I

BYRON *to* SHELLEY

Ravenna, *April* 26, 1821.

The child continues doing well, and the accounts are regular and favourable. It is gratifying to me that you and Mrs Shelley do not disapprove of the step which I have taken, which is merely temporary.

I am very sorry to hear what you say of Keats—is it *actually* true? I did not think criticism had been so killing. Though I

[1] These passages were the cause of a quarrel between Hazlitt and Hunt, who was even more offended by Hazlitt's strictures on his friend Shelley, than by the criticism of himself.

differ from you essentially in your estimate of his performances, I so much abhor all unnecessary pain, that I would rather he had been seated on the highest peak of Parnassus than have perished in such a manner. Poor fellow! though with such inordinate self-love he would probably have not been very happy. I read the review of *Endymion* in the *Quarterly*. It was severe—but surely not so severe as many reviews in that and other journals upon others.

I recollect the effect on me of the *Edinburgh* on my first poem; it was rage, and resistance, and redress—but not despondency nor despair. I grant that those are not amiable feelings; but, in this world of bustle and broil, and especially in the career of writing, a man should calculate upon his powers of *resistance* before he goes into the arena.

> Expect not life from pain nor danger free,
> Nor deem the doom of man reversed for thee.

You know my opinion of *that second-hand* school of poetry. You also know my high opinion of your own poetry,—because it is of *no* school. I read *Cenci*—but, besides that I think the *subject* essentially *undramatic*, I am not an admirer of our old dramatists *as models*. I deny that the English have hitherto had a drama at all. Your *Cenci*, however, was a work of power, and poetry. As to *my* drama, pray revenge yourself upon it, by being as free as I have been with yours.

I have not yet got your *Prometheus*, which I long to see. I have heard nothing of mine, and do not know that it is yet published. I have published a pamphlet on the Pope controversy, which you will not like. Had I known that Keats was dead—or that he was alive and so sensitive—I should have omitted some remarks upon his poetry, to which I was provoked by his *attack* upon *Pope*, and my disapprobation of *his own* style of writing.

You want me to undertake a great poem—I have not the inclination nor the power. As I grow older, the indifference—*not* to life, for we love it by instinct—but to the stimuli of life, increases. Besides, this late failure of the Italians has latterly disappointed me for many reasons—some public, some personal. My respects to Mrs S.

Yours ever,

B.

P.S.—Could not you and I contrive to meet this summer? Could not you take a run here *alone*?

II

Pisa, *May* 4, 1821.

My dear Lord Byron,

Your idea of our meeting this summer gives me the highest gratification....Will you come and spend this summer with us in our retirement under the mountains of Pisa? I live in my accustomed seclusion from society, which indeed I could not bear, even if it could bear me. You can easily imagine what pleasure a favourable reply will give both to Mary and to myself. If you come, bring whom you please, and make what arrangements are convenient to you, for we shall have "ample verge, and room enough"....

The account of Keats is, I fear, too true. Hunt tells me that in the first paroxysms of his disappointment he broke a blood-vessel; and thus laid the foundation of a rapid consumption. There can be no doubt but that the irritability which exposed him to this catastrophe was a pledge of future sufferings, had he lived. And yet this argument does not reconcile me to the employment of contemptuous and wounding expressions against a man merely because he has written bad verses; or, as Keats did, some good verses in a bad taste. Some plants, which require delicacy in rearing, might bring forth beautiful flowers if ever they should arrive at maturity. *Your* instance hardly applies. You felt the strength to soar beyond the arrows; the eagle was soon lost in the light in which it was nourished, and the eyes of the aimer were blinded. As to me, I am, perhaps, morbidly indifferent to this sort of praise or blame; and this, perhaps, deprives me of an incitement to do what now I never shall do, i.e. write anything worth calling a poem. Thanks to that happy indifference, I can yet delight in the

LIBRARY ST. MARY'S COLLEGE

productions of those who can; nor has ill-success yet turned me into an unfeeling, and malignant critic; that second degree in the descending scale of the Academy of Disappointed Authors. As to Keats' merits as a poet, I principally repose them upon the fragment of a poem entitled "Hyperion", which you may not, perhaps, have seen, and to which I think you would not deny high praise. The energy and beauty of his powers seem to disperse the narrow and wretched taste in which (most unfortunately for the real beauty which they hide) he has clothed his writings. I have not seen your pamphlet,[1] but have sent to Paris for it, where I see it has been republished. The tragedy I have not yet seen either; my anxiety to see it is very great. We look to you for substituting something worthy of the English stage, for the miserable trash which, from Milman to Barry Cornwall, has been intruded on it since the demand for tragical representation. I did not know that Keats had attacked Pope; I had heard that Bowles had done so, and that you had most severely chastised him therefor. Pope, it seems, has been selected as the pivot of a dispute in taste, on which, until I understand it, I must profess myself neuter. I certainly do not think Pope, or *any* writer, a fit model for any succeeding writer; if he, or they should be determined to be so, it would all come to a question as to under *what forms* mediocrity should perpetually reproduce itself, for true genius vindicates to itself an exemption from all regard to whatever has gone before—and in this question I feel no interest. My "Cenci" had, I believe, a complete failure—at least the silence of the bookseller would say so. I am aware of the unfitness of the subject, now it is written, but I had a different opinion in composition. I wish I could believe that it merited—or that anything of mine merited—the friendly commendations that you give them. The "Prometheus" is also a very imperfect poem. I begin to learn, "quid valeant humeri, quid ferre recusent". . . .

I expect with great anxiety your answer, as to whether I am to have the great delight of seeing you with me this

[1] *Letter to —— [John Murray], Esqre, on the Rev. W. L. Bowles's Strictures on the Life and Writings of Pope.*

summer. In the event of a disappointment, I shall certainly try to pay you a visit; but many circumstances will conspire to make it short, and inconvenient to me.

My dear Lord Byron,
Ever yours most faithfully,
P. B. Shelley

III

ADONAIS

In the death-chamber for a moment Death,
Shamed by the presence of that living Might,
Blushed to annihilation, and the breath
Revisited those lips, and Life's pale light
Flashed through those limbs, so late her dear delight.
"Leave me not wild and drear and comfortless,
As silent lightning leaves the starless night!
Leave me not!" cried Urania: her distress
Roused Death: Death rose and smiled, and met her vain caress.

"Stay yet awhile! speak to me once again;
Kiss me, so long but as a kiss may live;
And in my heartless breast and burning brain
That word, that kiss, shall all thoughts else survive,
With food of saddest memory kept alive,
Now thou art dead, as if it were a part
Of thee, my Adonais! I would give
All that I am to be as thou now art!
But I am chained to Time, and cannot thence depart!

"O gentle child, beautiful as thou wert,
Why didst thou leave the trodden paths of men
Too soon, and with weak hands though mighty heart
Dare the unpastured dragon in his den?
Defenceless as thou wert, oh, where was then

Wisdom the mirrored shield, or scorn the spear?
Or hadst thou waited the full cycle, when
Thy spirit should have filled its crescent sphere,
The monsters of life's waste had fled from thee like deer.

"The herded wolves, bold only to pursue;
The obscene ravens, clamorous o'er the dead;
The vultures to the conqueror's banner true
Who feed where Desolation first has fed,
And whose wings rain contagion;—how they fled,
When, like Apollo, from his golden bow
The Pythian of the age one arrow sped
And smiled!—The spoilers tempt no second blow,
They fawn on the proud feet that spurn them lying low.

"The sun comes forth, and many reptiles spawn;
He sets, and each ephemeral insect then
Is gathered into death without a dawn,
And the immortal stars awake again;
So is it in the world of living men:
A godlike mind soars forth, in its delight
Making earth bare and veiling heaven, and when
It sinks, the swarms that dimmed or shared its light
Leave to its kindred lamps the spirit's awful night."

Thus ceased she: and the mountain shepherds came,
Their garlands sere, their magic mantles rent:
The Pilgrim of Eternity,[1] whose fame
Over his living head like Heaven is bent,
An early but enduring monument,
Came, veiling all the lightnings of his song
In sorrow; from her wilds Ierne sent
The sweetest lyrist of her saddest wrong,[2]
And Love taught Grief to fall like music from his tongue.

Midst others of less note, came one frail Form,[3]
A phantom among men; companionless
As the last cloud of an expiring storm
Whose thunder is its knell; he, as I guess,

[1] Byron. [2] Moore. [3] Shelley himself.

Had gazed on Nature's naked loveliness,
Actaeon-like, and now he fled astray
With feeble steps o'er the world's wilderness,
And his own thoughts, along that rugged way,
Pursued, like raging hounds, their father and their prey.

A pardlike Spirit beautiful and swift—
A Love in desolation masked;—a Power
Girt round with weakness;—it can scarce uplift
The weight of the superincumbent hour;
It is a dying lamp, a falling shower,
A breaking billow;—even whilst we speak
Is it not broken? On the withering flower
The killing sun smiles brightly: on a cheek
The life can burn in blood, even while the heart may break.

His head was bound with pansies overblown,
And faded violets, white, and pied, and blue;
And a light spear topped with a cypress cone,
Round whose rude shaft dark ivy-tresses grew
Yet dripping with the forest's noonday dew,
Vibrated, as the ever-beating heart
Shook the weak hand that grasped it; of that crew
He came the last, neglected and apart;
A herd-abandoned deer struck by the hunter's dart.

All stood aloof, and at his partial moan
Smiled through their tears; well knew that gentle band
Who in another's fate now wept his own,
As in the accents of an unknown land
He sung new sorrow; sad Urania scanned
The Stranger's mien, and murmured: "Who art thou?"
He answered not, but with a sudden hand
Made bare his branded and ensanguined brow,
Which was like Cain's or Christ's—oh! that it should be so!

What softer voice is hushed over the dead?
Athwart what brow is that dark mantle thrown?
What form leans sadly o'er the white death-bed,

In mockery of monumental stone,
The heavy heart heaving without a moan?
If it be He,[1] who, gentlest of the wise,
Taught, soothed, loved, honoured the departed one,
Let me not vex, with inharmonious sighs,
The silence of that heart's accepted sacrifice.

Our Adonais has drunk poison—oh!
What deaf and viperous murderer could crown
Life's early cup with such a draught of woe?
The nameless worm would now itself disown:
It felt, yet could escape, the magic tone
Whose prelude held all envy, hate, and wrong,
But what was howling in one breast alone,
Silent with expectation of the song,
Whose master's hand is cold, whose silver lyre unstrung.

Live thou, whose infamy is not thy fame!
Live! fear no heavier chastisement from me,
Thou noteless blot on a remembered name!
But be thyself, and know thyself to be!
And ever at thy season be thou free
To spill the venom when thy fangs o'erflow:
Remorse and Self-contempt shall cling to thee;
Hot Shame shall burn upon thy secret brow,
And like a beaten hound tremble thou shalt—as now.

Nor let us weep that our delight is fled
Far from these carrion kites that scream below;
He wakes or sleeps with the enduring dead;
Thou canst not soar where he is sitting now.—
Dust to the dust! but the pure spirit shall flow
Back to the burning fountain whence it came,
A portion of the Eternal, which must glow
Through time and change, unquenchably the same,
Whilst thy cold embers choke the sordid hearth of shame.

[1] Leigh Hunt.

Peace, peace! he is not dead, he doth not sleep—
He hath awakened from the dream of life—
'Tis we, who lost in stormy visions, keep
With phantoms an unprofitable strife,
And in mad trance, strike with our spirit's knife
Invulnerable nothings.—*We* decay
Like corpses in a charnel; fear and grief
Convulse us and consume us day by day,
And cold hopes swarm like worms within our living clay.

He has outsoared the shadow of our night;
Envy and calumny and hate and pain,
And that unrest which men miscall delight,
Can touch him not and torture not again;
From the contagion of the world's slow stain
He is secure, and now can never mourn
A heart grown cold, a head grown gray in vain;
Nor, when the spirit's self has ceased to burn,
With sparkless ashes load an unlamented urn.

He lives, he wakes—'tis Death is dead, not he;
Mourn not for Adonais.—Thou young Dawn,
Turn all thy dew to splendour, for from thee
The spirit thou lamentest is not gone;
Ye caverns and ye forests, cease to moan!
Cease, ye faint flowers and fountains, and thou Air,
Which like a mourning veil thy scarf hadst thrown
O'er the abandoned Earth, now leave it bare
Even to the joyous stars which smile on its despair!

He is made one with Nature: there is heard
His voice in all her music, from the moan
Of thunder, to the song of night's sweet bird;
He is a presence to be felt and known
In darkness and in light, from herb and stone,
Spreading itself where'er that Power may move
Which has withdrawn his being to its own;
Which wields the world with never-wearied love,
Sustains it from beneath, and kindles it above.

He is a portion of the loveliness
Which once he made more lovely: he doth bear
His part, while the one Spirit's plastic stress
Sweeps through the dull dense world, compelling there,
All new successions to the forms they wear;
Torturing th' unwilling dross that checks its flight
To its own likeness, as each mass may bear;
And bursting in its beauty and its might
From trees and beasts and men into the Heaven's light.

The splendours of the firmament of time
May be eclipsed, but are extinguished not;
Like stars to their appointed height they climb,
And death is a low mist which cannot blot
The brightness it may veil. When lofty thought
Lifts a young heart above its mortal lair,
And love and life contend in it, for what
Shall be its earthly doom, the dead live there
And move like winds of light on dark and stormy air.

The inheritors of unfulfilled renown
Rose from their thrones, built beyond mortal thought,
Far in the Unapparent. Chatterton
Rose pale,—his solemn agony had not
Yet faded from him; Sidney, as he fought
And as he fell and as he lived and loved
Sublimely mild, a Spirit without spot,
Arose; and Lucan, by his death approved:
Oblivion as they rose shrank like a thing reproved.

And many more, whose names on Earth are dark,
But whose transmitted effluence cannot die
So long as fire outlives the parent spark,
Rose, robed in dazzling immortality.
"Thou art become as one of us," they cry,
"It was for thee yon kingless sphere has long
Swung blind in unascended majesty,
Silent alone amid an Heaven of Song.
Assume thy wingèd throne, thou Vesper of our throng!"

Who mourns for Adonais? Oh, come forth,
Fond wretch! and know thyself and him aright.
Clasp with thy panting soul the pendulous Earth;
As from a centre, dart thy spirit's light
Beyond all worlds, until its spacious might
Satiate the void circumference: then shrink
Even to a point within our day and night;
And keep thy heart light lest it make thee sink
When hope has kindled hope, and lured thee to the brink.

Or go to Rome, which is the sepulchre,
Oh, not of him, but of our joy: 'tis nought
That ages, empires, and religions there
Lie buried in the ravage they have wrought;
For such as he can lend,—they borrow not
Glory from those who made the world their prey;
And he is gathered to the kings of thought
Who waged contention with their time's decay,
And of the past are all that cannot pass away.

Go thou to Rome,—at once the Paradise,
The grave, the city, and the wilderness;
And where its wrecks like shattered mountains rise,
And flowering weeds, and fragrant copses dress
The bones of Desolation's nakedness
Pass, till the spirit of the spot shall lead
Thy footsteps to a slope of green access
Where, like an infant's smile, over the dead
A light of laughing flowers along the grass is spread;

And gray walls moulder round, on which dull Time
Feeds, like slow fire upon a hoary brand;
And one keen pyramid with wedge sublime,
Pavilioning the dust of him who planned
This refuge for his memory, doth stand
Like flame transformed to marble; and beneath,
A field is spread, on which a newer band
Have pitched in Heaven's smile their camp of death,
Welcoming him we lose with scarce extinguished breath.

Here pause: these graves are all too young as yet
To have outgrown the sorrow which consigned
Its charge to each; and if the seal is set,
Here, on one fountain of a mourning mind,
Break it not thou! too surely shalt thou find
Thine own well full, if thou returnest home,
Of tears and gall. From the world's bitter wind
Seek shelter in the shadow of the tomb.
What Adonais is, why fear we to become?

SHELLEY: *Adonais*

IV

Keats, when he died, had just completed his four-and-twentieth year. He was under the middle height; and his lower limbs were small in comparison with the upper, but neat and well turned. His shoulders were very broad for his size: he had a face in which energy and sensibility were remarkably mixed up; an eager power, checked and made patient by ill-health. Every feature was at once strongly cut, and delicately alive. If there was any faulty expression, it was in the mouth, which was not without something of a character of pugnacity. His face was rather long than otherwise; the upper lip projected a little over the under; the chin was bold, the cheeks sunken; the eyes mellow and glowing; large, dark, and sensitive. At the recital of a noble action, or a beautiful thought, they would suffuse with tears, and his mouth trembled. In this, there was ill-health as well as imagination, for he did not like these betrayals of emotion; and he had great personal as well as moral courage. He once chastised a butcher, who had been insolent, by a regular stand-up fight. His hair, of a brown colour, was fine, and hung in natural ringlets. The head was a puzzle for the phrenologists, being remarkably small in the skull; a singularity which he had in common with Byron and Shelley, whose hats I could not get on. Keats was sensible of the disproportion above noticed, between his upper and lower extremities; and he would look at his hand, which was faded, and swollen in the veins, and say it was the hand of a man of fifty.

LEIGH HUNT'S *Autobiography*

BYRON AT RAVENNA AND PISA

I

Shelley *to* Mrs Shelley

Ravenna, Friday [*August* 10, 1821].

We ride out in the evening, through the pine forests which divide this city from the sea. Our way of life is this, and I have accommodated myself to it without much difficulty:—L. B. gets up at two, breakfasts; we talk, read, etc., until six; then we ride, and dine at eight; and after dinner sit talking till four or five in the morning. I get up at twelve, and am now devoting the interval between my rising and his, to you.

L. B. is greatly improved in every respect. In genius, in temper, in moral views, in health, in happiness. The connexion with la Guiccioli has been an inestimable benefit to him. He lives in considerable splendour, but within his income which is now about £4000 a-year; £100 of which he devotes to purposes of charity. He has had mischievous passions, but these he seems to have subdued, and he is becoming what he should be, a virtuous man. The interest which he took in the politics of Italy, and the actions he performed in consequence of it, are subjects not fit to be *written*, but are such as will delight and surprise you. He is not yet decided to go to Switzerland—a place, indeed, little fitted for him: the gossip and the cabals of those anglicised coteries would torment him, as they did before, and might exasperate him into a relapse of libertinism, which he says he plunged into not from taste, but from despair. La Guiccioli and her brother (who is L. B.'s friend and confidant, and acquiesces perfectly in her connection with him) wish to go to Switzerland; as L. B. says, merely from the novelty of the pleasure of travelling. L. B. prefers Tuscany or Lucca, and is trying to persuade them to adopt his views. He has made *me* write a long letter to her to engage her to remain—an odd thing enough for an utter stranger to write on subjects of the utmost delicacy to his friend's mistress. But it seems destined that I am always to have some active part in everybody's affairs whom I approach. I have set down, in lame Italian, the strongest reasons I can think of against the Swiss emigration—to tell you the truth, I should be very glad to accept, as my fee, his establishment in Tuscany. Ravenna is a miserable place; the people are barbarous and wild, and their language the most infernal patois that you can imagine. He would be, in every respect, better among the Tuscans. I am afraid he would not like Florence, on account of the English there. There is Lucca, Florence, Pisa, Siena, and I think nothing more. What think you of Prato, or Pistoia, for him?—no Englishman approaches those towns; but I am afraid no house could be found good enough for him in that region.

He has read me one of the unpublished cantos of Don Juan, which is astonishingly fine. It sets him not only above, but far above, all the poets of the day—every word is stamped with immortality. I despair of rivalling Lord Byron, as well I may, and there is no other with whom it is worth contending. This canto is in the style, but totally, and sustained with incredible ease and power, like the end of the second canto. There is not a word which the most rigid asserter of the dignity of human nature would desire to be cancelled. It fulfils, in a certain degree, what I have long preached of producing—something wholly new and relative to the age, and yet surpassingly beautiful. It may be vanity, but I think I see the trace of my earnest exhortations to him to create something wholly new. He has finished his *life* up to the present time, and given it to Moore, with liberty for Moore to sell it for the best price he can get, with condition that the bookseller should publish it after his death. Moore has sold it to Murray for *two thousand pounds.* I have spoken to him of Hunt, but not with a direct view of demanding a contribution; and, though I am sure that if asked it would not be refused—yet there is something in me that makes it impossible. Lord Byron and I are excellent friends, and were I reduced to poverty, or were I a writer who had no claims to a higher station than I possess—or did I possess a higher than I deserve, we should appear in all things as such, and I would freely ask him any favour. Such is not the case. The demon of mistrust and pride lurks between two persons in our situation, poisoning the freedom of our intercourse. This is a tax, and a heavy one, which we must pay for being human. I think the fault is not on my side, nor is it likely, I being the weaker. I hope that in the next world these things will be better managed. What is passing in the heart of another, rarely escapes the observation of one who is a strict anatomist of his own....

Lord B. has here splendid apartments in the house of his mistress's husband, who is one of the richest men in Italy. *She* is divorced, with an allowance of 1200 crowns a year, a miserable pittance from a man who has 120,000 a-year.—Here are two monkeys, five cats, eight dogs, and ten horses, all of whom (except the horses), walk about the house like the masters of it. *Tita*, the Venetian is here, and operates as my valet; a fine fellow, with a prodigious black beard, and who has stabbed two or three people, and is one of the most good-natured looking fellows I ever saw.

We have good rumours of the Greeks here, and a Russian war. I hardly wish the Russians to take any part in it. My maxim is with Æschylus:—*τὸ δυσσεβὲς—μετὰ μὲν πλεῖονα τίκτει, σφετέρᾳ δ' εἰκότα γεννᾷ.* There is a Greek exercise for you. How should slaves produce anything but tyranny—even as the seed produces the plant?

Adieu, dear Mary,
Yours affectionately,
S

II

Shelley *to* Leigh Hunt

Pisa, *August* 26, 1821.

My dearest Friend,

Since I last wrote to you, I have been on a visit to Lord Byron at Ravenna. The result of this visit was a determination, on his part, to come and live at Pisa; and I have taken the finest palace on the Lung' Arno for him. But the material part of my visit consists in a message which he desires me to give you, and which, I think, ought to add to your determination—for such a one I hope you have formed—of restoring your shattered health and spirits by a migration to these "regions mild of calm and serene air".

He proposes that you should come out and go shares with him and me, in a periodical work, to be conducted here; in which each of the contracting parties should publish all their original compositions and share the profits. He proposed it to Moore, but for some reason it was never brought to bear. There can be no doubt that the *profits* of any scheme in which you and Lord Byron engage, must, from various, yet co-operating reasons, be very great. As for myself, I am for the present, only a sort of link between you and him, until you can know each other, and effectuate the arrangement; since (to entrust you with a secret which, for your sake, I withhold from Lord Byron) nothing would induce me to share in the profits, and still less, in the borrowed splendour of such a partnership. You and he, in different manners, would be equal, and would bring, in a different manner, but in the same proportion, equal stock of reputation and success. Do not let my frankness with you, nor my belief that you deserve it more than Lord Byron, have the effect of deterring you from assuming a station in modern literature which the universal voice of my contemporaries forbids me either to stoop or aspire to. I am, and I desire to be, nothing.

I did not ask Lord Byron to assist me in sending a remittance for your journey; because there are men, however excellent, from whom we would never receive an obligation, in the worldly sense of the word; and I am as jealous for my friend as for myself. I, as you know, have not it, but I suppose that I shall at last make up an impudent face, and ask Horace Smith to add to the many obligations he has conferred on me. I know I need only ask.

I think I have never told you how very much I like your *Amyntas*; it almost reconciles me to translations. In another sense I still demur. You might have written another such a poem as the *Nymphs*, with no great access of efforts. I am full of thoughts and plans, and should do something, if the feeble and irritable frame which encloses it, was willing to obey the spirit. I fancy that then I should do great things. Before this you will have seen *Adonais*. Lord Byron, I suppose from modesty, on account of his being mentioned in it, did not say a word of *Adonais*, though he was loud in his praise of *Prometheus*, and, what you will not agree with him in, censure of the *Cenci*. Certainly, if *Marino Faliero* is a drama, the *Cenci* is not—but that between ourselves. Lord Byron is reformed, as far as gallantry goes, and lives with a beautiful and sentimental Italian lady, who is as much attached to him as may be. I trust greatly to his intercourse with you, for his creed to become as pure as he thinks his conduct is. He has many generous and exalted qualities, but the canker of aristocracy wants to be cut out, and something, God knows, wants to be cut out of us all—except perhaps you.

III

In general, I do not draw well with literary men: not that I dislike them, but I never know what to say to them after I have praised their last publication. There are several exceptions, to be sure; but then they have either been men of the world, such as Scott, and Moore, etc., or visionaries out of it, such as Shelley, etc.: but your literary every day man and I never went well in company—especially your foreigner, whom I never could abide.

BYRON: *Detached Thoughts* (1821), no. 53

IV

SHELLEY *to* PEACOCK

Pisa, *January* [probably 11], 1822.

My dear Peacock,

Circumstances have prevented my procuring the certificate and signature which I enclose, so soon as I expected, and other circumstances made me even then delay. I enclose them, and should be much obliged by your sending them to their destination.—I am still at Pisa, where I have at length fitted up some rooms at the top of a lofty palace that overlooks the city and the surrounding region, and have collected books and plants about me, and established myself for some indefinite time, which, if I read the future, will not be short. I wish you to send my books by the very first opportunity, and I expect in them a great augmentation of comfort. Lord Byron is established here, and we are constant companions. No small relief this, after the dreary solitude of the understanding and the imagination in which we past the first years of our expatriation, yoked to all sorts of miseries and discomforts.

Of course you have seen his last volume, and if you before thought him a great poet, what is your opinion now that you have read "Cain"? The "Foscari" and "Sardanapalus" I have not seen; but as they are in the style of his later writings, I doubt not they are very fine. We expect Hunt here every day, and remain in great anxiety on account of the heavy gales which he must have encountered at Christmas. Lord Byron has fitted up the lower apartments of his palace for him, and Hunt will be agreeably surprised to find a commodious lodging prepared for him after the fatigues and dangers of his passage. I have been long idle, and, as far as writing goes, despondent; but I am now engaged in "Charles the First" and a devil of a nut it is to crack....

We live, as usual, tranquilly. I get up, or at least wake, early; read and write till two; dine; go to Lord B.'s, and ride, or play at billiards, as the weather permits; and sacrifice the evening either to light books or whoever happens to drop in. Our furniture, which is very neat, cost fewer shillings than that at Marlow did pounds sterling; and our windows are full of plants, which turn the sunny winter into spring. My health is better—my cares are lighter; and although nothing will cure the consumption of my purse, yet it drags on a sort of life in death, very like its master, and seems, like Fortunatus's, always empty yet never quite exhausted. You will have seen my "Adonais", and perhaps my "Hellas", and I think, whatever you may judge of the subject, the composition of the first poem will not wholly displease you. I wish I had something better to do than to furnish this jingling food for the hunger of oblivion, called verse, but I have not; and since you give me no encouragement about India, I cannot hope to have.

How is your little star, and the heaven which contains the milky way in which it glimmers?

Adieu—Yours ever; most truly,

S.

V

BYRON *to* SCOTT

Pisa, *January* 12, 1822.

My dear Sir Walter,—I need not say how grateful I am for your letter, but I must own my ingratitude in not having written to you again long ago. Since I left England (and it is not for all the usual term of transportation) I have scribbled to five hundred blockheads on business, etc., without difficulty, though with no great pleasure; and yet, with the notion of addressing you a hundred times in my head, and always in my heart, I have not done what I ought to have done. I can only account for it on the same principle of tremulous anxiety with which one sometimes makes love to a beautiful woman of our own degree, with whom one is enamoured in good earnest; whereas we attack a fresh-coloured housemaid without (I speak, of course, in earlier times) any sentimental remorse or mitigation of our virtuous purpose.

I owe to you far more than the usual obligation for the courtesies of literature and common friendship; for you went out of your way in 1817 to do me a service, when it required not merely kindness, but courage to do so: to have been recorded by you in such a manner would have been a proud memorial at any time, but at such a time, when "all the world and his wife", as the proverb goes, were trying to trample upon me, was something still higher to my self-esteem—I allude to the *Quarterly Review* of the Third Canto of *Childe Harold*, which Murray told me was written by you—and, indeed, I should have known it without his information, as there could not be *two* who *could* and *would* have done this at the time. Had it been a common criticism, however eloquent or panegyrical, I should have felt pleased, undoubtedly, and grateful, but not to the extent which the extraordinary good-heartedness of the whole proceeding must induce in any mind capable of such sensations. The very *tardiness* of this acknowledgement will, at least, show that I have not forgotten the obligation; and I can assure you that my sense of it has been out at compound interest during the delay. I shall only add one word upon the subject, which is, that I think that you, and Jeffrey, and Leigh Hunt, were the only literary men, of numbers whom I know (and some of whom I had served), who dared venture even an anonymous word in my favour just then: and that, of those three, I had never seen *one* at all—of the second much less than I desired—and that the third was under no kind of obligation to me, whatever; while the other *two* had been actually attacked by me on a former occasion; *one*, indeed, with some provocation, but the other wantonly enough. So you see you have been heaping "coals of fire", etc., in the true gospel manner, and I can assure you that they have burnt down to my very heart.

I am glad that you accepted the Inscription.[1] I meant to have inscribed *The Foscarini* to you instead; but, first, I heard that *Cain* was thought the least bad of the two as a composition; and, secondly, I have abused Southey like a pickpocket, in a note to *The Foscarini*, and I recollected that he is a friend of yours (though not of mine), and that it would not be the handsome thing to dedicate to one friend any thing containing such matters about another. However, I'll work the Laureate before I have done with him, as soon as I can muster Billingsgate therefor. I like a row, and always did from a boy, in the course of which propensity, I must needs say, that I have found it the most easy of all to be gratified, personally and poetically. You disclaim "jealousies"; but I would ask, as Boswell did of Johnson, "of *whom could* you be *jealous*?"—of none of the living certainly, and (taking all and all into

[1] *Cain* was dedicated to Scott.

consideration) of which of the dead? I don't like to bore you about the Scotch novels (as they call them, though two of them are wholly English, and the rest half so), but nothing can or could ever persuade me, since I was the first ten minutes in your company, that you are *not* the man. To me those novels have so much of "Auld lang syne" (I was bred a canny Scot till ten years old), that I never move without them; and when I removed from Ravenna to Pisa the other day, and sent on my library before, they were the only books that I kept by me, although I already have them by heart.

January 27, 1822.

I delayed till now concluding, in the hope that I should have got *The Pirate*, who is under way for me, but has not yet hove in sight. I hear that your daughter is married, and I suppose by this time you are half a grandfather—a young one, by the way. I have heard great things of Mrs Lockhart's personal and mental charms, and much good of her lord: that you may live to see as many novel Scotts as there are Scott's novels, is the very bad pun, but sincere wish of

Yours ever most affectionately, etc.

P.S.—Why don't you take a turn in Italy? You would find yourself as well known and as welcome as in the Highlands among the natives. As for the English, you would be with them as in London; and I need not add, that I should be delighted to see you again, which is far more than I shall ever feel or say for England, or (with a few exceptions "of kith, kin, and allies") any thing that it contains. But my heart warms to the "tartan", or to anything of Scotland, which reminds me of Aberdeen and other parts, not so far from the Highlands as that town, about Invercauld and Braemar, where I was sent to drink goat's *fey* in 1795–6, in consequence of a threatened decline after the scarlet fever. But I am gossiping, so, good night—and the gods be with your dreams!

Pray present my respects to Lady Scott, who may perhaps recollect having seen me in town in 1815.

I see that one of your supporters (for, like Sir Hildebrand, I am fond of Guillim) is a *mermaid*; it is my *crest* too, and with precisely the same curl of tail. There's concatenation for you. I am building a little cutter at Genoa, to go cruising in the summer. I know *you* like the sea too.

THE DEATH OF SHELLEY

I

From Monte Nero I returned to Leghorn; and, taking leave of our vessel, we put up at an hotel.[1] Mr Shelley then came to us from his *villeggiatura* at Lerici. His town abode, as well as Lord Byron's, was at Pisa. I will not dwell upon the moment.

Leghorn is a polite Wapping, with a square and a theatre. The country around is uninteresting when you become acquainted with it; but to a stranger the realization of anything he has read about is a delight, especially of such things as vines hanging from trees, and the sight of the Apennines. It is pleasant, too, to a lover of books, when at Leghorn, to think that Smollett once lived there; not, indeed, happily, for he was very ill, and besides living there, died there. But genius gives so much pleasure (and must also have received so much in the course of its life) that the memory of its troubles is overcome by its renown. Smollett once lived, as Lord Byron did, at Monte Nero; and he was buried in the Leghorn cemetery.

Mr Shelley accompanied us from Leghorn to Pisa, in order to see us fixed in our new abode. Lord Byron left Monte Nero at the same time, and joined us. We occupied the ground-floor of his lordship's house, the Casa Lanfranchi, on the river Arno, which runs through the city. Divided tenancies of this kind are common in Italy, where few houses are in possession of one family. The families in this instance, as in others, remained distinct. The ladies at the respective heads of them never exchanged even a word. It was set to the account of their want of acquaintance with their respective languages;

[1] The Hunts reached Italy early in July, 1822.

and the arrangement, I believe, which in every respect thus tacitly took place, was really, for many reasonable considerations, objected to by nobody.

In a day or two Shelley took leave of us to return to Lerici for the rest of the season, meaning, however, to see us more than once in the interval. I spent one delightful afternoon with him, wandering about Pisa, and visiting the cathedral. On the night of the same day he took a post-chaise for Leghorn, intending next morning to depart with his friend Captain Williams for Lerici. I entreated him, if the weather were violent, not to give way to his daring spirit and venture to sea. He promised me he would not; and it seems that he did set off later than he otherwise would have done, apparently at a more favourable moment. I never beheld him more.

The same night there was a tremendous storm of thunder and lightning, which made us very anxious; but we hoped our friend had arrived before then. When, some days later, Trelawny came to Pisa, and told us he was missing, I underwent one of the sensations which we read of in books, but seldom experience: I was tongue-tied with horror.

A dreadful interval took place of more than a week, during which, every inquiry and every fond hope were exhausted. At the end of that period our worst fears were confirmed. A body had been washed on shore, near the town of Via Reggio, which, by the dress and stature, was known to be our friend's. Keats's last volume also (the *Lamia*, &c.), was found open in the jacket pocket. He had probably been reading it when surprised by the storm. It was my copy. I had told him to keep it till he gave it me with his own hands. So I would not have it from any other. It was burnt with his remains. The body of his friend Mr Williams was found near a tower, four miles distant from its companion. That of the third party in the boat, Charles Vivian, the seaman, was not discovered till nearly three weeks afterwards.

LEIGH HUNT'S *Autobiography*

II

Leigh Hunt *to* Horace Smith

Pisa, *July* 25, 1822.

Dear Horace,

I trust that the first news of the dreadful calamity which has befallen us here will have been broken to you by report, otherwise I shall come upon you with a most painful abruptness; but Shelley, my divine-minded friend, your friend, the friend of the universe, he has perished at sea. He was in a boat with his friend Captain Williams, going from Leghorn to Lerici, when a storm arose, and it is supposed the boat must have foundered. It was on the 8th instant, about four or five in the evening, they guess. A fisherman says he saw the boat a few minutes before it went down: he looked again and it was gone. He saw the boy they had with them aloft furling one of the sails. We hope his story is true, as their passage from life to death will then have been short; and what adds to the hope is, that in S.'s pocket (for the bodies were both thrown on shore some days afterwards,—conceive our horrible certainty, after trying all we could to hope!) a copy of Keats's last volume, which he had borrowed of me to read on his passage, was found *open* and doubled back as if it had been thrust in, in the hurry of a surprise. God bless him! I cannot help thinking of him as if he were alive as much as ever, so unearthly he always appeared to me, and so seraphical a thing of the elements; and this is what all his friends say. But, what we all feel, your own heart will tell you.

I am only just stronger enough than Mrs S. at present to write you this letter; but shall do very well. Our first numbers[1] will shortly appear; though this, like everything else, however important to us, looks like an impertinence just now. God bless you. Mrs H. sends her best remembrances to you and Mrs Smith, and so does your obliged and sincere friend,

Leigh Hunt

[1] I.e. of the *Liberal.*

III

The remains of Shelley and Mr Williams were burnt after the good ancient fashion, and gathered into coffers. Those of Mr Williams were subsequently taken to England. Shelley's were interred at Rome, in the Protestant burial-ground, the place which he had so touchingly described in recording its reception of Keats. The ceremony of the burning was alike beautiful and distressing. Trelawny, who had been the chief person concerned in ascertaining the fate of his friends, completed his kindness by taking the most active part on this last mournful occasion. He and his friend Captain Shenley were first upon the ground, attended by proper assistants. Lord Byron and myself arrived shortly afterwards. His lordship got out of his carriage, but wandered away from the spectacle, and did not see it. I remained inside the carriage, now looking on, now drawing back with feelings that were not to be witnessed.

None of the mourners, however, refused themselves the little comfort of supposing, that lovers of books and antiquity, like Shelley and his companion, Shelley in particular with his Greek enthusiasm, would not have been sorry to foresee this part of their fate. The mortal part of him, too, was saved from corruption; not the least extraordinary part of his history. Among the materials for burning, as many of the gracefuller and more classical articles as could be procured—frankincense, wine, &c.—were not forgotten; and to these Keats's volume was added. The beauty of the flame arising from the funeral pile was extraordinary. The weather was beautifully fine. The Mediterranean, now soft and lucid, kissed the shore as if to make peace with it. The yellow sand and blue sky were intensely contrasted with one another: marble mountains touched the air with coolness; and the flame of the fire bore away towards heaven in vigorous amplitude, waving and quivering with a brightness of inconceivable beauty. It seemed as though it contained the glassy essence of vitality. You might have expected a seraphic countenance to look out of it, turning once more before it departed, to thank the friends that had done their duty.

Shelley, when he died, was in his thirtieth year. His figure was tall and slight, and his constitution consumptive. He was subject to violent spasmodic pains, which would sometimes force him to lie on the ground till they were over; but he had always a kind word to give to those about him, when his pangs allowed him to speak. In this organization, as well as in some other respects, he resembled the German poet, Schiller. Though well-turned, his shoulders were bent a little, owing to premature thought and trouble. The same causes had touched his hair with gray; and though his habits of temperance and exercise gave him a remarkable degree of strength, it is not supposed that he could have lived many years. He used to say that he had lived three times as long as the calendar gave out; which he would prove, between jest and earnest, by some remarks on Time,

> That would have puzzled that stout Stagyrite.

Like the Stagyrite's, his voice was high and weak. His eyes were large and animated, with a dash of wildness in them; his face small, but well shaped, particularly the mouth and chin, the turn of which was very sensitive and graceful. His complexion was naturally fair and delicate, with a colour in the cheeks. He had brown hair, which, though tinged with gray, surmounted his face well, being in considerable quantity, and tending to a curl. His side-face, upon the whole, was deficient in strength, and his features would not have told well in a bust; but when fronting and looking at you attentively his aspect had a certain seraphical character that would have suited a portrait of John the Baptist, or the angel whom Milton describes as holding a reed "tipt with fire". Nor would the most religious mind, had it known him, have objected to the comparison; for, with all his scepticism, Shelley's disposition was truly said to have been anything but irreligious. A person of much eminence for piety in our times has well observed, that the greatest want of religious feeling is not to be found among the greatest infidels, but among those who never think of religion except as a matter of course. The leading feature of Shelley's character may be said to have been a natural piety. He was pious towards nature, towards his friends, towards the whole human race, towards the meanest insect of the forest. He did himself an injustice with the public in using the popular name of the Supreme Being inconsiderately. He identified it solely with the most vulgar and tyrannical notions of a God made after the worst human fashion; and did not sufficiently reflect that it was often used by a juster devotion to express a sense of the great Mover of the universe. An impatience in contradicting worldly and pernicious notions of a supernatural power led his own aspirations to be misconstrued; for though, in the severity of his dialectics, and particularly in moments of despondency, he sometimes appeared to be hopeless of what he most desired—and though he justly thought that a Divine Being would prefer the increase of benevolence and good before any praise, or even recognition of himself (a reflection worth thinking of by the intolerant), yet there was in reality no belief to which he clung with more fondness than that of some great pervading "Spirit of Intellectual Beauty"; as may be seen in his aspirations on that subject. He assented warmly to an opinion which I expressed in the cathedral at Pisa, while the organ was playing, that a truly divine religion might yet be established, if charity were really made the principle of it, instead of faith.

Music affected him deeply. He had also a delicate perception of the beauties of sculpture. It is not one of the least evidences of his conscientious turn of mind that, with the inclination and the power to surround himself in Italy with all the graces of life, he made no sort of attempt that way; finding other uses for his money, and not always satisfied with himself for indulging even in the luxury of a boat. When he bought elegancies of any kind it was to give them away. Boating was his great amusement. He loved the mixture of action and repose which he found in it; and delighted to fancy himself gliding away to Utopian isles and bowers of enchantment. But he would give up any pleasure to do a deed of kindness. Indeed, he may be said to have made the whole comfort of his life a sacrifice to what he thought the wants of society.

Temperament and early circumstances conspired to make

him a reformer, at a time of life when few begin to think for themselves; and it was his misfortune, as far as immediate reputation was concerned, that he was thrown upon society with a precipitancy and vehemence which rather startled others with fear for themselves, than allowed them to become sensible of the love and zeal that impelled him. He was like a spirit that had darted out of its orb, and found itself in another world. I used to tell him that he had come from the planet Mercury. When I heard of the catastrophe that overtook him it seemed as if this spirit, not sufficiently constituted like the rest of the world to obtain their sympathy, yet gifted with a double portion of love for all living things, had been found in a solitary corner of the earth, its wings stiffened, its warm heart cold; the relics of a misunderstood nature, slain by the ungenial elements.

LEIGH HUNT'S *Autobiography*

IV

BYRON *to* MOORE

Pisa, *August* 27, 1822.

It is boring to trouble you with "such small gear"; but it must be owned that I should be glad if you would enquire whether my Irish subscription ever reached the committee in Paris from Leghorn. My reasons, like Vellum's, "are threefold":—First, I doubt the accuracy of all almoners, or remitters of benevolent cash; second, I do suspect that the said Committee, having in part served its time to time-serving, may have kept back the acknowledgement of an obnoxious politician's name in their lists; and third, I feel that I shall one day be twitted by the government scribes for having been a professor of love for Ireland, and not coming forward with the others in her distresses.

It is not, as you may opine, that I am ambitious of having my name in the papers, as I can have that any day of the week gratis. All I want is to know if the Reverend Thomas Hall did or did not remit my subscription (200 scudi of Tuscany, or about a thousand francs, more or less,) to the Committee at Paris.

The other day at Viareggio, I thought proper to swim off to my schooner (the Bolivar) in the offing, and thence to shore again—about three miles, or better, in all. As it was at mid-day, under a broiling sun, the consequence has been a feverish attack, and my whole skin's coming off, after going through the process of one large continuous blister, raised by the sun and sea together. I have suffered much pain; not being able to lie on my back, or even side; for my shoulders and arms were equally St Bartholomewed. But it is over, and I have got a new skin, and am as glossy as a snake in its new suit.

We have been burning the bodies of Shelley and Williams on the sea-shore, to render them fit for removal and regular interment. You can have no idea what an extraordinary effect such a funeral pile has, on a desolate shore, with mountains in the back-ground and the sea before, and the singular appearance the salt and frankincense gave to the flame. All of Shelley was consumed, except his *heart*, which would not take the flame, and is now preserved in spirits of wine.

Your old acquaintance Londonderry has quietly died at North Cray! and the virtuous De Witt was torn in pieces by the populace! What a lucky * * the Irishman has been in his life and end. In him your Irish Franklin *est mort*!

Leigh Hunt is sweating articles for his new Journal; and both he and I think it somewhat shabby in *you* not to contribute. Will you become one of the *properrioters*? "Do, and we go snacks." I recommend you to think twice before you respond in the negative.

I have nearly (*quite three*) four new cantos of *Don Juan* ready. I obtained permission from the female Censor Morum of *my* morals to continue it,[1] provided it were immaculate; so I have been as decent as need be. There is a deal of war—a siege, and all that, in the style, graphical and technical, of the shipwreck in Canto Second, which "took", as they say in the Row.

Yours, etc.

P.S.—That * * * Galignani[2] has about ten lies in one

[1] Byron had given up *Don Juan* at the entreaty of the Countess Guiccioli, who had been shocked by its tone.

[2] The famous Paris bookseller.

paragraph. It was not a Bible that was found in Shelley's pocket, but John Keats's poems. However, it would not have been strange, for he was a great admirer of Scripture as a composition. *I* did not send my bust to the academy of New York; but I sat for my picture to young West, an American artist, at the request of some members of that Academy to *him* that he would take my portrait,—for the Academy, I believe.

I had, and still have, thoughts of South America, but am fluctuating between it and Greece. I should have gone, long ago, to one of them, but for my liaison with the Countess G.; for love, in these days, is little compatible with glory. *She* would be delighted to go too; but I do not choose to expose her to a long voyage, and a residence in an unsettled country, where I shall probably take a part of some sort.

AFTER SHELLEY'S DEATH

I

Our manner of life was this. Lord Byron, who used to sit up at night writing *Don Juan* (which he did under the influence of gin and water), rose late in the morning. He breakfasted; read; lounged about, singing an air, generally out of Rossini; then took a bath, and was dressed; and coming down stairs, was heard, still singing, in the court-yard, out of which the garden ascended, by a few steps, at the back of the house. The servants, at the same time, brought out two or three chairs. My study, a little room in a corner, with an orange-tree at the window, looked upon this court-yard. I was generally at my writing when he came down, and either acknowledged his presence by getting up and saying something from the window, or he called out "Leontius!" (a name into which Shelley had pleasantly converted that of "Leigh Hunt") and came up to the window with some jest or other challenge to conversation. His dress, as at Monte Nero, was a nankin jacket, with white waistcoat and trousers, and a cap, either velvet or linen, with a shade to it. In his hand was a tobacco-box, from which he helped himself occasionally to what he thought a preservative from getting too fat. Perhaps, also, he supposed it good for the teeth. We then lounged about, or sat and talked, Madame Guiccioli, with her sleek tresses, descending after her toilet to join us. The garden was small and square, but plentifully stocked with oranges and other shrubs; and, being well watered, it looked very green and refreshing under the Italian sky. The lady generally attracted us up into it, if we had not been there before. Her appearance might have reminded an English spectator of Chaucer's heroine—

> Yclothed was she, fresh for to devise.
> Her yellow hair was braided in a tress
> Behind her back, a yardè long, I guess:
> And in the garden (as the sun uprist)
> She walketh up and down, where as her list:

and then, as Dryden has it:

> At every turn she made a little stand,
> And thrust among the thorns her lily hand.

In the evening we sometimes rode or drove out, generally into the country. The city I first walked through in company with Shelley, but speedily, alas! explored it by myself, or with my children.

LEIGH HUNT'S *Autobiography*

II

Genoa again!—With what different feelings we beheld it from those which enchanted us the first time! Mrs Shelley, who preceded us, had found houses both for Lord Byron's family and my own at Albaro, a neighbouring village on a hill. We were to live in the same house with her; and in the Casa Negrotto we accordingly found an English welcome. There were forty rooms in it, some of them such as would be con sidered splendid in England, and all neat and new, with borders and arabesques. The balcony and staircase were of marble; and there was a little flower-garden. The rent of this house was twenty pounds a year. Lord Byron paid four-and-twenty for his, which was older and more imposing, and a good piece of ground. It was called the Casa Saluzzi. Mr Landor and his family had occupied a house in the same village—the Casa Pallavicini. He has recorded an interesting dialogue that took place in it.

The Genoese post brought us the first number of our new quarterly, the *Liberal*, accompanied both with hopes and fears, the latter of which were too speedily realized. Living now in a separate house from Lord Byron, I saw less of him than before; and, under all the circumstances, it was as well: for though we had always been on what are called "good terms", the cordiality did not increase. His friends in England, who, after what had lately taken place there in his instance, were opposed, naturally enough, to his opening new fields of publicity, did what they could to prevent his taking a hearty interest in the *Liberal*; and I must confess that I did not mend the matter by my own inability to fall in cordially with his ways, and by a certain jealousy of my position, which prevented me, neither very wisely nor justly, from manifesting the admiration due to his genius, and reading the manuscripts he showed me with a becoming amount of thanks and good words. I think he had a right to feel this want of accord in a companion, whatever might be its value. A dozen years later, reflection would have made me act very differently. At the same time, though the *Liberal* had no mean success, he unquestionably looked to its having a far greater; and the result of all these combined circumstances was, that the interest he took in it cooled in proportion as it should have grown warm, and after four numbers it ceased. They were all published during our residence in this part of Italy. Lord Byron contributed some poems, to which his customary publisher had objected on account of their fault-finding in Church and State, and their critical attacks on acquaintances. Among them was the *Vision of Judgment*, the best satire since the days of Pope. Churchill's satires, compared with it, are bludgeons compared with steel of Damascus. Hazlitt contributed some of the most entertaining of his vigorous essays; and Shelley had left us his masterly translation of the *May-Day Night* in *Faust*. As to myself, if I may speak of my own articles after these, I wrote by far the greater number,—perhaps nearly half the publication; but I was ill; and with the exception of one or two, I hope they were not among my best. This, however, did not hinder great puzzlement among the critics of that day. I say it with not the slightest intention of self-compliment; and I should think him a very dull fellow who supposed it.

LEIGH HUNT'S *Autobiography*

III

BYRON *to* JOHN MURRAY

Byron's aristocratic friends in England had been alarmed at his association with the "atheist" Shelley and the "Cockney" Hunt in the *Liberal*, and had tried their hardest to persuade him to withdraw. Furthermore, it was not long after Shelley's death that a coolness sprang up between him and Hunt, who was now practically dependent on Byron for support.

Genoa, *December* 25, 1822.

I had sent you back the *Quarterly*, without perusal, having resolved to read no more reviews, good, bad, or indifferent; but "who can control his fate?" Galignani, to whom my English studies are confined, has forwarded a copy of at least one half of it in his indefatigable catch-penny weekly compilation; and as, "like honour, it came unlooked for", I have looked through it. I must say that, upon the *whole*, that is, the whole of the *half* which I have read (for the other half is to be the segment of Galignani's next week's circular), it is extremely handsome, and anything but unkind or unfair. As I take the good in good part, I must not, nor will not, quarrel with the bad. What the writer says of *Don Juan* is harsh, but it is inevitable. He must follow, or at least not directly oppose, the opinion of a prevailing, and yet not very firmly seated, party. A Review may and will direct and "turn awry" the currents of opinion, but it must not directly oppose them. *Don Juan* will be known by and by, for what it is intended, a *Satire* on *abuses* of the present states of society, and not an eulogy of vice. It may be now and then voluptuous: I can't help that. Ariosto is worse; Smollet ten times worse; and Fielding no better. No girl will ever be seduced by reading *Don Juan*:—no, no; she will go to Little's poems and Rousseau's *romans* for that, or even to the immaculate De Staël. They will encourage her, and not the Don, who laughs at that, and—and—most other things. But never mind—*ça ira*!...

Now, do you see what you and your friends do by your injudicious rudeness?—actually cement a sort of connection which you strove to prevent, and which, had the Hunts *prospered*, would not in all probability have continued. As it is, I will not quit them in their adversity, though it should cost me character, fame, money, and the usual *et cetera*.

My original motives I already explained (in the letter which you thought proper to show): they are the *true* ones, and I abide by them, as I tell you, and I told Leigh Hunt when he questioned me on the subject of that letter. He was violently hurt, and never will forgive me at bottom; but I can't help that. I never meant to make a parade of it; but if he chose to question me, I could only answer the plain truth: and I confess I did not see anything in the letter to hurt him, unless I said he was "a *bore*", which I don't remember. Had their Journal gone on well, and I could have aided to make it better for them, I should then have left them, after my safe pilotage off a lee shore, to make a prosperous voyage for themselves. As it is, I can't, and would not, if I could, leave them among the breakers.

As to any community of feeling, thought, or opinion, between Leigh Hunt and me, there is little or none. We meet rarely, hardly ever; but I think him a good-principled and able man, and must do as I would be done by. I do not know what world he has lived in, but I have lived in three or four; but none of them like his Keats and kangaroo terra incognita. Alas! poor Shelley! how we would have laughed had he lived, and how we used to laugh, now and then, at various things which are grave in the suburbs!

You are all mistaken about Shelley. You do not know how mild, how tolerant, how good he was in society; and as perfect a gentleman as ever crossed a drawing-room, when he liked, and where he liked.

I have some thoughts of taking a run down to Naples (*solus*, or, at most, *cum sola*) this spring, and writing, when I have studied the country, a Fifth and Sixth Canto of Childe Harold; but this is merely an idea for the present, and I have other excursions and voyages in my mind....

Yours, &c. N. B.

P.S. Mrs Shelley is residing with the Hunts at some distance from me. I see them very seldom, and generally on account of their business. Mrs Shelley, I believe, will go to England in the spring....

IV

BYRON *to* MRS SHELLEY

[Undated.]

...I presume that you, at least, know enough of me to be sure that I could have no intention to insult Hunt's poverty. On the contrary, I honour him for it; for I know what it is, having been as much embarrassed as ever he was, without perceiving aught in it to diminish an honourable man's self-respect. If you mean to say that, had he been a wealthy man, I would have joined in this Journal, I answer in the negative....I engaged in the Journal from good-will towards him, added to respect for his character, literary and personal; and no less for his political courage, as well as regret for his present circumstances: I did this in the hope that he might, with the same aid from literary friends of literary contributions (which is requisite for all journals of a mixed nature), render himself independent....

I have always treated him, in our personal intercourse, with such scrupulous delicacy, that I have forborne intruding advice which I thought might be disagreeable, lest he should impute it to what is called "taking advantage of a man's situation".

As to friendship, it is a propensity in which my genius is very limited. I do not know the *male* human being, except Lord Clare, the friend of my infancy, for whom I feel any thing that deserves the name. All my others are men-of-the-world friendships. I did not even feel it for Shelley, however much I admired and esteemed him; so that you see not even vanity could bribe me into it, for, of all men, Shelley thought highest of my talents,—and, perhaps, of my disposition.

I will do my duty by my intimates, upon the principle of doing as you would be done by. I have done so, I trust, in most instances. I may be pleased with their conversation—rejoice in their success—be glad to do them service, or to receive their counsel and assistance in return. But as for friends and friendship, I have (as I already said) named the only remaining male for whom I feel anything of the kind, excepting, perhaps, Thomas Moore. I have had, and may have still, a thousand friends, as they are called, in *life*, who are like one's partners in the waltz of this world—not much remembered when the ball is over, though very pleasant for the time. Habit, business, and companionship in pleasure or in pain, are links of a similar kind, and the same faith in politics is another....

LAMB TO COLERIDGE

March 9, 1822.

Dear C.,—It gives me great satisfaction to hear that the pig turned out so well—they are interesting creatures at a certain age—what a pity such buds should blow out into the maturity of rank bacon! You had all some of the crackling—and brain sauce—did you remember to rub it with butter, and gently dredge it a little, just before the crisis? Did the eyes come away kindly with no Œdipean avulsion? Was the crackling the colour of the ripe pomegranate? Had you no complement of boiled neck of mutton before it, to blunt the edge of delicate desire? Did you flesh maiden teeth in it? Not that I sent the pig, or can form the remotest guess what part Owen could play in the business. I never knew him give anything away in my life. He would not begin with strangers. I suspect the pig, after all, was meant for me; but at the unlucky juncture of time being absent, the present somehow went round to Highgate. To confess an honest truth, a pig is one of those things I could never think of sending away. Teals, wigeons, snipes, barn-door fowl, ducks, geese—your tame villatic things—Welsh mutton, collars of brawn, sturgeon, fresh or pickled, your potted char, Swiss cheeses, French pies, early grapes, muscadines, I impart as freely unto my friends as to myself. They are but self-extended; but pardon me if I stop somewhere—where the fine feeling of benevolence giveth a higher smack than the sensual rarity—there my friends (or any good man) may command me; but pigs are pigs, and I myself therein am nearest to myself. Nay, I should think it an affront, an undervaluing done to Nature who bestowed such a boon upon me, if in a churlish mood I parted with the precious gift. One of the bitterest pangs of remorse I ever felt was when a child—when my kind old aunt had strained her pocket-strings to bestow a sixpenny whole plum-cake upon me. In my way home through the Borough, I met a venerable old man, not a mendicant, but thereabouts—a look-beggar, not a verbal petitionist; and in the coxcombry of taught-charity I gave away the cake to him. I walked on a little in all the pride of an Evangelical peacock, when of a sudden my old aunt's kindness crossed me—the sum it was to her—the pleasure she had a right to expect that I—not the old impostor—should take in eating her cake—the cursed ingratitude by which, under the colour of a Christian virtue, I had frustrated her cherished purpose. I sobbed, wept, and took it to heart so grievously, that I think I never suffered the like—and I was right. It was a piece of unfeeling hypocrisy, and proved a lesson to me ever after. The cake has long been masticated, consigned to dunghill with the ashes of that unseasonable pauper.

But when Providence, who is better to us all than our aunts, gives me a pig, remembering my temptation and my fall, I shall endeavour to act towards it more in the spirit of the donor's purpose.

Yours (short of pig) to command in everything,

C. L.

LIBRARY ST. MARY'S COLLEGE

LAMB TO BERNARD BARTON

East India House, *October* 9, 1822.

Dear Sir,—I am asham'd not sooner to have acknowledged your letter and poem. I think the latter very temperate, very serious, and very seasonable. I do not think it will convert the club at Pisa, neither do I think it will satisfy the bigots on our side the water. Something like a parody on the song of Ariel would please them better:—

Full fathom five the Atheist lies,
Of his bones are hell-dice made.

I want time, or fancy, to fill up the rest. I sincerely sympathize with you on your doleful confinement. Of Time, Health, and Riches, the first in order is not last in excellence. Riches are chiefly good, because they give us Time. What a weight of wearisome prison hours have I to look back and forward to, as quite cut out of life—and the sting of the thing is, that for six hours every day, I have no business which I could not contract into two, if they would let me work Task-work. I shall be glad to hear that your grievance is mitigated.

Shelley I saw once. His voice was the most obnoxious squeak I ever was tormented with, ten thousand times worse than the Laureat's, whose voice is the worst part about him, except his Laureatcy. Lord Byron opens upon him on Monday in a Parody (I suppose) of the *Vision of Judgment*, in which latter the Poet I think did not much show *his*. To award his Heaven and his Hell in the presumptuous manner he has done, was a piece of immodesty as bad as Shelleyism.

I am returning a poor letter. I was formerly a great scribbler in that way, but my hand is out of order. If I said my head too, I should not be very much out, but I will tell no tales of myself. I will therefore end, (after my best thanks, with a hope to see you again some time in London,) begging you to accept this Letteret for a Letter—a Leveret makes a better present than a grown hare, and short troubles (as the old excuse goes) are best.

I hear that C. Lloyd is well, and has returned to his family. I think this will give you pleasure to hear.

I remain, dear sir, yours truly,
C. Lamb

BYRON ON HIS CONTEMPORARIES

In twice five years the "greatest living poet",
Like to the champion in the fisty ring,
Is called on to support his claim, or show it,
Although 't is an imaginary thing.
Even I—albeit I'm sure I did not know it,
Nor sought of foolscap subjects to be king,—
Was reckoned a considerable time
The grand Napoleon of the realms of rhyme.

But Juan was my Moscow, and Faliero
My Leipsic, and my Mont Saint Jean seems Cain:
La Belle Alliance of dunces down at zero,
Now that the Lion's fallen, may rise again:
But I will fall at least as fell my hero;
Nor reign at all, or as a *monarch* reign;
Or to some lonely isle of gaolers go,
With turncoat Southey for my turnkey Lowe.

Sir Walter reigned before me; Moore and Campbell
Before and after; but now grown more holy,
The Muses upon Sion's hill must ramble
With poets almost clergymen, or wholly;
And Pegasus has a psalmodic amble
Beneath the reverend Rowley Powley,[1]
Who shoes the glorious animal with stilts,
A modern Ancient Pistol—"by these hilts"!

[1] The Rev. George Croly.

Still he excels that artificial hard
  Labourer in the same vineyard, though the vine
Yields him but vinegar for his reward.—
  That neutralised dull Dorus of the Nine;[1]
That swarthy Sporus, neither man nor bard;
  That ox of verse, who *ploughs* for every line:—
Cambyses' roaring Roman beat at least
The howling Hebrews of Cybele's priest.—

Then there's my gentle Euphues,[2]—who, they say,
  Sets up for being a sort of *moral me*;
He'll find it rather difficult some day
  To turn out both, or either, it may be.
Some persons think that Coleridge hath the sway;
  And Wordsworth has supporters, two or three;
And that deep-mouthed Bœotian "Savage Landor"
Has taken for a swan rogue Southey's gander.

John Keats, who was killed off by one critique,
  Just as he really promised something great,
If not intelligible, without Greek
  Contrived to talk about the gods of late,
Much as they might have been supposed to speak.
  Poor fellow! His was an untoward fate;
'T is strange the mind, that very fiery particle,
Should let itself be snuffed out by an article.

The list grows long of live and dead pretenders
  To that which none will gain—or none will know
The conqueror at least; who, ere Time renders
  His last award, will have the long grass grow
Above his burnt-out brain, and sapless cinders.
  If I might augur, I should rate but low
Their chances;—they're too numerous, like the thirty
Mock tyrants, when Rome's annals waxed but dirty.

This is the literary *lower* empire,
  Where the praetorian bands take up the matter;—
A "dreadful trade", like his who "gathers samphire",
  The insolent soldiery to soothe and flatter,

[1] Dean Milman. [2] Barry Cornwall.

With the same feelings as you'd soothe a vampire.
  Now, were I once at home, and in good satire,
I'd try conclusions with those Janizaries,
And show them *what* an intellectual war is.

BYRON: *Don Juan*, canto XI, stanzas 55–62

LAMB ON BYRON

1823.

January 8th.—Went in the evening to Lamb. I have seldom spent a more agreeable few hours with him. He was serious and kind—his wit was subordinate to his judgment, as is usual in *tête-à-tête* parties. Speaking of Coleridge, he said, "He ought not to have a wife or children; he should have a sort of diocesan care of the world—no parish duty". Lamb reprobated the prosecution of Byron's "Vision of Judgment". Southey's poem of the same name is more worthy of punishment, for his has an arrogance beyond endurance. Lord Byron's satire is one of the most good-natured description—no malevolence.

HENRY CRABB ROBINSON'S *Diary*

LAMB TO WORDSWORTH

[*January*, 1823.]

Dear Wordsworth,

I beg your acceptance of Elia, detached from any of its old companions which might have been less agreeable to you. I hope your eyes are better, but if you must spare them, there is nothing in my pages which a Lady may not read aloud without indecorum, *which is more than can be said of Shakespeare.*

What a nut this last sentence would be for Blackwood!

You will find I availed myself of your suggestion, in curtailing the dissertation on Malvolio.

I have been on the Continent since I saw you.

I have eaten frogs.

I saw Monkhouse tother day, and Mrs M. being too poorly to admit of company, the annual goosepye was sent to Russell

Street, and with its capacity has fed "A hundred head" (not of Aristotle's) but "of Elia's friends".

Mrs Monkhouse is sadly confined, but chearful.—

This packet is going off, and I have neither time, place, nor solitude for a longer Letter.

Will you do me the favour to forward the other volume to Southey?

Mary is perfectly well, and joins me in kindest remembrances to you all.

WORDSWORTH, LAMB AND MOORE

1823.

April 2nd.—An interesting day. After breakfasting at Monkhouse's, I walked out with Wordsworth, his son John, and Monkhouse. We first called at Sir George Beaumont's to see his fragment of Michael Angelo—a piece of sculpture in bas and haut relief—a holy family....Sir George is a very elegant man, and talks well on matters of art. Lady Beaumont is a gentlewoman of great sweetness and dignity; I should think among the most interesting by far of persons of quality in the country. I should have thought this even had I not known of their great attachment to Wordsworth.

We then called on Moore, and had a very pleasant hour's chat with him. Politics were a safer topic than poetry, though on this the opinions of Wordsworth and Moore are nearly as adverse as their poetic character. Moore spoke freely and in a tone I cordially sympathised with about France and the Bourbons. He considers it quite uncertain how the French will feel at any time on any occasion, so volatile and vehement are they at the same time. Yet he thinks that, as far as they have any thought on the matter, it is in favour of the Spaniards and liberal opinions. Notwithstanding this, he says he is disposed to assent to the notion, that of all the people in Europe, the French alone are unfit for liberty. Wordsworth freely contradicted some of Moore's assertions, but assented to the last. Of French poetry Moore did not speak highly....

Moore's person is very small, his countenance lively rather than intellectual. I should judge him to be kind-hearted and friendly.

Wordsworth and I went afterwards to the Society of Arts, and took shelter during a heavy rain in the great room. Wordsworth's curiosity was raised and soon satisfied by Barry's pictures.

Concluded my day at Monkhouse's. The Lambs were there.

April 4th.—Dined at Monkhouse's. Our party consisted of Wordsworth, Coleridge, Lamb, Moore, and Rogers. Five poets of very unequal worth and most disproportionate popularity, whom the public probably would arrange in a different order. During this afternoon, Coleridge alone displayed any of his peculiar talent. I have not for years seen him in such excellent health, and with so fine a flow of spirits. His discourse was addressed chiefly to Wordsworth, on points of metaphysical criticism—Rogers occasionally interposing a remark. Moore seemed conscious of his inferiority. He was attentive to Coleridge, but seemed to relish Lamb, to whom he sat next.

[1] I have a distinct recollection of more than I have put in my journal, as is often the case. I can still recall to my mind the look and tone with which Lamb addressed Moore, when he could not articulate very distinctly: "Mister Moore, will you drink a glass of wine with me?"—suiting the action to the word, and hobnobbing. Then he went on: "Mister Moore, till now I have always felt an antipathy to you, but now that I have seen you, I shall like you ever after". Some years after I mentioned this to Moore. He recollected the fact, but not Lamb's amusing manner.

HENRY CRABB ROBINSON'S *Diary*

[1] Added by Crabb Robinson in 1853.

LEIGH HUNT IN FLORENCE

On Byron's departure from Italy to take part in the struggle for Greek independence Leigh Hunt was left practically stranded. He lived near Florence for about two years, writing for the journals in England (the *Liberal* did not outlast its fourth number) until he managed to raise sufficient money to return.

Notwithstanding these amusements at Maiano, I passed a very disconsolate time; yet the greatest comfort I experienced in Italy (next to writing a book which I shall mention) was living in that neighbourhood, and thinking, as I went about, of Boccaccio. Boccaccio's father had a house at Maiano, supposed to have been situated at the Fiesolan extremity of the hamlet. That many-hearted writer (whose sentiment outweighed his levity a hundredfold, as a fine face is oftener serious than it is merry) was so fond of the place, that he has not only laid the two scenes of the *Decameron* on each side of it, with the valley which his company resorted to in the middle, but has made the two little streams that embrace Maiano, the Affrico and the Mensola, the hero and heroine of his *Nimphale Fiesolano.* A lover and his mistress are changed into them, after the fashion of Ovid. The scene of another of his works is on the banks of the Mugnone, a river a little distant; and the *Decameron* is full of the neighbouring villages. Out of the windows of one side of our house we saw the turret of the Villa Gherardi, to which, according to his biographers, his "joyous company" resorted in the first instance. A house belonging to the Macchiavelli was nearer, a little to the left; and farther to the left, among the blue hills, was the white village of Settignano, where Michael Angelo was born. The house is still in possession of the family. From our windows on the other side we saw, close to us, the Fiesole of antiquity and of Milton, the site of the Boccaccio-house before mentioned still closer, the *Decameron's* Valley of Ladies at our feet; and we looked over towards the quarter of the Mugnone and of a house of Dante, and in the distance beheld the mountains of Pistoia. Lastly, from the terrace in front, Florence lay clear and cathedralled before us, with the scene of Redi's *Bacchus* rising on the other side of it, and the Villa of Arcetri, illustrious for Galileo. Hazlitt, who came to see me there (and who afterwards, with one of his felicitous images, described the state of mind in which he found me, by saying that I was "moulting"), beheld the scene around us with the admiration natural to a lover of old folios and great names, and confessed, in the language of Burns, that it was a sight to enrich the eyes.

But I had other friends, too, not far off, English, and of the right sort. My friend, Charles Armitage Brown (Keats's friend, and the best commentator on Shakspeare's Sonnets), occupied for a time the little convent of San Baldassare, near Maiano, where he represented the body corporate of the former possessors, with all the joviality of a comfortable natural piety. The closet in his study, where it is probable the church treasures had been kept, was filled with the humanities of modern literature, not the less Christian for being a little sceptical: and we had a zest in fancying that we discoursed of love and wine in the apartments of the Lady Abbess.

Our friend Brown removed to Florence, and, together with the books and newspapers, made me a city visitor. I there became acquainted with Landor, to whose genius I had made the *amende honorable* the year before; and with Mr Kirkup, an English artist, who was not poor enough, I fear, either in purse or accomplishment, to cultivate his profession as he ought to have done; while at the same time he was so beloved by his friends, that they were obliged to get at a distance from him before they could tell him of it. Yet I know not why they should; for a man of a more cordial generosity, with greater delicacy in showing it, I never met with: and such men deserve the compliment of openness. They know how to receive it.

LEIGH HUNT'S *Autobiography*

LAMB'S FRIENDS

In 1824 Lamb was offended at what seemed to be a reflection on his religious principles and on those of his friends in a reference to the *Essays of Elia* in one of Southey's articles in *The Quarterly*. He replied in the *London Magazine* with the *Letter of Elia to Robert Southey, Esquire*, from which the following passages are taken. Southey apologized for the unintentional offence he had given, and Lamb immediately repented his hot-headedness, so that the incident caused no breach between them.

In more than one place, if I mistake not, you have been pleased to compliment me at the expense of my companions. I cannot accept your compliment at such a price. The upbraiding a man's poverty naturally makes him look about him, to see whether he be so poor indeed as he is presumed to be. You have put me upon counting my riches. Really, Sir, I did not know I was so wealthy in the article of friendships. There is —, and —, whom you never heard of, but exemplary characters both, and excellent church-goers; and N[orris], mine and my father's friend for nearly half a century; and the enthusiast for Wordsworth's poetry, T. N. T[alfourd], a little tainted with Socinianism, it is to be feared, but constant in his attachments, and a capital critic; and —, a sturdy old Athanasian, so that sets all to rights again; and W[ainewright], the light, and warm-as-light hearted Janus of the *London*; and the translator of Dante, still a curate, modest and amiable C[ary]; and Allan C[unningham], the large-hearted Scot; and P[rocter], candid and affectionate as his own poetry; and A[llsop], Coleridge's friend; and G[illma]n, his more than friend; and Coleridge himself, the same to me still, as in those old evenings, when we used to sit and speculate (do you remember them, Sir?) at our old Salutation tavern, upon Pantisocracy and golden days to come on earth; and W[ordswor]th (why, Sir, I might drop my rent-roll here; such goodly farms and manors have I reckoned up already. In what possessions has not this last-named alone estated me!—but I will go on)—and M[onkhouse], the noble-minded kinsman, by wedlock, of W[ordswor]th; and H. C. R[obinson], unwearied in the offices of a friend; and Clarkson, almost above the narrowness of that relation, yet condescending not seldom heretofore from the labours of his world-embracing charity to bless my humble roof; and the high-minded associate of Cook, the veteran Colonel [Phillips], with his lusty heart still sending cartels of defiance to old Time; and, not least, W. A[yrton], the last and steadiest left to me of that little knot of whist-players, that used to assemble weekly, for so many years, at the Queen's Gate (you remember them, Sir?) and called Admiral Burney friend.

I will come to the point at once. I believe you will not make many exceptions to my associates so far. But I have purposely omitted some intimacies, which I do not yet repent of having contracted, diametrically opposed to yourself in principles. You will understand me to allude to the authors of Rimini and of the Table Talk. And first, of the former.—

Accident introduced me to the acquaintance of Mr L. H.—and the experience of his many friendly qualities confirmed a friendship between us. You, who have been misrepresented yourself, I should hope, have not lent an idle ear to the calumnies which have been spread abroad respecting this gentleman. I was admitted to his household for some years, and do most solemnly aver that I believe him to be in his domestic relations as correct as any man. He chose an ill-judged subject for a poem; the peccant humours of which have been visited on him tenfold by the artful use, which his adversaries have made, of an *equivocal term.* The subject itself was started by Dante, but better because brieflier treated of. But the crime of the Lovers, in the Italian and the English poet, with its aggravated enormity of circumstance, is not of a kind (as the critics of the latter well knew) with those conjunctions, for which Nature has provided no excuse, because no temptation.—It has nothing in common with the black horrors, sung by Ford and Massinger. The familiarising of it in tale or fable may be for that reason incidentally more contagious. In spite of Rimini, I must look upon its author as a man of taste, and a poet. He is better than so, he is one of the most cordial-minded men I ever knew, and matchless as a fire-side companion.

I mean not to affront or wound your feelings when I say that, in his more genial moods, he has often reminded me of you. There is the same air of mild dogmatism—the same condescending to a boyish sportiveness—in both your conversations. His hand-writing is so much the same with your own, that I have opened more than one letter of his, hoping, nay, not doubting, but it was from you, and have been disappointed (he will bear with my saying so) at the discovery of my error. L. H. is unfortunate in holding some loose and not very definite speculations (for at times I think he hardly knows whither his premises would carry him) on marriage—the tenets, I conceive, of the Political Justice, carried a little further. For any thing I could discover in his practice, they have reference, like those, to some future possible condition of society, and not to the present times. But neither for these obliquities of thinking (upon which my own conclusions are as distant as the poles asunder)—nor for his political asperities and petulancies, which are wearing out with the heats and vanities of youth—did I select him for a friend; but for qualities which fitted him for that relation. I do not know whether I flatter myself with being the occasion, but certain it is, that, touched with misgiving for sundry harsh things which he had written aforetime against our friend C[oleridge], —before he left this country he sought a reconciliation with that gentleman (himself being his own introducer), and found it.

L. H. is now in Italy; on his departure to which land with much regret I took my leave of him and of his little family—seven of them, Sir, with their mother—and as kind a set of little people (T. H. and all), as affectionate children, as ever blessed a parent. Had you seen them, Sir, I think you could not have looked on them as so many little Jonases—but rather as pledges of the vessel's safety, that was to bear such a freight of love.

I wish you would read Mr H.'s lines to that same T. H., "six years old, during a sickness":

Sleep breaks at last from out thee,
My little patient boy—

(they are to be found on the 47th page of "Foliage")—and ask yourself how far they are out of the spirit of Christianity. I have a letter from Italy, received but the other day, into which L. H. has put as much heart, and as many friendly yearnings after old associates, and native country, as, I think, paper can well hold. It would do you no hurt to give that perusal also.

From the *other gentleman* I neither expect nor desire (as he is well assured) any such concessions as L. H. made to C. What hath soured him, and made him to suspect his friends of infidelity towards him, I know not. I stood well with him for fifteen years (the proudest of my life), and have ever spoke my full mind of him to some, to whom his panegyric must naturally be least tasteful. I never in thought swerved from him, I never betrayed him, I never slackened in my admiration of him, I was the same to him (neither better nor worse) though he could not see it, as in the days when he thought fit to trust me. At this instant, he may be preparing for me some compliment, above my deserts, as he has sprinkled many such among his admirable books, for which I rest his debtor; or, for any thing I know, or can guess to the contrary, he may be about to read a lecture on my weaknesses. He is welcome to them (as he was to my humble hearth), if they can divert a spleen, or ventilate a fit of sullenness. I wish he would not quarrel with the world at the rate he does; but the reconciliation must be effected by himself, and I despair of living to see that day. But, protesting against much that he has written, and some things which he chooses to do; judging him by his conversation which I enjoyed so long, and relished so deeply; or by his books, in those places where no clouding passion intervenes—I should belie my own conscience, if I said less, than that I think W. H. to be, in his natural and healthy state, one of the wisest and finest spirits breathing. So far from being ashamed of that intimacy, which was betwixt us, it is my boast that I was able for so many years to have preserved it entire; and I think I shall go to my grave without finding, or expecting to find, such another companion.

LAMB: *Letter of Elia to Robert Southey, Esquire*

LAMB'S RETIREMENT

To WORDSWORTH

Colebrook Cottage, *April* 6, 1825.

Dear Wordsworth, I have been several times meditating a letter to you concerning the good thing which has befallen me, but the thought of poor Monkhouse came across me. He was one that I had exulted in the prospect of congratulating me. He and you were to have been the first participators, for indeed it has been ten weeks since the first motion of it. Here I am then after 33 years' slavery, sitting in my own room at 11 o'Clock this finest of all April mornings a freed man, with £441 a year for the remainder of my life, live I as long as John Dennis, who outlived his annuity and starved at 90. £441, i.e. £450, with a deduction of £9 for a provision secured to my sister, she being survivor, the Pension guaranteed by Act Georgii Tertii, &c.

I came home for ever on Tuesday in last week. The incomprehensibleness of my condition overwhelm'd me. It was like passing from life into Eternity. Every year to be as long as three, i.e. to have three times as much real time, time that is my own, in it! I wandered about thinking I was happy, but feeling I was not. But that tumultuousness is passing off, and I begin to understand the nature of the gift. Holydays, even the annual month, were always uneasy joys: their conscious fugitiveness—the craving after making the most of them. Now, when all is holyday, there are no holydays. I can sit at home in rain or shine without a restless impulse for walkings. I am daily steadying, and shall soon find it as natural to me to be my own master, as it has been irksome to have had a master. Mary wakes every morning with an obscure feeling that some good has happened to us.

Leigh Hunt and Montgomery after their releasements describe the shock of their emancipation much as I feel mine. But it hurt their frames. I eat, drink, and sleep sound as ever. I lay no anxious schemes for going hither and thither, but take things as they occur. Yesterday I excursioned 20 miles, to day I write a few letters. Pleasuring was for fugitive play days: mine are fugitive only in the sense that life is fugitive. Freedom and life co-existent.

At the foot of such a call upon you for gratulation, I am ashamed to advert to that melancholy event. Monkhouse was a character I learnd to love slowly, but it grew upon me, yearly, monthly, daily. What a chasm has it made in our pleasant parties! His noble friendly face was always coming before me, till this hurrying event in my life came, and for the time has absorpt all interests. In fact it has shaken me a little. My old desk companions with whom I have had such merry hours seem to reproach me for removing my lot from among them. They were pleasant creatures, but to the anxieties of business, and a weight of possible worse ever impending, I was not equal. Tuthill and Gillman gave me my certificates. I laughed at the friendly lie implied in them, but my sister shook her head and said it was all true. Indeed this last winter I was jaded out, winters were always worse than other parts of the year, because the spirits are worse, and I had no daylight. In summer I had daylight evenings. The relief was hinted to me from a superior power, when I poor slave had not a hope but that I must wait another 7 years with Jacob—and lo! the Rachel which I coveted is bro^{t}—to me.

Communicate my news to Southey, and beg his pardon for my being so long acknowledging his kind present of the "Church", which circumstances I do not wish to explain, but having no reference to himself, prevented at the time. Assure him of my deep respect and friendliest feelings.

Divide the same, or rather each take the whole to you—I mean you and all yours. To Miss Hutchinson I must write separate. What's her address? I want to know about Mrs M.

Farewell! and end at last, long selfish Letter!

C. Lamb

BLAKE

1827.

February 2nd.—Götzenberger, the young painter from Germany, called, and I accompanied him to Blake. We looked over Blake's Dante. Götzenberger was highly gratified by the designs. I was interpreter between them. Blake seemed gratified by the visit, but said nothing remarkable.

Rem.[1]—It was on this occasion that I saw Blake for the last time. He died on the 12th of August. His genius as an artist was praised by Flaxman and Fuseli, and his poems excited great interest in Wordsworth. His theosophic dreams bore a close resemblance to those of Swedenborg. I have already referred to an article written by me, on Blake, for the Hamburg "Patriotic Annals". My interest in this remarkable man was first excited in 1806. Dr Malkin, our Bury Grammar School head-master, published in that year a memoir of a very precocious child, who died. An engraving of a portrait of him, by Blake, was prefixed. Dr Malkin gave an account of Blake, as a painter and poet, and of his visions, and added some specimens of his poems, including the "Tiger". I will now gather together a few stray recollections. When, in 1810, I gave Lamb a Catalogue of the paintings exhibited in Carnaby Street, he was delighted, especially with the description of a painting afterwards engraved, and connected with which there is a circumstance which, unexplained, might reflect discredit on a most excellent and amiable man. It was after the friends of Blake had circulated a subscription paper for an engraving of his "Canterbury Pilgrims", that Stothard was made a party to an engraving of a painting of the same subject, by himself. But Flaxman considered this as done wilfully. Stothard's work is well known; Blake's is known by very few. Lamb preferred the latter greatly, and declared that Blake's description was the finest criticism he had ever read of Chaucer's poem....[Blake] illustrated Blair's "Grave", the "Book of Job", and four books of Young's "Night Thoughts". The last I once showed to William Hazlitt. In

[1] Added in 1852.

the designs he saw no merit; but when I read him some of Blake's poems, he was much struck, and expressed himself with his usual strength and singularity. "They are beautiful", he said, "and only too deep for the vulgar. As to God, a worm is as worthy as any other object, all alike being to him indifferent; so to Blake the chimney-sweeper, etc. He is ruined by vain struggles to get rid of what is on his brain; he attempts impossibilities." I added: "He is like a man who lifts a burthen too heavy for him; he bears it an instant—it then falls and crushes him".

I lent Blake the 8vo edition, 2 vols., of Wordsworth's poems, which he had in his possession at the time of his death. They were sent me then. I did not at first recognise the pencil notes as his, and was on the point of rubbing them out when I made the discovery. In the fly-leaf, vol. i, under the words *Poems referring to the Period of Childhood*, the following is written:—"I see in Wordsworth the natural man rising up against the spiritual man continually; and then he is no poet, but a heathen philosopher, at enmity with all true poetry or inspiration". On the lines,

> And I could wish my days to be
> Bound each to each by natural piety,

he wrote, "There is no such thing as natural piety, because the natural man is at enmity with God". On the verses "To H.C., Six Years Old" (p. 43) the comment is, "This is all in the highest degree imaginative, and equal to any poet—but not superior. I cannot think that real poets have any competition. None are greatest in the kingdom of heaven. It is so in poetry". At the bottom of page 44, "On the Influence of Natural Objects", is written: "Natural objects always did and now do weaken, deaden, and obliterate imagination in me. Wordsworth must know that what he writes valuable is not to be found in nature. Read Michael Angelo's Sonnet, vol. ii, p. 179". That is, the one beginning—

> No mortal object did these eyes behold,
> When they met the lucid light of thine.

It is remarkable that Blake, whose judgments were in most points so very singular, should nevertheless, on one subject closely connected with Wordsworth's poetical reputation, have taken a very commonplace view. Over the heading of the "Essay Supplementary to the Preface", at the end of the volume, he wrote: "I do not know who wrote these Prefaces. They are mischievous, and directly contrary to Wordsworth's own practice" . . . . And at the end of the essay he wrote: "It appears to me as if the last paragraph, beginning, 'Is it the right of the whole, etc.', was written by another hand and mind from the rest of these Prefaces. They give the opinions of [word effaced] landscape painter. Imagination is the divine vision, not of the world, nor of man, nor from man as he is a natural man, but only as he is a spiritual man. Imagination has nothing to do with memory".

A few months after Blake's death, Barron Field and I called on Mrs Blake. The poor old lady was more affected than I expected she would be at the sight of me. She spoke of her husband as dying like an angel. She informed us that she was going to live with Linnell as his housekeeper. She herself died within a few years. She seemed to be the very woman to make her husband happy. She had been formed by him. Indeed, otherwise, she could not have lived with him. Notwithstanding her dress, which was poor and dingy, she had a good expression on her countenance, and with a dark eye, the remains of youthful beauty. She had the wife's virtue of virtues—an implicit reverence for her husband. It is quite certain that she believed in all his visions. On one occasion, speaking of his visions, she said, "You know, dear, the first time you saw God was when you were four years old, and he put his head to the window, and set you a-screaming". In a word, she was formed on the Miltonic model, and, like the first wife, Eve, worshipped God in her husband.

> He for God only, she for God in him.

HENRY CRABB ROBINSON'S *Diary*

THE LAST NIGHT AT ABBOTSFORD

On September 17th [1831] the old splendour of Abbotsford was, after a long interval, and for the last time, revived. Captain James Glencairn Burns, son of the poet, had come home from India, and Sir Walter invited him (with his wife, and their cicerones Mr and Mrs M'Diarmid of Dumfries) to spend a day under his roof. The neighbouring gentry were assembled, and having his son to help him, Sir Walter did most gracefully the honours of the table.

On the 20th Mrs Lockhart set out for London to prepare for her father's reception there; and on the following day Mr Wordsworth and his daughter arrived from Westmoreland to take farewell of him. This was a very fortunate circumstance: nothing could have gratified Sir Walter more, or sustained him better, if he needed any support from without. On the 22nd—his arrangements being all completed, and Laidlaw having received a paper of instructions, the last article of which repeats the caution to be "very careful of the dogs"—these two great poets, who had through life loved each other well, and, in spite of very different theories as to art, appreciated each other's genius more justly than inferior spirits ever did either of them, spent the morning together in a visit to Newark. Hence *Yarrow Revisited*—the last of the three poems by which Wordsworth has connected his name to all time with the most romantic of Scottish streams.

Sitting that evening in the library, Sir Walter said a good deal about the singularity that Fielding and Smollett had both been driven abroad by declining health, and never returned;—which circumstance, though his language was rather cheerful at this time, he had often before alluded to in a darker fashion; and Mr Wordsworth expressed his regret that neither of those great masters of romance appeared to have been surrounded with any due marks of respect in the close of life. I happened to observe that Cervantes, on his last journey to Madrid, met with an incident which seemed to have given him no common satisfaction. Sir Walter did not remember the passage, and desired me to find it out in the life by Pellicer which was at hand, and translate it. I did so, and he listened with lively though pensive interest. Our friend Allan, the historical painter, had also come out that day from Edinburgh, and he since told me that he remembers nothing he ever saw with so much sad pleasure as the attitudes and aspect of Scott and Wordsworth as the story went on. Mr Wordsworth was at that time, I should notice—though indeed his noble stanzas tell it—in but a feeble state of general health. He was, moreover, suffering so much from some malady in his eyes, that he wore a deep green shade over them. Thus he sat between Sir Walter and his daughter: *absit omen*—but it was no wonder that Allan thought as much of Milton as of Cervantes. The anecdote of the young student's raptures on discovering that he had been riding all day with the author of *Don Quixote*, is introduced in the Preface to *Count Robert* and *Castle Dangerous*, which—(for I may not return to the subject)—came out at the close of November in four volumes, as the Fourth Series of *Tales of My Landlord*.

The following sonnet was, no doubt, composed by Mr Wordsworth that same evening:—

A trouble, not of clouds, or weeping rain,
Nor of the setting sun's pathetic light
Engendered, hangs o'er Eildon's triple height:
Spirits of power assembled there complain
For kindred power departing from their sight;
While Tweed, best pleased in chanting a blithe strain,
Saddens his voice again, and yet again.
Lift up your hearts, ye mourners! for the might
Of the whole world's good wishes with him goes;
Blessings and prayers, in nobler retinue
Than sceptred King or laurelled Conqueror knows,
Follow this wondrous potentate. Be true,
Ye winds of Ocean, and the Midland Sea,
Wafting your charge to soft Parthenope.

LOCKHART: *Life of Scott*

LANDOR AND LAMB

I

1832.

September 28th.—Landor breakfasted with me, and also Worsley, who came to supply Hare's place. After an agreeable chat, we drove down to Edmonton, and walked over the fields to Edmonton, where Charles Lamb and his sister were ready dressed to receive us. We had scarcely an hour to chat with them; but it was enough to make both Landor and Worsley express themselves delighted with the person of Mary Lamb, and pleased with the conversation of Charles Lamb; though I thought him by no means at his ease, and Miss Lamb was quite silent. Nothing in the conversation recollectable. Lamb gave Landor White's "Falstaff's Letters". Emma Isola just showed herself. Landor was pleased with her, and has since written verses on her.

HENRY CRABB ROBINSON'S *Diary*

II

LAMB *to* LANDOR

[*October*, 1832.]

Dear Sir,—Pray accept a little volume. 'Tis a legacy from Elia, you'll see. Silver and Gold had he none, but such as he had left he you. I do not know how to thank you for attending to my request about the Album. I thought you would never remember it. Are not you proud and thankful, Emma? Yes; *very, both.* [Signed.] Emma Isola.

Many things I had to say to you, which there was not time for. One, why should I forget? 'tis for Rose Aylmer, which has a charm I cannot explain. I lived upon it for weeks. Next, I forgot to tell you I knew all your Welsh annoyances, the measureless Beethams. I knew a quarter of a mile of them. Seventeen brothers and sixteen sisters, as they appear to me in memory. There was one of them that used to fix his long legs on my fender, and tell a story of a shark every night, endless, immortal. How have I grudged the salt sea ravener not having had his gorge of him! The shortest of the daughters measured five foot eleven without her shoes. Well, some day we may confer about them. But they were tall. Truly, I have discover'd the longitude. Sir, if you can spare a moment, I should be happy to hear from you. That rogue Robinson, detained your verses till I call'd for them. Don't entrust a bit of prose to the rogue; but believe me,

Your obliged, C. L.

My sister sends her kind regards.

W. S. Landor, Esq.
From Ch. Lamb.

COLERIDGE ON WORDSWORTH

I

Of all the men I ever knew, Wordsworth has the least femineity in his mind. He is *all* man. He is a man of whom it might be said,—"It is good for him to be alone".

II

I cannot help regretting that Wordsworth did not first publish his thirteen books on the growth of an individual mind—superior, as I used to think, upon the whole, to *The Excursion.* You may judge how I felt about them by my own poem upon the occasion. Then the plan laid out, and, I believe, partly suggested by me, was, that Wordsworth should assume the station of a man in mental repose, one whose principles were made up, and so prepared to deliver upon authority a system of philosophy. He was to treat man as man,—a subject of eye, ear, touch, and taste, in contact with external nature, and informing the senses from the mind, and not compounding a mind out of the senses; then he was to describe the pastoral and other states of society, assuming something of the Juvenalian spirit as he approached the high civilisation of cities and towns, and opening a melancholy picture of the present state of degeneracy and vice; thence he was to infer and reveal the proof of, and necessity for, the whole state of man and society being subject to, and illustrative of, a redemptive process in operation, showing how this idea reconciled all the anomalies, and promised future glory and restoration. Something of this sort was, I think, agreed on. It is, in substance, what I have been all my life doing in my system of philosophy.

I think Wordsworth possessed more of the genius of a great philosophic poet than any man I ever knew, or, as I believe, has existed in England since Milton; but it seems to me that he ought never to have abandoned the contemplative position, which is peculiarly—perhaps I might say exclusively—fitted for him. His proper title is *Spectator ab extra*.

COLERIDGE: *Table Talk*

ELIA

Once, and once only, have I seen thy face,
Elia! once only has thy tripping tongue
Run o'er my breast, yet never has been left
Impression on it stronger or more sweet.
Cordial old man! what youth was in thy years,
What wisdom in thy levity, what truth
In every utterance of that purest soul!
Few are the spirits of the glorified
I'd spring to earlier at the gate of Heaven.

LANDOR

TO SOUTHEY, 1833

Indweller of a peaceful vale,
Ravaged erewhile by white-hair'd Dane;
Rare architect of many a wondrous tale,
Which, till Helvellyn's head lie prostrate, shall remain!

From Arno's side I hear thy Derwent flow,
And see methinks the lake below
Reflect thy graceful progeny, more fair
And radiant than the purest waters are,
Even when gurgling in their joy among
The bright and blessed throng
Whom, on her arm recline,
The beauteous Proserpine
With tenderest regretful gaze,
Thinking of Enna's yellow field, surveys.

Alas! that snows are shed
Upon thy laurell'd head,
Hurtled by many cares and many wrongs!
Malignity lets none
Approach the Delphic throne;
A hundred lane-fed curs bark down Fame's hundred tongues.
But this is in the night, when men are slow
To raise their eyes, when high and low,
The scarlet and the colourless, are one;
Soon Sleep unbars his noiseless prison,
And active minds again are risen;
Where are the curs? dream-bound, and whimpering in the sun.

At fife's or lyre's or tabor's sound
The dance of youth, O Southey, runs not round,
But closes at the bottom of the room
Amid the falling dust and deepening gloom,
Where the weary sit them down,
And Beauty too unbraids, and waits a lovelier crown.

We hurry to the river we must cross,
And swifter downward every footstep wends;
Happy, who reach it ere they count the loss
Of half their faculties and half their friends!
When we are come to it, the stream
Is not so dreary as they deem
Who look on it from haunts too dear;
The weak from Pleasure's baths feel most its chilling air!

No firmer breast than thine hath Heaven
To poet, sage, or hero given:
No heart more tender, none more just
To that He largely placed in trust:
Therefore shalt thou, whatever date
Of years be thine, with soul elate
Rise up before the Eternal throne,
And hear, in God's own voice, "Well done".

Not, were that submarine
Gem-lighted city mine,
Wherein my name, engraven by thy hand,
Above the royal gleam of blazonry shall stand;
Not, were all Syracuse
Pour'd forth before my Muse,
With Hiero's cars and steeds, and Pindar's lyre
Brightening the path with more than solar fire,
Could I, as would beseem, requite the praise
Showered upon my low head from thy most lofty lays.

LANDOR

THE DEATH OF COLERIDGE

1834.

When I heard of the death of Coleridge, it was without grief. It seemed to me that he long had been on the confines of the next world,—that he had a hunger for eternity. I grieved then that I could not grieve. But since, I feel how great a part he was of me. His great and dear spirit haunts me. I cannot think a thought, I cannot make a criticism on men or books, without an ineffectual turning and reference to him. He was the proof and touchstone of all my cogitations. He was a Grecian (or in the first form) at Christ's Hospital, where I was deputy Grecian; and the same subordination and deference to him I have preserved through a life-long acquaintance. Great in his writings, he was greatest in his conversation.

In him was disproved that old maxim, that we should allow every one his share of talk. He would talk from morn to dewy eve, nor cease till far midnight, yet who ever would interrupt him,—who would obstruct that continuous flow of converse, fetched from Helicon or Zion? He had the tact of making the unintelligible seem plain. Many who read the abstruser parts of his "Friend" would complain that his works did not answer to his spoken wisdom. They were identical. But he had a tone in oral delivery, which seemed to convey sense to those who were otherwise imperfect recipients. He was my fifty years old friend without a dissension. Never saw I his likeness, nor probably the world can see again. I seemed to love the house he died at more passionately than when he lived. I love the faithful Gillmans more than while they exercised their virtues towards him living. What was his mansion is consecrated to me a chapel.

Chs. Lamb

Edmonton.

W. S. LANDOR TO H. C. ROBINSON

[1835.]

The death of Charles Lamb has grieved me very bitterly. Never did I see a human being with whom I was more inclined to sympathise. There is something in the recollection that you took me with you to see him which affects me greatly more than writing or speaking of him could do with any other. When I first heard of the loss that all his friends, and many that never were his friends, sustained in him, no thought took possession of my mind except the anguish of his sister. That very night, before I closed my eyes, I composed this:

To the sister of Charles Lamb

Comfort thee, O thou mourner! yet awhile
 Again shall Elia's smile
Refresh thy heart, whose heart can ache no more.
 What is it we deplore?
He leaves behind him, freed from griefs and years,
 Far worthier things than tears.

The love of friends, without a single foe;
    Unequalled lot below!
His gentle soul, his genius, these are thine;
    Shalt thou for these repine?
He may have left the lowly walks of men;
    Left them he has: what then?
Are not his footsteps followed by the eyes
    Of all the good and wise?
Though the warm day is over, yet they seek,
    Upon the lofty peak
Of his pure mind, the roseate light, that glows
    O'er Death's perennial snows.
Behold him! From the Spirits of the Blest
    He speaks; he bids thee rest.

If you like to send these to Leigh Hunt, do it. He may be pleased to print in his *Journal* this testimony of affection to his friend—this attempt at consolation to the finest genius that ever descended on the heart of woman....

AFTERMATH

1838.

May 20th.—My breakfast-party went off very well indeed, as far as talk was concerned. I had with me Landor, Milnes, and Serjeant Talfourd. A great deal of rattling on the part of Landor. He maintained Blake to be the greatest of poets; that Milnes is the greatest poet now living in England; and that Scott's "Marmion" is superior to all that Byron and Wordsworth have written, and the description of the battle better than anything in Homer!!! But Blake furnished chief matter for talk.

May 22nd.—A delightful breakfast with Milnes—a party of eight, among whom were Rogers, Carlyle, who made himself very pleasant indeed, Moore, and Landor. The talk very good, equally divided. Talleyrand's recent death and the poet Blake were the subjects. Tom Moore had never heard of Blake, at least not of his poems. Even he acknowledged the beauty of such as were quoted.

HENRY CRABB ROBINSON'S *Diary*

INDEX

INDEX

INDEX

LIBRARY ST. MARY'S COLLEGE

INDEX